THE
EVERYTHING
NATURAL HEALTH
FOR DOGS
BOOK

Dear Reader,

Our dogs have our hearts and we want to do everything we possibly can to provide them with the best toys, food, bedding, and health care available. Naturally, we think they deserve a quality life and want them to share our lives forever. Helping them live a natural lifestyle is the most important step we can take to achieve that goal.

As an experienced dog lover, I will lead you through the maze of canine holistic health care. In this book, you'll find the latest information about all types of natural health maintenance and prevention techniques. You'll learn the basics of nutrition and care, and you can be aware of any changes in your dog's health or behavior and seek treatment at the first signs of trouble. When you know what questions to ask your veterinarian or what remedies you can give your dog yourself, you are in the best position to safeguard his health.

What's wonderful about providing holistic health care for your dog is the wide range of options that are available to treat a problem. Many of these alternatives have been tested over generations and go a long way toward keeping your dog in tip-top shape for many years to come.

Elaine Waldorf Gewirtz

Welcome to the EVERYTHING® Series!

These handy, accessible books give you all you need to tackle a difficult project, gain a new hobby, comprehend a fascinating topic, prepare for an exam, or even brush up on something you learned back in school but have since forgotten.

You can choose to read an *Everything*® book from cover to cover or just pick out the information you want from our four useful boxes: e-questions, e-facts, e-alerts, and e-ssentials.

We give you everything you need to know on the subject, but throw in a lot of fun stuff along the way, too.

We now have more than 400 *Everything*® books in print, spanning such wide-ranging categories as weddings, pregnancy, cooking, music instruction, foreign language, crafts, pets, New Age, and so much more. When you're done reading them all, you can finally say you know *Everything*®!

E-QUESTION

Answers to common questions

FACTS

Important snippets of information

ALERTS!

Urgent warnings

ESSENTIALS

Quick handy tips

PUBLISHER Karen Cooper

DIRECTOR OF ACQUISITIONS AND INNOVATION Paula Munier

MANAGING EDITOR, EVERYTHING SERIES Lisa Laing

COPY CHIEF Casey Ebert

ACQUISITIONS EDITOR Katrina Schroeder

ASSOCIATE DEVELOPMENT EDITOR Elizabeth Kassab

SENIOR DEVELOPMENT EDITOR Brett Palana-Shanahan

EDITORIAL ASSISTANT Hillary Thompson

Visit the entire Everything® series at *www.everything.com*

THE
EVERYTHING®
NATURAL HEALTH FOR DOGS BOOK

The healthy, affordable way to ensure a long,
happy life for your pet

Elaine Waldorf Gewirtz
with Jordan Herod Nuccio, DVM, CVA

Adamsmedia
Avon, Massachusetts

An Everything® Series Book.
Everything® and everything.com® are registered trademarks of F+W Media, Inc.

Published by Adams Media, a division of F+W Media, Inc.
57 Littlefield Street, Avon, MA 02322 U.S.A.
www.adamsmedia.com

ISBN 10: 1-59869-991-1
ISBN 13: 978-1-59869-991-3

Printed in the United States of America.

J   I   H   G   F   E   D   C   B   A

Library of Congress Cataloging-in-Publication Data
is available from the publisher.

The Everything® Natural Health for Dogs Book is intended as a reference volume only, not as a medical manual. In light of the complex, individual, and specific nature of health problems, this book is not intended to replace professional veterinary advice. The ideas, procedures, and suggestions in this book are intended to supplement, not replace, the advice of a trained veterinary professional. Consult your dog's veterinarian before adopting the suggestions in this book, as well as about any condition that may require diagnosis or medial attention. The authors and publisher disclaim any liability arising directly or indirectly from the use of this book.

This publication is designed to provide accurate and authoritative information with regard to the subject matter covered. It is sold with the understanding that the publisher is not engaged in rendering legal, accounting, or other professional advice. If legal advice or other expert assistance is required, the services of a competent professional person should be sought.

—From a *Declaration of Principles* jointly adopted by a Committee of the American Bar Association and a Committee of Publishers and Associations

Many of the designations used by manufacturers and sellers to distinguish their products are claimed as trademarks. Where those designations appear in this book and Adams Media was aware of a trademark claim, the designations have been printed with initial capital letters.

This book is available at quantity discounts for bulk purchases.
For information, please call 1-800-289-0963.

Contents

Acknowledgments

Special thanks to my agent, Kate Epstein, for going the distance for me in a kind and gentle manner, and to my editor, Katrina Schroeder, for her utmost support and patience.

Dedication

Kudos to my family, especially to my husband, Steve, and to my children Beth-Jo, Seth, Sameya, and Sara and her husband Ryan, for their understanding when I was too busy to come play. Roses to my mother, father, and sister, Rosalie, Leo, and Beverlee-Jo Waldorf for sharing the wonderful memories of our first dogs, and finally to today's Dalmatians, Bob, Jill, Will, Halle, and Kota, who have their leashes on and are waiting at the door to go for a walk.

Top Ten Ways to Keep Your Dog Naturally Healthy

1. Choose a healthy dog to bring home and begin house training and regular training as soon as he arrives.

2. Locate a holistic or integrative veterinarian that you feel comfortable with and provide preventive health care by taking your dog to the doctor regularly.

3. Give your dog plenty of water daily and feed her a natural high-quality diet with fresh, wholesome ingredients, supplements, and vitamins.

4. Give your dog some exercise every day; exercise should be appropriate for his age and growth stage.

5. Spay your female dog before her first season to prevent mammary cancer and neuter your male by his first birthday to prevent testicular cancer.

6. Give the core set of vaccines only to puppies, or comply with the legal requirements of your state; after that use blood tests, called vaccine titers, to determine immunity levels before vaccinating.

7. Keep your dog free of parasites and your environment clear of toxins.

8. Ask your veterinarian about using homeopathy, traditional Chinese medicine, acupuncture, massage, aromatherapy, and herbs when appropriate.

9. Maintain your dog's oral health.

10. Learn the early warning signs of illness and seek preventive treatment when necessary.

Introduction

▶ FROM THE TOP of his huggable head to the tip of his furry tail, your dog needs you to keep him healthy. While he has no trouble figuring out creative ways to bring you tulips from the garden or unhinge the trash can lid, there's no way he can live strong without your assistance. You are his cook, chauffeur, barber, nurse, personal trainer, activities director, and pest control specialist. And when you walk through the door with a bagful of new toys, you are his main squeeze.

That you've made the decision to help your dog live a natural lifestyle is a credit to how much you care about her. Maybe you've been thinking for a while that the way your parents or grandparents raised their dogs is outdated, and that the days of feeding your canine whatever bag of dog food is on sale at the supermarket, buying her only one toy every five years, and leaving him alone in the yard 24/7 are over. You want more for your dog and she's only too happy to oblige you spoiling rights.

Today, people treat their dogs like treasured members of the family and they want to give them the healthiest and longest lives possible. Many folks are opting to make their own dog food, and when you combine this with other alternative therapies and the many new advances in veterinary medicine, it's no wonder that dogs are living better lives a whole lot longer.

Going holistic (or integrative or complementary) with your four-footed friend is the big buzz these days. This means taking advantage of all forms of veterinary medicine—alternative techniques as well as conventional methods. More veterinarians are incorporating the old, natural ways of treating their patients and using the least invasive and the least harmful cures.

Acupuncture, for example, has been used in China for 3,500 years and is the main treatment for a quarter of the world's human population. Veterinarians are using it today for a wide variety of canine ailments, including arthritis, gastrointestinal disorders, respiratory problems, and allergies. The holistic veterinarian considers all aspects of canine life before making a diagnosis and looks at the cause rather than just the symptom.

The key to having a healthy dog the holistic way isn't anything fancy, and not that much different than maintaining your own good health. It all comes down to eating a well-balanced, and fresh diet, getting plenty of exercise, being happy, and staying stress-free.

The *Everything® Natural Health for Dogs Book* will help you understand what holistic (or integrative or complementary) health care for your dog is all about. Here you'll discover the healthiest ways to feed your dog; the latest developments in major health issues, such as allergies, arthritis, cancer, and epilepsy; and new ways to use some old therapies like homeopathy, herbs, Chinese medicine, acupuncture, and massage. The question of whether or not to vaccinate your dog will be answered, and you'll discover some easy ways to keep your dog allergy- and parasite-free and find out why brushing his teeth may very well save his life.

The goal of this book is not to overwhelm you with a lot of high-tech medical jargon and time-consuming therapies to use on your dog. Instead, it should empower you with the basic knowledge that will allow you to enrich your dog's health and make your lives as meaningful as possible.

CHAPTER 1

Assessing Your Situation

Learning how to take care of your new four-footed friend is an adventure. It helps if you begin with a healthy puppy or dog. If you're looking for a pure-bred, buying one from a reputable breeder who cares about the pups' health will cut down on trips to the veterinarian later on. If a rescue dog is for you, look for the signs of strength and vigor. Keep your environment safe and free of toxins and you'll be going a long way toward keeping your dog healthy.

Already Have a Dog?

If this is your first puppy or adult dog, perhaps you're always wondering if you're taking care of him properly. You're anxious every time he coughs and you rush him to the veterinarian if an odd bump pops up on his stomach. Don't worry. This is what all good new owners do. You care about your dog and you want him to be strong and healthy. As time goes by, you'll begin to recognize when a condition warrants an emergency trip to the veterinarian and when you can treat your dog at home.

It helps to have a holistic or a traditional veterinarian who is knowledgeable and likes your dog. You should feel comfortable talking to the veterinarian. She will help teach you the ins and outs of canine health care. An integrative veterinarian who uses all types of therapies can give you the best of both medical worlds.

More people are turning to natural forms of treatment for both themselves and their dogs. Both traditional and holistic veterinarians agree that the best way to keep a dog healthy is to prevent illness in the first place, but they differ on the best way to accomplish that. Holistic veterinarians are more conservative when using products, and they often use natural alternatives they feel are healthier and pose less potential harm than standard medications.

Getting a New Dog?

If you're thinking about adding the patter of puppy or adult paws to your household, don't rush into purchasing or adopting the first cute canine that licks your face or is sitting off in the corner and seems lonely. Getting a dog is a choice and there are many dogs that need good homes.

FACT

Taking care of a dog is expensive. The American Pet Products Manufacturers Association estimates that pet owners spend $41 billion a year on their pets. That breaks down to about $25,000 to care for a dog during her lifetime. This includes routine veterinary care, medications or natural health products, grooming, food, toys, bedding, collars, and leashes.

Choosing a dog that is healthy and mentally stable right from the start means you'll spend less on veterinary expenses and remedies to care for your dog. This leaves you with time and money to have a quality experience with your canine so you can truly enjoy your years with him.

Before you bring a new dog home, consider all that will be involved in caring for him over the next ten to fifteen years. Take some time to research breeds or check out different shelters to learn as many details as you can about canine health.

Choosing a Hardy Breed

No breed is immune to health problems and every breed is prone to developing some medical condition during its lifetime. While it's true that some breeds have more than their share of health issues, even mixed-breed dogs will need to see the veterinarian for medical issues.

If you have a certain breed in mind, find out as much as you can about the breed's predisposition to certain health problems. Research the breed's health issues by talking with breeders, asking your veterinarian, and reading.

One way to learn about a breed's health issues is to go to the American Kennel Club website (*www.akc.org*) and click on the breed's national club. Every club provides the latest information on the breed's health issues and ways to treat their conditions. Most clubs have health education committees who report the latest technology and treatments available.

If you know what diseases your breed may be prone to develop, you can be on the lookout for early warning signs and obtain treatment right away. You'll also know what to do to prevent them. Some health issues are preventable with the right diet and care, while others may require extensive and expensive treatment and ongoing care. It helps to know ahead of time what medical issues may lie ahead.

Finding a Breeder or Rescue

It doesn't matter if you're looking for a show-stopping purebred or a loving pet that lives to dig up the garden and sleep on your best chair. Your first step is finding a healthy, quality pup either from a conscientious breeder or a reputable rescue.

Where to Look

You'll find breeders almost everywhere. The Internet is loaded with breeder websites, and you can find purebreds listed in newspaper and magazine advertisements. Unfortunately, some of these breeders may not be as good as they sound. Although many breeders will offer a health guarantee that promises to replace the puppy if he becomes ill, not many people will return a dog once they fall in love with it.

ALERT!

Never buy a puppy or dog through a website or advertisement without seeing it yourself. Talking to someone on the phone or seeing pictures is not the same as actually seeing the pup or dog. The pup should be raised in clean conditions and should be healthy.

Ask your veterinarian for the name of a good breeder. She knows if there are breeders in the area who produce healthy or unhealthy puppies. Even if she doesn't know anyone in the breed you're interested in, she may have an associate who does. The American Kennel Club's breeder referral program is also a good source of information. You can contact any AKC national breed club for its list of good breeders and club rescue groups for both puppies and adult dogs that need a new home.

A Reputable Breeder

When it comes to buying a healthy purebred puppy, it's all about choosing the best breeder you can find. A good breeder has devoted years to producing the best puppies possible, and really cares about what happens to their puppies for the rest of their lives.

The breeder will probably screen you to make sure that you can offer the dog or pup the best home possible, so expect to be quizzed. A good breeder will freely offer information on the breed's behavior, care, health, and training. This comes in handy if you come across a problem later on. Your breeder will be more than willing to share her expertise, and most are happy to hear from owners with questions and anecdotes. It helps to select a breeder you like and feel comfortable talking to.

Health Clearances

A reputable breeder chooses the healthiest breeding stock before she breeds them. If tests are available for the genetic health issues her breed is prone to developing, such as hip or elbow dysplasia, she'll test the male and female to make sure they are clear of problems. Adult dogs with health problems should never be bred.

When you're out puppy shopping, ask to see proof of health clearances or even the parents' health files. When you're spending anywhere from $500 to $2,500 for a purebred puppy, you have a right to make sure it's healthy. Many breeders will provide a health guarantee.

These guarantees typically provide a replacement puppy in case she develops a genetic, life-threatening illness within the first two years, and a few breeders may offer a monetary reimbursement for a major problem. A good health guarantee includes a letter from the breeder's veterinarian stating that the puppy has been examined and is healthy.

Adopting a Healthy Puppy

If you're interested in adopting a breed from a shelter, do some homework before you bring the dog home. Research the genetic weaknesses this breed may be prone to developing and decide if you want to take these on. With mixed breeds there's no way of knowing what hereditary problems your dog may have. Either way, observe your dog for any signs of respiratory disease. Coughing may indicate kennel cough, which is contagious but treatable. Ask when the dog was examined by a veterinarian and if the dog is clear of intestinal parasites. If the dog comes with a medical history, this is helpful. Look the dog over carefully and run your hands over his entire body to look for any tumors, fleas, hair loss, and inflamed skin, which may be signs of allergic dermatitis. Skin conditions are not life threatening but are often difficult to treat, so think carefully before adopting a dog with this problem.

Selecting a Healthy Puppy or Adult Dog

There are ways to tell if a puppy or adult dog is healthy. Learn to recognize the signs of good health before you decide to give a dog a home. After all, it's just as easy to fall in love with a strong, healthy puppy as a weak, ill one.

Activity Level

While you're only buying one puppy, insist on seeing all of the puppies in the litter if they're still on the breeder's premises. By five weeks of age, healthy pups will begin playing with one another and should be lively and energetic.

Visit long enough to see the puppies when they're awake. Every pup in the litter should be rambunctious and eager to engage one another in puppy games. A pup that does otherwise could be ill.

If you're acquiring a rescue dog, ask to take him out of his enclosure and take him for a walk on a leash. He should be able to walk without limping. If there's a big fenced-in yard, let him run freely. Not every dog enjoys chasing a ball or Frisbee, but if he wants to engage you in play this is a good sign that he wants your approval and is healthy enough to run.

Shy or Outgoing

A pup or adult dog should be happy and eager to interact with you. The dog that's off in the corner is not only shy, but could also be ill. While you may feel sorry for a dog that seems afraid to meet you, this behavior could mean major veterinary bills later on.

Even if she's physically healthy, shyness could mean a mentally unhealthy animal, which can become a great burden. Although some introverted pups come out of their shells later on, many do not. These pups in the corner can easily grow up to become fearful adults and are not good choices for an active, noisy family or for people who have never had a dog before and are still learning about how to train one.

These dogs can develop separation anxiety and cry and carry on every time you leave them alone. They may be afraid of noises and inanimate objects, including their own shadows. They may develop obsessive-compulsive habits that include licking and biting themselves and running in circles. Some fearful dogs may actually become aggressive and may bite to overcompensate for their fear. They may well require a tremendous amount of training and socialization in order to live a happy life.

Signs of a Healthy Pup

When choosing a puppy, it's easy to get caught up in his looks. Instead, focus on evaluating his overall condition and look at the pup through a veterinarian's eyes. Look for these signs:

- Skin should be smooth, clean, and shiny without any sores or bumps.
- Puppies should not be biting or scratching at themselves continuously, which could signal fleas.
- At ten to twelve days of age, eyes should be open and clear without any redness or discharge.
- Pups should not be scratching at their eyes, which may mean there's an infection or irritation.
- Vomiting or coughing more than once is not normal and may indicate the pup is ill.
- Stools should be firm without being watery or bloody; abnormalities may be a sign of illness or worms.
- Pups should run or walk freely without limping.
- You should be able to slightly feel a pup's ribs if you rub his sides, but you should not be able to see the ribs protruding through the skin.

Health Records

A good breeder should provide you with records of your puppy's health. These should include the dates of your puppy's first vaccines, when she was dewormed, and the results of her first examination by a veterinarian. Hopefully the veterinarian listened to the puppy's heart and noted any signs of a heart murmur or an umbilical hernia. This information should be revealed to you if you are interested in purchasing the pup.

The parents' test results for the absence of hip or elbow dysplasia (dislocation), cardiac problems, and slipped patellas (kneecaps) should also be given to you. Any history of cancer, allergies, or digestion problems should also be noted. These problems may be an early indicator of health issues your puppy may inherit. The best breeders take great pride in handing over a thick notebook full of the latest behavior, care, health, and training information on your puppy. Be sure to read it and feel free to ask the breeder questions. It will prove invaluable when it comes to raising your puppy. Once you've chosen a puppy, plan to take her to your own veterinarian for a checkup within two days of bringing her home.

Signs of a Healthy Dog

A reputable rescue organization will have all dogs temperamentally and medically screened to make sure you are getting a healthy dog. Check her over yourself anyway for these signs of good health:

- Eyes should be clear and not runny or cloudy.
- Coat should not be thin or patchy.
- Skin should be clear and free of bumps; run your hands underneath the coat to make sure.
- No fleas or ticks.
- Dog should be able to move freely.
- Dog should not be coughing or wheezing.
- Dog should not be rubbing or pawing at her ears or eyes; this could mean ear or eye infection.
- Dog should not be biting at her skin or licking one area obsessively; this could signal allergy problems.
- Dog should be a healthy weight; protruding ribs means she's too thin, a solid round shape without any definition of her waist means she's overweight.

Building a Bond with Your Puppy

Hopefully you've picked up your puppy early in the morning and plan to be home for at least the first two days. This will give you some special time to bond with your new pup.

The first few days with your new puppy will set the stage for your future. You're learning what makes him tick and letting him know that he can rely on you to care for him. Take lots of pictures! The memories of this special time with your new puppy will last a lifetime.

Limit Visitors

Ask neighbors and friends who are anxious to meet your pup to wait a few days until your dog has had a chance to settle in. They mean well and are naturally excited about the new addition to your family, but you'll want to focus on your dog's needs without having to entertain company.

Try to stay off the phone too and resist taking on noisy or complicated home improvement projects for the first few days. All this commotion may frighten a young pup and will inhibit your efforts to get to know your new little four-footed friend.

No Distractions

Turn off the computer and other distractions and take your pup outdoors for a daily walk and play session. Talk to your pup—even sing your favorite song to him so he has a chance to become accustomed to your voice and begin the bonding process.

Bed Buddies

One of the best ways to build a relationship with your new pup is to have him sleep in his crate at the side of your bed. He will inhale your scent and hear every sound you make all night long. You'll also be able to hear him if he needs to go outside to eliminate, which helps when trying to housetrain him.

Besides the fun of just spending time with your new puppy, the goal of bonding is to have a healthy, happy dog for many years to come.

CHAPTER 2

Basic Natural Care

Enjoying good health is a hot topic these days. What's the secret of having a healthy dog? Start with a good foundation, add a holistic approach, and maintain a balanced lifestyle for her. By providing wholesome nutrition, a nurturing environment, and the opportunity for your dog to safely interact with the world around her, she's bound to thrive. Add conventional and alternative veterinary care and voilá: natural wellness!

Going Holistic

Holistic medicine is a natural healing philosophy, sometimes referred to as alternative medicine, which has been practiced for thousands of years. Today, more veterinarians and dog owners are recognizing its benefits. Holistic medicine focuses on preventing illness and maintaining health. Holistic practices are gentle and minimally invasive, and emphasize love and respect for the patient.

Holistic medical care is easy on your budget. Many natural therapies are generally less expensive than conventional veterinary care over the long-term, especially when you seek treatment as soon as you bring your dog home. Many pet insurance companies offer the same coverage for holistic practices as they do for conventional veterinary health care.

Holistic medicine views health as a balance of body systems—mental, emotional, physical, and spiritual. Whether directed at humans or dogs, it considers the whole picture and provides support to the body so that it can correct itself. Practitioners devise a treatment plan involving many different kinds of therapies.

The holistic veterinarian believes the dog's emotional and spiritual state can affect his condition. She looks for the true root of the disease or the collection of symptoms by evaluating everything about the dog. What often seems like a simple problem on the surface really has several layers beneath it. The practitioner combines healing arts and medical skills and performs a thorough examination, takes a complete medical history, and asks detailed questions about your dog. These include his ancestry, environment, diet, daily life, and causes of any stress.

Types of Holistic Treatments

When it comes to treating patients, the holistic veterinarian is a strong advocate of preventive medicine. She may use modern veterinary techniques such as medication, laboratory tests, ultrasound, and surgery as well as alternative methods. These treatments may involve:

- Acupuncture
- Acupressure
- Aromatherapy
- Chinese herbs
- Chiropractic adjustments
- Diet and nutritional therapy
- Flower essences
- Homeopathy
- Lifestyle changes
- Massage

Holistic therapies have the advantage of fewer side effects than conventional treatments. Sometimes there may be no conventional treatments available for a particular condition, or holistic therapies may succeed where traditional medicine has failed.

E-QUESTION

What is allopathic medicine?
While *allopathic medicine* may sound like a highly specialized medical term, it's actually just another name for Western or conventional medicine. It refers to treatments that control, stop, or inhibit symptoms of the disease. It comes from two Greek words: *allos*, meaning "other," and *pathos*, meaning "suffering" or "disease." Allopathy defines health as the absence of disease.

Natural Medicine

Natural veterinary medicine depends upon the body's ability to heal and maintain itself. Many therapies may use herbs and foods rather than surgery or drugs.

Preventive Care

Obtain holistic veterinary care before your dog actually needs help. Since many diseases progress slowly, a visit to the veterinarian for a routine exam, a blood test, and a urinalysis can catch many problems in the early stages. Before your visit, observe and take notes about your dog's eating and bathroom habits, his activity level, and any unusual behavior, such as excessive scratching or licking. This information will help the practitioner evaluate your dog's health. She may be able to identify problems before they become serious and recommend dietary changes, nutritional supplements, and acupuncture as part of an overall preventive treatment plan.

Conventional and Alternative Medicine

Alternative or holistic medicine views disease as an imbalance in the body and treatments work to eliminate the source of the imbalance. But there are times when conventional tests come in handy. These are used as diagnostics. Conventional veterinary treatments may include:

- Antibiotics
- Anti-inflammatory drugs
- Chemotherapy
- Parasite control
- Steroids
- Surgery
- Vaccination

Alternative therapies help relieve discomfort and treat the cause of the problem. Most therapies don't have any side effects and they provide nutrients that strengthen the immune system.

Integrative: The Best of Both Worlds

Integrative medicine uses all therapies to prevent and treat disease. This approach minimizes adverse effects, maximizes successful outcomes, and improves quality of life.

A growing number of veterinarians are specializing in holistic medicine, while conventional veterinarians are incorporating alternative techniques into their practices. You may notice the words *integrative* or *complementary care* listed on their office stationery or included in directories. This means they will choose the best of both worlds. If you have a conventional veterinarian but think that you'd like to try some alternative therapies, discuss your thoughts with your vet. He may be very willing to explore these options.

The Veterinary Institute of Integrative Medicine (*www.viim.org*) in Arvada, Colorado, helps educate conventional veterinarians about the benefits of alternative medicine. Formed by a prominent group of holistic veterinarians, it maintains a directory of holistic veterinarians throughout the United States and publishes *The Veterinarians' Desk Reference of Natural Medicines*, which provides information for treating more than 100 conditions with natural products.

It's About Balance

Staying on an even keel may sound like a simple cliché, but it expresses what the holistic perspective means—balance. Natural healing relies on maintaining balance; when the body is out of balance other ailments will likely follow. Your dog's body is connected at all levels. If one area isn't up to par, other areas that may seem unrelated on the surface will be thrown off kilter. From skin inflammation to chronic diarrhea, all problems result from imbalance.

Traditional Chinese medicine views the condition of the body to be determined by a balance between yin and yang and the flow of energy called qi. When there is disease, it means there is an imbalance in the body. Holistic practitioners seek to restore the balance in the body and eliminate "dis-ease," or malfunctions of the body, so the body can repair itself.

Nutrition 101

Good nutrition is one of the basics of a holistic lifestyle. Perhaps you pick your dog's commercial food with care or maybe you've heard about the benefits of feeding your dog raw food and wouldn't mind doing a little home cooking for your pet. With so many choices, however, choosing the right natural dietary care for your dog can be confusing.

First and foremost, a wholesome diet maintains good health and supports your dog's immune system. It provides natural healing energies and can make a monumental difference in easing the symptoms of some mild conditions such as allergies. Poor diets that are too high in saturated fats and carbohydrates or too low in fiber are often responsible for obesity, cancer, and heart and liver disease.

When considering your dog's diet, you should also consider her eating habits. While some canines will gobble up everything in sight, others will pick and choose their tidbits carefully. Giving your dog the very best food is pointless if she doesn't eat it.

If you only give your dog raw meat and bones, there is no guarantee that he is receiving the right nutrition. His food should have the correct proportions of carbohydrates, fats, minerals, protein, and vitamins. Many holistic veterinary clinics offer homemade diets with the right amount of ingredients.

After seeing their dogs walk away from half-eaten meals time after time, it's no wonder many well-meaning owners are ready to put just about anything in their dogs' bowls to get them to eat. This may include canned dog food, treats, or leftovers from the dinner table. While these additions usually make owners feel better because their dogs are eating, feeding a dog an unbalanced diet is not healthy in the long run.

Observing Your Dog's Appetite

One of the first questions your holistic veterinarian will ask you is about your dog's appetite. Having a picky eater is not unusual. If you are concerned your dog may be too fat or too thin, it helps to take notes or keep a log about how much or how little your dog eats. This will allow you to help your veterinarian spot a problem early. A healthy dog looks forward to dining and will usually lick up every last morsel. If he walks away from a meal it may be a sign of illness.

Meal Options

There are several ways to feed your dog healthy meals. If you want to use a high quality commercial dry food, switch off between a few different high-quality brands every few months as long as your dog can tolerate the transition without vomiting or diarrhea. Feeding your dog a variety of foods will prevent dietary imbalances and the development of food allergies from overexposure to one protein or carbohydrate source.

If you'd rather stick with the same quality brand, try adding fresh food to it. The vitamins and minerals contained in fresh fruits and puréed vegetables make a big difference. You can also prepare a home-cooked or raw foods diet for your dog. All it takes is a little planning and organization on your part, and the results are well worth the effort.

A Raw Diet

Holistic veterinarians, websites, and many owners tout the raw food diet. They argue that a balanced raw diet significantly increases the nutritional quality of the food. According to this line of thinking, cooking or extruding foods changes their biochemical structure and reduces their nutritional value, so raw foods are logically healthier. Before making a decision on switching the menu, discuss the pros and cons with your veterinarian.

Why Environment Matters

Creating a safe and loving home for your dog is a natural part of caring for him. Ordinary household items can be deadly if your dog gets his paws or his mouth on them. He doesn't know that chewing and swallowing the wrong thing can cause an electrical shock or a life-threatening intestinal blockage. It's your responsibility to dog-proof your house to avoid potentially harmful accidents.

If you have a puppy, limit the area he has access to. It will be easier to keep an eye on him and prevent him from getting into trouble and finding dangerous things to chew. If you have an adult dog, use baby gates or keep him out of rooms that are strewn with small objects that he can swallow. The best way to dog-proof the house is to go through every room and to get down on all fours and check around. You'll be able to see what things look like at your dog's level on the floor or carpet.

The following list contains objects that often send dogs to emergency clinics. Check for these items in your home and be sure to take precautions to keep your dog from harm:

❑ Electrical cords
❑ Small metal, wood, or plastic objects, such as screws, pins, needles, wire, pens, pencils, markers, jewelry, buttons, and children's toys
❑ Socks, shoes, underwear, pantyhose, clothing, baby bottles, and pacifiers
❑ Pedestal lamps and wobbly furniture
❑ Poisonous houseplants and wall air fresheners
❑ Toilet bowl and household cleaners
❑ Trashcans without lids
❑ Unused electrical outlets

Outdoor Hazards

Don't forget to check your garage and yard for any dangerous objects lying around. Check for and pick up or put away the following:

❑ Antifreeze and oil containers
❑ Blue-green pond algae
❑ Broken glass and sharp objects
❑ Cocoa mulch
❑ Compost piles
❑ Exposed wiring
❑ Pool and garden chemicals and supplies
❑ Rinds and seeds from falling fruits

❑ Slug and snail baits
❑ Small nails and screws

Your dog's safety also depends on having a safe place to exercise in. It's the one place where he can run around freely off-leash and be able to potty. If you have landscaping that you take special pride in, make sure the area is off limits to him. Make sure that your yard is fully fenced and that your gates are closed securely. Check the bottom of the fence and the gate for any holes or gaps that he may be able to slip through. Make sure the fence is tall enough that he can't jump over it.

Emotional Needs

Providing a safe and nurturing environment for your dog is vital to his health. When dogs lived in the wild, they remained with their pack and relied on the group for food and shelter. Today dogs are companion animals and they rely on their modern packs—their families—to give them the basics. This is the reason your dog has a strong need to interact with you. You are his pack. He's happiest when you give him attention and he's able to follow you around the house.

ALERT!

Dogs love to chew plants and flowers, but many are toxic. A few poisonous plants that you'd never suspect are lilies, sago palm, tulip and narcissus bulbs, azaleas, and oleander. The Department of Animal Science at Cornell University has a list of more than seventy-five poisonous plants with photographs at *www.ansci.cornell.edu/plants*. The ASPCA also maintains a list of plants toxic to dogs on their website, *www.aspca .org/pet-care/poison-control*.

Being left alone all day or abandoned in the yard for long periods is the worst thing for a dog, both emotionally and physically. When dogs are denied social interaction and physical exercise, they will develop behavioral problems such as digging, barking, aggression, or destructive chewing. Make sure your dog gets plenty of the right attention at home.

Reducing Stress

You're probably aware of the negative effect stress has on your own body. Compared to your responsibility-laden life, you might figure your dog must be totally relaxed. But as odd as it sounds, stress is a problem for dogs too.

Dogs feel stress over different things. Your dog may not know your schedule and may worry every time you leave the house. Try to maintain a regular schedule and take her for a walk before and/or after you get home to help both of you relax.

Take a few minutes when you get home to give her your total attention. Playing a few rounds of catch or grooming her for just a few minutes reassures her that she matters to you. If you're pressed for time and have to go on errands, take her along. She'll appreciate the opportunity to check out new surroundings and have a breath of fresh air.

Socializing Your Dog

One of the best things about having a dog is showing him off to your friends and family and sharing your favorite outdoor activities with him. Meeting new friends and exploring the world around him is great for your dog's physical and emotional health and provides a solid foundation for the rest of his life. Dogs that never leave the house or yard grow up distrustful of people and the sights and sounds outside their familiar environment because they don't know these things won't hurt them.

ALERT!

Stay away from grassy areas or the dog park, especially if you have a young dog. These places aren't the cleanest, as dogs defecate and urinate here and your pup is at risk for picking up all sorts of nasty things until her immune system fully kicks in. While she'll see other dogs, there's no guarantee that the encounters will be positive ones.

Hopefully your dog's breeder began the socialization process by handling him the day the litter was born and introducing the pups to normal household sounds and experiences. Once you take your dog home, it's your job to introduce him to new stimuli so he can continue building his confidence. When it comes to encountering new experiences, young dogs are open to accepting everything you expose them to. Good socialization will give your dog the chance to learn about other people and dogs in his environment.

Choosing the Best Age

Veterinarians suggest waiting to begin taking puppies outside their home environment until after they've had their vaccinations, beginning at nine weeks of age. From seven to twelve weeks, puppies are especially receptive to people and experiences and eagerly embrace all things new and exciting. After that age they're a little more wary and may need additional time to feel comfortable with anything they're not accustomed to seeing.

Deciding How Much to Do

Every puppy is different and has different needs. The behaviors your puppy exhibits will be a combination of nature and nurture. Since you can only influence the nurture part of the equation, it is best to use a gentle but consistent approach. Allow your puppy to socialize and expose him to new experiences several times a week, but try to avoid situations that are frightening or overwhelming. If he shows signs of nervousness, help him gain confidence by taking it slower next time and reassure him with treats and lots of praise. At the very least, take your dog out several times a week. You don't need to spend hours doing this. Frequent, short jaunts of ten to fifteen minutes work nicely as long as you choose different places to go.

Where to Go

A brief walk around the neighborhood is a good beginning, but don't limit your outings to this location. Open-air shopping centers are great places to encounter children and adults, noisy skateboarders and whirling bike riders, and enticing food smells. Many public places such as the dry cleaners, car wash, and even some banks and department stores heartily welcome well-behaved dogs coming to visit. Just remember not to overwhelm your dog with too many new experiences all at once.

What to Do

When you take your dog to a new place to socialize, always have him on a leash. Not only does this begin the leash training process, but walking on his own and not being carried helps build his confidence. (Your community also may require it by law.) Casually stroll around the area and take a few minutes to greet anyone who comes up to admire your dog. It helps to bring along some treats with you. If someone stops to pet your dog, ask if they would like to give your dog a treat. This way your dog will begin to associate a new face with a positive reward.

If your dog shies away from people by hiding behind your legs, shrinking down to the ground, or shaking, resist the urge to coddle your dog. It's best to just ignore his behavior. If you don't make a fuss over his reluctance, he'll realize he's not receiving any rewards for his insecurity. The more you take him out, the more he'll become accustomed to new people and experiences.

CHAPTER 3

Homeopathic Energy

3

You would think that a kinder, gentler remedy that's
been effective for 200 years would be an appreciated
option for health care. But when it comes to homeopathy, this wasn't always the case. This natural healing modality is actually the most misunderstood.
Although it was popular in Europe during the 1800s, it
never quite hit the mark with American medical doctors. It's possible that the definition of *homeopathy*—
"like cures like"—confused people, but fortunately
this has changed. Today more dog owners are redis-
covering this powerful way to heal their dogs.

What Is Homeopathy?

Homeopathy may seem like a mysterious form of medicine, but it's actually a very effective healing process. Practitioners and owners say that homeopathic remedies have helped their dogs heal from injuries, diseases, and stressful situations.

This treatment is effective and soothes separation and travel anxiety as well as fear of thunderstorms and loud noises. Trips to the veterinarian's office and the grooming salon are less intimidating with homeopathic remedies, especially when they are paired with behavioral conditioning. Homeopathy can also be used to treat:

- Allergies
- Chronic diseases and illness
- Inflammation
- Poisoning
- Respiratory and urinary tract infections
- Skin problems

Origin

The word *homeopathy* comes from the Greek root *homeo*, which means similar, and *pathos*, which means suffering or disease. Referred to as the law of similars or "like cures like," homeopathy certainly sounds vague at best and downright confusing at worst. Basically, homeopathy means that the very substance that produces signs of illness in a healthy dog can be used in small amounts to cure a sick dog. A trained homeopathic veterinarian matches the symptoms of the dog to the remedy.

Homeopathic remedies are diluted in stages to produce different strengths of the substance. Different strengths produce specific benefits without being toxic. They isolate any energy blockages that cause the illness and restore the balance. This relieves the symptoms and cures the problem.

Before prescribing any remedies, homeopathic practitioners evaluate the dog's total condition by looking at his emotional and physical state. When they choose a treatment, it is specific to each dog's needs. Owners who utilize this unique natural therapy see amazing results in their dogs.

History of Homeopathy

In Germany during the late 1700s, available medical treatments were harsh—purging, bloodletting, and blistering. Looking for a less threatening way to practice medicine, Samuel Hahnemann (1755–1843), a physician, chemist, and linguist, experimented with cinchona bark, which was used to cure malaria. Hahnemann was healthy, yet when he administered some of this to himself he developed symptoms of malaria.

FACT

Homeopathy was extremely popular in the late nineteenth and early twentieth centuries, with about 14,000 homeopathic practitioners and twenty-two homeopathic schools in the United States. But the trend was short-lived. The rise of modern traditional medicine, including antiseptic techniques, antibiotics, and anesthesia, attracted physicians' interest and the use of homeopathic practices declined.

This proved that a substance could cause the same symptoms it could also relieve—like cures like. Known to cause vomiting in a healthy person, it actually treats vomiting when taken in tiny homeopathic doses.

In other words, like cures like means that symptoms are the body's attempt to heal itself. For example, you develop a fever as an immune response to an infection, and coughing helps you avoid mucus buildup and congestion.

Current Homeopathy

Today homeopathy is making a comeback, and many European veterinarians have active homeopathic practices. Founded in 1982, the British Association of Homeopathic Veterinary Surgeons (BAHVS) supports veterinary homeopathy.

In the United States, Richard Pitcairn DVM, PhD, is responsible for advancing homeopathy. He leads training programs for veterinarians interested in learning more about this modality, and he is one of the founders of the Academy of Veterinary Homeopathy (AVH), a nonprofit professional organization.

E-QUESTION

What are the benefits of homeopathy?
Perfectly safe for dogs of all ages, homeopathic remedies have no side effects, are nonaddictive, and are relatively inexpensive. Available without a prescription, they are effective in treating both serious conditions and common first aid situations.

As a result, more American veterinarians are incorporating homeopathic techniques into their practices and there are more than 100 veterinarians in the Academy of Veterinary Homeopathy. Pitcairn's book *Natural Health for Dogs and Cats* is considered the bible of holistic medicine.

Basic Principles

There are many reasons to consider using homeopathy, including the following:

- Your dog's symptoms will be carefully observed before any treatment is given.
- Every treatment is individualized.
- Homeopathy is noninvasive and promotes your dog's capacity for self-healing.
- There are no side effects.
- When successful treatment is completed, symptoms do not return.

The primary principle of homeopathy is that an animating force exists within all living things—the divine spark or breath that is the difference between life and death.

The sustaining energy called the vital force maintains harmony and equilibrium in people and in animals. When this is fully functioning, the body is nourished and healthy. If it is off kilter, the homeopathic practitioner seeks to restore it.

In homeopathy, less is definitely more. Homeopathy asserts that the more diluted a remedy, the more powerful it is. Regardless of how many times a substance is diluted, it's still effective. Some remedies are so highly diluted that very little of the original substance is left.

ALERT!

When making a plant remedy, the best specimens of the species should be accurately identified and used. This ensures consistency. Plants should come from their natural environment, free from pesticides or artificial fertilizers. They should be harvested in the spring or summer when the part of the plant that is going to be used is at its peak.

Homeopathy treats the whole patient rather than the disease. Before the practitioner treats a patient, she evaluates all aspects of the patient's condition. This encompasses everything—the type and amount of food and exercise the dog gets, his sleep patterns, and what's happening in his environment. The reason for this screening is that two dogs with the same disease may be treated with different remedies.

How Homeopathic Medicines Are Made

Homeopathic remedies use very diluted substances used to stimulate and encourage the body's own reserves of recovery. These remedies themselves do not heal, but they help the body heal itself. While homeopathic remedies may look like conventional medicines on the surface, they are prepared differently and may take a little longer to effect change than traditional methods.

The Source

Seventy percent of homeopathic remedies have an herbal origin. The most effective remedies are derived from minerals, but plants and animal sources are also used. Whether these remedies are prepared using healing substances such as flowers, neutral substances such as table salt, or toxic materials such as arsenic, all are safe. Homeopathic medicines are very delicate and there is a very specific way to prepare them. If a plant or a part of plant is going to be used, it is washed before its juice is extracted and added to water.

Regardless of what source is used, no measurable amount remains after dilution. Only the life force that is responsible for the healing properties of the remedy remains.

Using Water and Alcohol

To make a remedy, the pharmacist dissolves a small amount of the original substance in water or alcohol. Although the ratio of substance to water and alcohol varies according to the condition of the substance, 90 percent pure alcohol and 10 percent distilled water is the usual ratio. The solution is left to dissolve for two to four weeks and is vigorously shaken a few times throughout that period. The resulting liquid, known as a mother tincture, is then strained.

FACT

In the nineteenth century, lighthouse keepers were hired to tend to some of the homeopathic potencies. The long lonely hours on the job watching over the light and the sea were ideal for performing the rhythmic and repeated motions of shaking and diluting the remedies.

This mother tincture is diluted again and more alcohol and water is added to produce different potencies of the remedy. Between each stage of dilution, the tinctures are shaken. The process is repeated a few more times until the desired dilution is achieved. This is called the potentized solution. It contains the tiniest amount of the original substance. The more the homeopathic remedy is diluted, the more effective it will be.

Shake It Up

The process of forceful vigorous shaking, or succussion, was originally done by hand. Today a machine does the job, but it can still take ten to twelve weeks to prepare a tincture with a high potency (the more diluted a tincture, the higher the potency).

Each succussion should come to a brief stop before continuing again. This allows the liquid to fall in the laboratory test tube via natural inertia. While machines handle this action, they need to be carefully regulated and regularly maintained to guarantee that the succussion is always the same.

Storing

Homeopathic remedies should be carefully stored and handled. If they are not, they lose their potency and are ineffective. The medicines should last indefinitely if you keep them in a cool, dry, and closed drawer or cabinet away from food, strong odors, or electronics.

If your dog has a chronic condition or if you're giving him a homeopathic remedy for the first time, schedule a consultation with your veterinarian or a trained homeopath before administering any medicine. She will evaluate your dog's personality and condition and prescribe the right treatment. Time and experience will teach you when these remedies are okay to use on your own.

Avoid placing them in extreme temperatures or near highly aromatic substances or electromagnetic radiation. Keep remedies out of the refrigerator because food smells can neutralize them. Don't store them near spices or windows either. Computers, televisions, and all other electronics have an energy field that can disrupt the remedy's chemistry.

Everyday Remedies

There's no shortage of homeopathic remedies to choose from. There are hundreds available and many are basic enough to give your dog for everyday conditions such as diarrhea or insect bites. None should be substituted for a visit to the veterinarian if a serious situation develops. Here are just a few basic homeopathic remedies:

- **Aconitum napellus (aconite or monkshood).** For shock or fever, uncontrollable fear, or panic. It also treats canine distemper, snake bites, infections, and eye injuries.
- **Apis mellifica (honeybee venom).** For allergic reactions from insect stings, inflammation, and fluid retention.
- **Arnica montana (leopard's bane).** For everyday first aid, especially when applied to strains and fractures.
- **Belladonna (deadly nightshade).** For fevers, ear infections, heat, and sunstroke. It's also effective against liver disease, eclampsia, canine distemper, and boils.
- **Calendula officinalis (marigold).** For healing wounds and cuts.
- **Camomilla (chamomile).** For soothing oral pain.
- **Nux vomica (poison nut).** For treating severe overstimulation of the nervous system that results in stomach aches, indigestion, constipation, and gastric upsets. It also treats bloat and pancreatitis.
- **Mercurius solubilis (mercury, quicksilver).** For treating gingivitis and mucousy diarrhea.
- **Rhus toxicodendron (poison ivy).** For treating skin eruptions, blistering, itching, rashes, and hives from poison ivy. It is also effective in alleviating the pain from sprains and strains.
- **Sulphur.** For skin conditions such as mange and allergic reactions. It is also used to treat coughing, infected ears, gas, and diarrhea.

Multitask Remedies

Many remedies are effective for several different conditions. That's the beauty of homeopathic medicine. The goal of a practitioner is to look up the ideal remedy from the *materia medica* in order to prevent further complications.

Works Alone

Homeopathy is not a complementary therapy. It's not designed to work with conventional medications or other holistic modalities, as these may offset the benefits of potency.

Picking the Potency

Homeopathic remedies have a wide range of potencies. At first glance the labeling can be confusing, but once you know what the letters and numbers mean it's easy to figure out the remedy's potency.

Potency Range

Potencies are labeled with a number and a letter—for example, Arnica 6X or Cantharis 30C. The number indicates how many dilutions the tincture has undergone. There are two main dilution scales: centesimal or C potencies and X potencies. The letter X is a Roman numeral and shows the proportions used in each dilution. The Roman numeral X signifies that the substance was diluted by a factor of 10 at each step, and the Roman numeral C signifies dilution by a factor of 100 at each step, along with the number of successions each solution undergoes.

E-QUESTION

What is a *materia medica*?
This is a collection of the effects of homeopathic medicines—a remedy reference guide. *Materia medica* is a Latin medical term for collected knowledge about therapeutic properties of healing substances. This differs from other medical guides in that it is organized by the remedy's name and description, instead of the illness.

Basically, the more dilutions and successions a substance undergoes, the higher the number on the label. The higher the number, the higher the potency and the more powerful and deeper acting it is.

A remedy labeled 3X means that one part of the substance was diluted in ten parts water; one part of the resulting substance was mixed in ten additional parts water, and finally, one part of that resulting substance was mixed in another ten parts water. A 6X strength signifies that the mother tincture was diluted in ten parts water six times. The common potencies are 6X, 3C, 6C, 12C, 30C, and 1M. (The Roman numeral M means one part mother tincture was diluted in 1,000 parts water.)

When a practitioner is deciding which potency to use, she will consider the strength of the dog and the severity of his illness. With a critical condition, she will opt for a remedy with a higher potency.

FACT

If a dog is weak or frail he will receive a remedy with a lower potency that is gentler on his system. Potencies 3X, 6X, or 12X are usually prescribed for older dogs or dogs with a mild injury or illness. Strong dogs or dogs with severe injuries or illnesses will receive high potency remedies, such as 200C or IM.

Considering the Potency

When your practitioner is choosing potency for your dog she will take several factors of your dog's condition into consideration. These will include:

- ❑ The dog's vulnerability
- ❑ The root of the illness (the dog's mental, emotional, and physical condition)
- ❑ The nature and intensity of the illness
- ❑ The duration of the illness
- ❑ The history of previous treatments
- ❑ The dog's age
- ❑ The dog's temperament
- ❑ The dog's daily routine
- ❑ The pathology of the illness

If the practitioner is not sure if the remedy selected is the right one for your dog and his illness or injury, she may start with a lower potency, such as 12X or 6C, and steadily increase it.

Using a Remedy

In the beginning you may not know what products to try, but a veterinary homeopath can advise you. He will match your dog's symptom with the appropriate remedy. In time you'll come to know the common ones.

Working with a Homeopathic Veterinarian

A homeopathic veterinarian will closely assess your dog's total condition and monitor the results. Your veterinarian should be certified by the Academy of Veterinary Homeopathy to insure that he is trained in using homeopathy to treat chronic illnesses and injuries. You should feel comfortable with your veterinarian and be confident that he knows how to treat your dog.

Homeopathic remedies are absorbed more quickly into the system if you give them to your dog an hour before or an hour after he has a meal. Don't mix a remedy into foods because they will neutralize it. Unlike traditional medications, homeopathic remedies shouldn't be swallowed, but rather dissolved in the mouth.

Although some veterinary homeopaths will discuss your dog's case over the telephone, it's best to meet with a veterinarian so he can see the dog for himself. However, if you don't live near a veterinarian who is trained in homeopathy, a phone call will have to do.

To choose the best prescription, your doctor will depend on you, as your dog's primary caregiver, to provide as much information about your dog's condition as you possibly can. You'll need to pay close attention to everything your dog does. Ask your doctor what information he needs exactly. Most likely he'll want you to observe every physical symptom your dog shows and how she acts. Be sure to jot down the time of day and how often you observe a behavior, such as every other day or once a week.

Take note of any conditions that improve or worsen the symptoms, such as changes in your dog's food, weather, and the presence of other dogs. Note whether she craves affection from you or prefers to be left alone. It helps if you can be as objective as possible. You might be tempted to interpret your dog's actions as signals that the homeopathic remedies are working, but your job is to write down what you see and let the veterinarian make the judgments. The more objective information your veterinarian has, the easier it is for him to evaluate your dog's treatment.

Buying a Remedy

Many veterinary homeopaths can supply you with the remedy you need, but if you need to buy them on your own, you can find most homeopathic remedies at any local well-stocked health food store. They typically come in two forms: liquid and small pellets or pills. The pellets are coated with a few drops of an alcohol stock solution.

Administering

There are three ways to administer a homeopathic remedy. Drop the pellets in his mouth, dissolve the liquid or the pellets in a small amount of distilled water, or grind them into a powder between two spoons and add to milk and let him lick it out of a bowl or pour into your dog's mouth. If you decide to pop a few into your dog's mouth, don't pour them directly into your hand as this may lessen their effectiveness. Instead, put them into the bottle cap, and then into the dog's mouth.

If you dissolve them in water, use an eyedropper or a spoon to give them to your dog. To give your dog either the liquid or the powder, gently pull his lower lip away from his teeth and place the eyedropper or pellets between the cheek and the gum. The remedy is absorbed in the mucous membranes and the healing energy works its way into the system.

Train your dog to allow you to touch his mouth. Start by petting him gently beneath his chin and around his face and lips for a few minutes each day. Progress to lifting the lip on one side of his mouth for just a brief minute and lower it. Be sure to tell your dog he's a good boy after each handling so he knows this is what you want him to do.

Unlike conventional drugs, homeopathic remedies are pleasant-tasting so you don't have to worry too much that your dog will spit them out. Fortunately, there are many homeopathic remedies that can be applied topically, such as arnica gel and calendula.

Doses

Dosing your dog with the correct frequency is even more important than finding the right potency. The frequency depends on the severity of her condition. If your dog has an acute problem, such as shock, infection, or high fever, she needs to see the veterinarian right away. Until you transport her to the doctor, you can give her a remedy every fifteen minutes to help her condition. Call your veterinarian and ask what the correct dosage is.

E-QUESTION

Does homeopathy really work?
Although there's no hard science that proves the effectiveness of homeopathic remedies, 200 years worth of clinical experience from practitioners and owner testimonials provides strong evidence of success.

With less serious cases, a dose once or twice a day should suffice. You should see some relief within a day. If not, it's possible you've chosen the wrong remedy and you'll need to re-evaluate your dog's symptoms, consult with your veterinarian, and pick another one.

If your dog has a chronic condition and a veterinarian has examined her, the recommended dose may be given once a day. You should see some relief within two to three days. For dogs that have been sick for several days, the signs of improvement may not be readily apparent. If, after four to five days, you don't notice any improvement, consult your veterinarian to see if you should increase the number of doses to twice a day.

Observe your dog's condition and if you still don't notice any improvement within three days, try a higher potency. If your dog's condition has not improved after a week, consult with your veterinarian. She will most likely recommend another remedy. If your dog improves, reduce the number of doses. Occasionally, the original symptoms may return. If so, one dose of the remedy should help the condition.

Signs of Healing

When you use a homeopathic remedy the results are a little different than what you may have experienced after giving your dog traditional medication.

Evaluating the Outcome

To detect clues to his overall condition, observe your dog carefully for subtle changes in his symptoms. Sometimes the symptoms continue even though your dog is actually improving. If the same symptoms persist and his condition is deteriorating it may mean he's been given the wrong remedy. Your veterinarian will be able to diagnose the different reactions.

After your veterinarian has recommended giving your dog a few doses and he still shows no improvement, the remedy may need to be changed. If the dog's condition returns after repeated doses, perhaps the remedy is keeping the condition under control but it isn't addressing the cause.

Here's where the experience of your homeopathic veterinarian is worth its weight in gold. She can evaluate the remedies and start the healing process all over again.

Physical Reactions

If your dog is acting his old happy self and has more energy and better eating and sleeping habits, you can deduce that the treatment you've given is successful. Don't be alarmed if your dog experiences an episode of diarrhea or vomiting; this may be your dog's normal healing process. His vital force is beginning the healing process by resisting the disease. However, persistent diarrhea and vomiting should be brought to the attention of your veterinarian.

CHAPTER 4

Your Holistic Health Practitioner

Sometimes it takes a village to keep a dog in top shape. As diligent as you are about caring for your canine companion, your veterinarian is a valuable partner in the process. Together you create a supportive, healing environment for your dog. When selecting a physician, you'll find different treatment philosophies, specializations, and office practices to choose from. Interview the vets as carefully as you would select your family doctor. When your dog goes in for his first visit he needs to like the veterinarian. You do too.

Choosing a Holistic Veterinarian

When it comes to picking a veterinarian, you may have many choices. At first glance they may all look alike, but ask a few questions about the services they offer and you'll discover some differences. There are conventional (also called Western), nonconventional (also called holistic), and complementary practices. Before you rush into making your first appointment, take some time to think about what kind of treatment you want your dog to have. Then narrow down the choices and choose a veterinarian whose medical philosophy agrees with your own.

Western Approaches

Conventional veterinarians are also known as traditional or Western veterinarians. They focus on treating the disease. They generally limit their practice to the forms of medicine you're probably already familiar with, such as drug therapy and yearly immunizations.

The traditional physician examines the dog and gathers information about his medical history and may use modern veterinary techniques to determine a diagnosis. These include blood and urine testing, X-rays, ultrasounds, cultures, and CT or MRI scans. Once the cause of the problem is identified, the conventional veterinarian will use traditional treatments such as medication or surgery to treat the patient. Some doctors won't consider using any natural therapies.

Eastern Approaches

A holistic veterinarian uses a nonconventional approach and will look carefully at the dog for signs of what might be wrong. When you take your dog to a holistic veterinarian, the appointment may take a little longer than what you've experienced in the past with a conventional doctor. The first visit can last an hour or so and the doctor will ask you a lot of questions about your dog's physical and emotional life and what the dog is like at home.

You are part of the problem-solving process, and you can help the doctor discover nuances in the dog's condition that may reveal what may be troubling your canine. The detailed consultations give the holistic veterinarian cues beyond prescribing medication. You might discuss training techniques or dietary changes, for example. It's all part of evaluating stresses that can cause imbalances in the body.

E-QUESTION

What is a naturopathic veterinarian?
The naturopathic veterinarian believes that nature isn't toxic and opts for herbal treatments over conventional drugs. While there are many advantages to using herbs, there are a few, such as ephedra, black walnut, and comfrey, which can be toxic in high dosages.

For this reason, it helps to keep a daily log of your observations of what your dog is doing so that you can provide your veterinarian with an accurate picture. Otherwise, it's easy for a busy owner to forget the small things that a dog does every day.

Complementary or Integrative Approach

Some veterinarians will describe their practice as complementary or integrative. These are just other terms for nonconventional medicine. The integrative or complementary veterinarian uses alternative therapies as an adjunct to traditional methods. These complement the standard treatment but do not replace it.

Your Choice

If you're wondering what kind of veterinarian to take your dog to, think optimum care. A good holistic veterinarian uses the best modalities available and often combines conventional with alternative treatments if they are helpful. With more dog owners expressing interest in natural health remedies for their dogs, it helps to have a veterinarian who is open-minded to using a wide range of therapies and whose treatment philosophy matches your own.

Choose a doctor who views your dog in his entirety and with the idea of disease prevention in mind. Your veterinarian shouldn't focus exclusively on the symptoms of a problem. Together you and your holistic doctor will devise a preventive treatment plan that will focus on your dog's total wellness.

Training for Holistic Vets

A good holistic veterinarian knows about Western science, attends one of the twenty-eight veterinary colleges or universities in the United States, and earns the same degrees as other veterinarians. With the exception of chiropractic and acupuncture methods, holistic medicine isn't taught at veterinary schools, although there's a growing emphasis on disease prevention programs.

FACT

More veterinary schools are acknowledging wellness. The American Holistic Veterinary Association sponsors Holistic Veterinary Medicine Clubs on veterinary school campuses. These student chapters provide opportunities for students to learn about acupuncture, homeopathy, medicinal herbs, chiropractic, nutritional therapy, and other complementary therapies. The AHVMA sponsors symposiums, organizes speakers, and helps students locate integrative/holistic practitioners who are willing to mentor students.

Following their traditional education, holistic veterinarians learn more about chiropractic, acupuncture, acupressure, massage, or herbs through holistic veterinary medicine programs or alongside other doctors who agree to mentor them.

Locating a Veterinarian

If you've moved to a different area, acquired a new dog, or think you want a second medical opinion, finding a veterinarian is a top priority. It's a good idea to select a doctor before your dog actually needs one. The last thing you want to do is have to find a veterinarian in an emergency. This will give you a chance to take your time and interview a few doctors that you think you and your dog will like.

Word of Mouth

If you bought a puppy from a local breeder, you may want to use the breeder's veterinarian. No doubt this doctor treated your pup when he administered the first set of vaccines and is familiar with your pup's other relatives and their health issues.

If you're too far away from this veterinarian, ask your breeder if she knows a good doctor in your community. Reputable breeders often have a large network of other breeders, and someone will more than likely know a good practitioner you can call.

If you've acquired your dog from an animal shelter or breed rescue, a coordinator may be able to recommend a doctor. Another option is to contact your local kennel or breed club. Members in these organizations are only too happy to refer a physician they trust. Groomers are another good source for veterinarian recommendations. They hear stories about them from their clients and will surely know which ones to call or avoid.

While you can probably open a phone directory and find listings for several veterinarians in your area, one of the best ways to find one is through a referral from someone who takes his dog to a veterinarian he likes. Don't overlook coworkers, friends with dogs, or other dog owners you meet while walking your dog or at a dog park. These people will be eager to share the names of doctors they like or dislike. Be specific with your questions and ask people why they like their veterinarian, how the physician handled a medical crisis if they've had one, and what they would improve about the doctor or the office.

Check out the Internet too. There are dog message boards where people extol the virtues of their veterinarians or warn others about practices they didn't like.

Veterinary Associations and Organizations

You can contact the following national veterinary associations for the names of holistic veterinarians or specialists in your area:

- American Holistic Veterinary Medicine Association (*www.ahvma.org*)
- International Veterinary Acupuncture Society (*www.ivas.org*)

- American Academy of Veterinary Acupuncture (*www.aava.org*)
- American Veterinary Chiropractic Association (*www.animalchiropractic.org*)
- Academy of Veterinary Homeopathy (*www.theavh.org*)
- Veterinary Institute of Integrative Medicine (*www.viim.org*)
- Veterinary Botanical Medicine Association (*www.vbma.org*)

In addition to providing names of veterinarians, these organizations are a valuable source of holistic medical information. Many of their websites have reference sections that define terms and procedures, and they keep member veterinarians informed about upcoming continuing education symposiums.

Vetting the Doctor

Once you've compiled a list of potential veterinarians, your next step is to choose one whose opinion you respect and with whom you feel an emotional connection. To narrow your choices, schedule a consultation appointment with every veterinarian you're interested in. Leave your dog at home so you can focus on your discussion without having to worry about what your dog is doing.

Expect to pay a fee for the veterinarian's time, but this is a wise investment. Meeting the doctor and chatting in a relaxed atmosphere gives you a chance to get to know her and to ask questions about her background and treatment philosophy.

Questions to Ask

You may know you like a doctor from the moment you shake hands. If not, here are a few questions you can ask that will help you break the ice and narrow your choices.

- **Why did you want to become a veterinarian?** The doctor's passion for animals should be readily apparent.
- **What are your veterinary credentials?** This is a good way to find out if your veterinarian has a specialty.

- **How long have you practiced veterinary medicine?** A doctor with a few years of experience is more likely to know the latest treatments and procedures. A doctor who's been in practice for a few decades may not be as familiar with the most recent developments but will have a firm background in veterinary medicine.
- **Do you attend veterinary conferences throughout the year?** This lets you know that your veterinarian learns about the newest advances in veterinary medicine and networks with other veterinarians about unusual cases.
- **What diagnostic equipment do you use?** The office should have an ultrasound and X-ray machine, and the veterinarian should use conventional methods, such as surgery, pharmaceutical drugs, and blood tests, to help diagnose and monitor your dog's condition.
- **What do you think about using pharmaceutical drugs when treating a problem?** Medications should be limited to cases that are not helped by natural therapies or at least consistently monitored for possible side effects that may occur.
- **What modalities do you use to treat chronic diseases?** The veterinarian should feel comfortable using conventional medications if they are necessary, as well as a range of natural treatments.
- **What kind of food do you recommend?** The veterinarian should emphasize your dog's health requirements and a natural diet without animal and plant byproducts with as few chemicals and artificial ingredients as possible.
- **Who monitors the dogs after surgery, and who is in charge of the hospital facility?** Your veterinarian's office should have qualified veterinary technicians and ideally one or more doctors who supervise this area.
- **Are you or another veterinarian in the office on call for emergencies?** If your dog ever needs to be rushed to the veterinarian, you need to know who will take care of him.

Attributes to Consider

Besides having all the right answers to your questions and keeping up with the latest developments in the veterinary field, you'll want to choose a veterinarian you like. This physician should be easy to talk to and doesn't rush through his explanations or use a lot of medical jargon you may not understand.

He's kind, patient, and willing to listen to your concerns, and is responsive to all of your inquiries. You should feel comfortable asking him anything. Although most veterinarians are usually very busy, you should never feel rushed through your appointment time.

Your veterinarian's office and personnel is important too. The staff should be friendly, helpful, and seem to genuinely like being around dogs. The facility should be clean.

Your Dog's First Examination

The day you bring your new puppy or dog home is an exciting one, but plan on taking her to see the veterinarian within seventy-two hours. You want to know that your dog is healthy and the physician can identify health defects and any medical problems that you might not have noticed when you picked up your dog.

If you have a puppy, carry her in and out of the veterinarian's office either in your arms or in a crate. Her immunity isn't fully established yet and you don't want your puppy to come in contact with something from another dog.

Be sure to schedule your initial visit when you have plenty of time and don't have to leave early to do something else. Your first holistic veterinary appointment is going to take longer than what you might expect— often more than an hour. If time is a consideration, call ahead to ask the receptionist to estimate about how long you might have to wait for the doctor and plan accordingly.

What to Bring

A puppy should be carried or in a crate when you visit the veterinarian. An adult dog must be on a leash when you enter the veterinarian's office. Other dogs in the waiting room may not be very friendly and you can keep your dog away from trouble by containing your pup or controlling the leash.

It's normal for your dog to be frightened in the doctor's office. There are new sights and smells he's unaccustomed to experiencing. Just don't coddle him and tell him, "It's okay!" This just affirms your dog's fears. A better thing to do is to ignore his behavior and stay calm yourself. Your dog will pick up on your cues and relax.

You probably have saved up a list of questions or issues to discuss with your veterinarian about your new dog's health or behavior. If you didn't talk about vaccines with your veterinarian during your initial interview, now's the time to discuss her views. Remember that no question is off limits! This is your time to have everything explained.

Be sure to bring along your dog's health record, including a list of any medications he is currently taking. Your veterinarian should know about any prior vaccines and dewormings.

Let your vet know what kind of food your dog is eating. If you're feeding him a commercial diet be sure to give her the name of the brand and its ingredients.

A few hours before you leave for the vet's office, collect a small stool sample from your dog and place it in a plastic bag or a small disposable food container with a lid. Bring it with you to your appointment. To make sure that it's not accidentally mixed up with another dog's at the office, write your name on the bag or container. Your veterinarian will check the stool for the presence of internal parasites.

The Exam

When the doctor enters the exam room he'll greet your dog and begin establishing a relationship with her right away. Gaining your dog's trust enables him to examine her without causing a fearful or stressed reaction in the dog.

E-QUESTION

How do you collect a stool sample?
It should be fresh, so collect it soon after your dog leaves it. Wrap a new plastic bag around your hand or use a small clean shovel to pick up a tablespoon of your dog's stool. You don't need to take all of it. Keep it chilled until you leave.

Your veterinarian will take a detailed history of your dog and will want to know everything about her day-to-day activities—how much and where she sleeps, what she eats, how much physical activity she has, and any behavior issues. Your observations help the veterinarian assess your dog's condition, so don't leave out any details. Most veterinarians, however, can take one look at their patients and know right away if something isn't quite right.The physical examination includes checking your dog's:

- **Weight.** This establishes a baseline as your puppy grows and continues to gain weight and makes sure she doesn't get too heavy.
- **Temperature.** A dog's normal body temperature ranges from 100°F–102.5°F.
- **Eyes.** While some breeds have more eye problems than others, your dog's eyes should be checked for signs of glaucoma, cataracts, cloudiness of the lens, and discoloration, discharge, or swelling.
- **Ears.** The inside should not be red or have an odor or discharge, and your dog should not be scratching her ears or shaking her head, which may indicate an ear infection.
- **Mouth.** Teeth are not impacted, gums are a healthy pink, and there are no unusual sores.

- **Skin and coat.** Feel the body for any growths, abnormalities, unusual spots, or hair loss.
- **Heart and lungs.** The heart rate should be normal without any murmurs, which may be a sign of heart disease, and there is normal and unobstructed airflow through the lungs.
- **Anal area.** There should be no obstruction or infection.

If you have a puppy who is nine weeks of age or older who has not already been vaccinated, your veterinarian will administer distemper and parvovirus vaccines. More information about vaccines is found in Chapter 9.

The veterinarian may also want to take blood and urine samples to detect any problems in the kidneys, liver, pancreas, and thyroid gland. This diagnostic testing is especially important as your dog gets older.

When Emergency Strikes

Hopefully your dog will never have a traumatic injury, but if he does it helps to know what to do and where to go. When you're choosing a veterinarian, ask if the office is open after hours for emergencies. If not, ask the doctor to recommend an emergency clinic near your home. Keep the phone number and address of the facility where you can quickly locate it. Be sure to visit the facility before your dog actually needs to go there.

To find an emergency facility nearby, contact the American College of Veterinary Emergency and Critical Care (*www.acvecc.org*). This organization provides specialized emergency training for veterinarians and maintains a list of veterinarians who are specialists in emergency and critical care treatment. The clinic you select should have a fully staffed emergency room and an intensive care unit with a life support team.

Choose an emergency clinic as carefully as you would your primary care veterinarian. Meet the doctor and office staff and make sure this is a place that you would want to take your dog if you had to.

Ask about fees. After-hours emergency veterinary care is often very expensive—sometimes double or triple the cost of what daytime services might be. You should never sacrifice your dog's health for a few extra dollars, but sometimes it helps to weigh the nature of the emergency against the cost of the services. You don't want to take your dog to the doctor at midnight and pay extra fees if the problem can wait until normal operating hours. If you're ever in doubt whether or not to take your dog to the veterinarian, call the office and ask.

Spaying and Neutering

Healthy dogs have no problem conceiving. If left to themselves, they will constantly reproduce. Therefore, it's up to you to leave breeding to those dedicated individuals who responsibly breed quality purebred dogs on a limited basis. Many of these breeders spend years studying pedigrees and the hereditary issues in their breed and consistently work on improving the health and temperament of their stock to preserve the breed for future generations.

FACT

When females are spayed before their first heat cycle, their chances of developing mammary cancer, ovarian cysts, or uterine infections are minimal. If your dog goes through more than two heat cycles there's a 25 percent chance she will develop mammary cancer. Males who are neutered do not develop testicular cancer and there's less chance for prostate enlargement and tumors of the glands around the anus.

If you're not breeding for this purpose, it's up to you to prevent your dog from breeding and adding to the canine overpopulation problem. Animal shelters in the United States are overcrowded and there are not enough homes for all of the unwanted puppies and dogs. As a result, millions of healthy dogs are euthanized each year.

Dog Breeding 101

A female is receptive to a male's sexual advances and can conceive only during a few days in her heat cycle (estrus). This occurs once every six to nine months and lasts about twenty-one days. Male dogs are strongly attracted to females when they are in estrus and will go to extraordinary lengths to breed a female.

Once bred, a female will deliver a litter of puppies about sixty-three days later. Depending upon the female's breed and size, there could be as few as one or two pups or as many as ten or twelve in a litter. If you're the breeder, just imagine what it must be like to help take care of so many pups and then try to find homes for them!

If every owner spayed or neutered their dogs, fewer would need homes. When a female is spayed, her ovaries and uterus are removed, which eliminates her heat cycles and prevents pregnancy. When a male is neutered or castrated, his testes are removed, leaving the scrotum or sac. This prevents sperm production, and renders the male sterile.

The Surgery

Spaying, or ovario-hysterectomy, of the female and neutering of the male requires surgery under general anesthesia. Before performing the procedure your veterinarian will want to know that your dog is healthy. This can be determined with a simple blood chemistry panel. This provides information that the kidneys, liver, muscles, glandular, and digestive functions are normal.

The surgery can be performed when a puppy is as young as six weeks of age, although many veterinarians prefer to wait until the puppy just reaches puberty at about five or six months of age. With the help of improved monitoring equipment, anesthesia is much safer than it once was.

The recovery time is quick, and many dogs are up and about the same day or the next, although they will need to recuperate to facilitate the healing process. You will need to restrict their activity for a few days and keep them confined to a crate or a separate room away from other dogs and any roughhousing.

Following the surgery your dog will need to wear a large protective collar that prohibits him from biting, licking, and scratching the stitches as they begin to heal. One collar type is a large, plastic, cone-shaped model known as an Elizabethan collar, which most dogs hate.

ALERT!

Some veterinarians recommend that dogs spend the night of the surgery in the hospital. For the first twelve to twenty-four hours, any little movement causes pain and swelling. To reduce discomfort the dog's activities should be restricted. Many dogs have an easier time healing if their pain is managed and they can rest.

An inflatable collar design is just as effective and dogs seem to tolerate it much better. It has a canvas-lined outer jacket that is scratch- and bite-resistant and is adjustable with a Velcro strap. When the stitches come off, the collar can come off too.

Benefits

Besides avoiding pregnancy, there are other good reasons to spay and neuter your dog. For one thing, it's healthier. Females are less likely to develop cancer, cysts, and infections, and males have a reduced chance of developing cancer, tumors, and enlarged prostates. Neutering also reduces the male's urge to go roaming in search of female dogs and lessens aggression toward other dogs. Some people claim that their dogs—both males and females—are a lot calmer after spaying or neutering, but others hardly notice any difference.

Side Effects

Many owners complain that after spaying or neutering, their dogs tend to gain a lot of weight and become more lethargic. Removing reproductive organs does affect the body by slowing metabolism by about 15 percent, but this can be managed.

Increasing your dog's exercise with daily walks or runs—even chasing a ball—revs up the metabolism. Being more active also helps alleviate your dog's boredom and prevents destructive behavior. To prevent obesity, cut down on the amount you feed your dog and limit the number of treats you give throughout the day.

Another side effect is a small amount of sporadic urinary incontinence in some large breed females. The chances of this happening can be reduced if you keep your dog at a healthy weight and provide daily exercise; good muscle tone exerts less pressure on the bladder. Dogs should be given unlimited opportunity to empty their bladders throughout the day and evening so there's less chance of leakage later on.

CHAPTER 5

Natural Healing

Developed thousands of years ago in China, Eastern medicine has withstood the test of time. The practice includes a wide range of holistic treatments that take the patient's body, mind, and spirit into consideration, and it is effective in treating many canine ailments. Qi or chi (pronounced "chee"), the energy in your dog's system, is the life force within it. A holistic veterinarian who uses traditional Chinese medicine to treat your dog assesses his qi with a combination of acupuncture, acupressure, massage, and herbs.

Traditional Chinese Medicine (TCM)

It takes two texts of eighty-one chapters apiece to explain the full theoretical foundation of Chinese medicine. *The Inner Canon of the Yellow Emperor* from China dates to the first century B.C.E. It is a question and answer discussion between the mythical Yellow Emperor and his advisors concerning methods of diagnosis and treatment methods.

Traditional Chinese medicine can be used with Western medicine. For some diseases, using Chinese herbal medicine, acupuncture, dietary changes, drugs, and/or surgery in addition to Western treatments will achieve a far better outcome than if only one modality is used.

According to this ancient belief, diet, lifestyle, emotions, environment, age, and heredity are responsible for illness and disease. It's no wonder that many Western physicians today believe the same factors are behind numerous ailments, and that prevention is half the cure.

Traditional Chinese medicine has layers of concepts and metaphors and can be somewhat confusing to new students. It takes practitioners years to study and fully understand it, but the results are rewarding.

Qi

The theory behind traditional Chinese medicine is that the body—and the greater universe—consists of a life force. This animating energy flows in an orderly fashion and is known as qi. Qi flows throughout the world and within individuals and TCM works to balance this energy flow to create harmony.

Good health depends upon this balance. Disease results when there is a disturbance in the flow. Imagine the qi as following a path that winds gently up a mountain and around trees, caves, and creeks. When a large boulder falls on the path, no one can continue along the route.

Meridians

Qi courses through the body through channels, or meridians. Each meridian corresponds to a different part of the body, but they are all interconnected. A blockage or disruption in one meridian can have an effect in a distant meridian. Each meridian has both yin and yang energy.

There are seven yang meridians that flow along the top and outer sides of the body and extremities:

- Stomach
- Large intestine
- Urinary bladder
- Gall bladder
- Small intestine
- Triple heater channel. This meridian begins at the tip of the toe and ends at the outside edge of the eyebrow.
- Governing vessel. This meridian runs along the back midline.

There are seven yin meridians coursing through the underside, inner thighs, and forelegs of the body:

- Spleen
- Lung
- Kidney
- Liver
- Heart
- Pericardium
- Conception vessel. This meridian travels the full length of the dog's body.

Yin and Yang

The yin and yang are polar opposites that are dependent upon one another. Yin qualities are expressed as soft, calm, substantial, cold, conserving, and tranquil female energy. Yang qualities are expressed as hot, fire, hard, dry, restless, and active male energy. Yin is water and the moon, while yang is fire and the sun. Never static, the yin and yang are constantly shifting within the body, both within a meridian and within an organ. When a holistic veterinarian assesses your dog's condition, she locates and adjusts any imbalances of yin and yang.

Five Elements Theory

According to traditional Chinese medicine, there are five different elements in the world of nature. Each has its own properties, yet all are related. The five elements theory is a methodology in TCM that is used to interpret the relationship between the natural environment and the body's physiology and pathology. It correlates the organs in the body and the meridians that course through them with the five elements of nature—metal, water, wood, fire, and earth. These correlations explain the relationships of the various organs to one another.

The Power of Acupuncture

Overall, acupuncture helps the body heal itself by rebalancing energy and correcting the flow of energy. This ancient technique uses stimulation of specific points on the body, namely the acupuncture points on the meridians, to relieve pain and muscle spasms, increase circulation, and release neurotransmitters and neurohormones. Acupuncture is useful as a primary or a backup therapy for arthritis, spinal injury, hip dysplasia, digestive disorders, epilepsy, kidney and liver disease, allergies, heart problems, and respiratory problems.

Preparing for Acupuncture

If you or your veterinarian is contemplating acupuncture treatment on your dog, your veterinarian will perform a complete physical examination first. Expect to provide information on your dog's dietary history, his level of activity, how much and what kind of exercise he receives, and where he spends his time at night and during the day. The veterinarian will ask about your dog's history of allergies and any major surgeries, illnesses, or traumatic incidents.

How Acupuncture Works

To perform acupuncture, the practitioner inserts thin, pliable steril-ized stainless steel needles at specific points on the surface of the body. These points allow access to the energy channels of the body. The needle increases or decreases the energy flow where the practitioner places it, bal-ancing the qi. The needles slide into the tissue very easily and smoothly and it's usually a painless process.

Depending on the condition your dog is being treated for and the method used, acupuncture treatments may last from 10 seconds to 30 minutes one to three times a week. Typical acupuncture treatment is once a week for four to six weeks. Follow-up maintenance therapy is once every two to six months, although some dogs never need acupuncture again after their condition is resolved.

Most dogs seem surprised at first by the strange objects penetrating their skin, but they usually relax once the needles are in place. Some dogs are so comfortable that they even fall asleep during the treatment. Others appear restless and it may take a few treatments before they become comfortable enough to relax during the process.

Acupuncture is very safe and has few side effects. If a dog is particularly weak, the practitioner will limit the number of acupuncture points for the first few sessions and wait to add additional points when the dog is stronger.

Types of Acupuncture

The practitioner chooses from several types of acupuncture depending upon the dog's condition:

- **Electroacupuncture.** For dogs in severe pain, an electric current is sent through acupuncture needles to provide extra stimulation.
- **Laser acupuncture.** For borderline aggressive dogs or for very sensi-tive dogs, infrared lasers are used to stimulate pressure points.

- **Aquapuncture.** For dogs that won't tolerate traditional acupuncture, a saline solution of vitamin B_{12} and distilled water is inserted at a meridian and used to stimulate the area.
- **Moxibustion.** For some dogs with intervertebral disc disease or any condition that requires warming or improved circulation, the herb mugwort is burned over acupuncture points to stimulate the area and increase circulation through the meridians.
- **Sonapuncture.** For all dogs, this uses ultrasound to stimulate the acu-points in areas that are too difficult for needles to reach.

Expectations

The earlier your dog's disease is diagnosed and he receives acupuncture, the better the response will be. If you're anticipating a miraculous cure for your dog after he receives the first acupuncture treatment, you should probably readjust your thinking. Acupuncture is not a cure-all and may not be the answer to some diseases. Several treatments are usually necessary to achieve the desired result. Be aware too that because acupuncture decreases pain, your dog will feel better after a treatment and may overuse his injured limb and possibly reinjure it.

Acupuncture and Cancer

If your pet has had cancer or is currently battling it, your acupuncturist will want to know that too. Care should be taken when choosing to treat cancer with acupuncture. With some dogs, improving the blood flow and flow of energy in the body may help the cancer grow instead of reducing it. You and your veterinarian should discuss the options and decide whether or not to proceed with the acupuncture treatment as part of the cancer treatment.

For other dogs with cancer, acupuncture has been known to relieve the pain, nausea, and diarrhea that often accompany radiation and chemotherapy treatments. Acupuncture may help balance the energy flow throughout the body and direct the healing system to fight the tumor. It reduces muscle spasms without drugs, but if it does not provide relief after five treatments, you and your vet should discuss whether it is time to discontinue it.

Your veterinarian will also want to know about any physical changes your dog has during or after all of her acupuncture treatments.

Acupressure

Acupressure is a variation of acupuncture. It uses touch—your fingers instead of needles—to balance the energy system and activate the acupuncture points. A very safe procedure, this user-friendly technique is something you can learn how to do for your dog in your own home.

Once you become proficient in the basic technique, you can use acupressure to support healing, reduce muscles spasms, strengthen your dog's immune system, and relieve his joint pain. Located along meridians, each pressure point treats a different condition. These points are the same as those used in acupuncture.

Massage

You don't need to take your dog to a fancy spa for him to enjoy a relaxing massage. You can do it for him in your own home. By physically manipulating the soft tissues of your dog's body, you relieve muscle tension and increase circulation. Think of it as upgrading your everyday petting to a therapeutic technique.

ALERT!

Be careful not to massage over an open wound, area of infection, insect bite, or incision. Avoid swollen areas. Skip the procedure if your dog has a fever, is seriously ill, or has cancer. Applying pressure to these areas may worsen the condition.

Other than just plain pampering, massage helps the flow of the lymphatic system that removes waste products and toxins. For dogs with arthritis, regular massages can ease joint pain, but they can also be used to help recovery after an injury or just to promote relaxation.

Assuming he is healthy, giving your dog a massage has many benefits. If you have a puppy, massage will help him accept your touch during his early socialization period. When it comes time to groom your dog he'll be very comfortable with you or a groomer handling him during brushing and bathing, and especially when touching his feet.

During massage you may detect a health problem, such as a tumor, swollen area, or a cut in early stages, and will be able to obtain treatment for your dog before it worsens. Massage is a wonderful thing to do when you need to calm your overactive dog, and it relieves environmental stress from a move or a boarding situation. Best of all, you're building a loving bond between you and your dog that will last a lifetime.

Massage Techniques

Massage techniques vary, depending upon the system you want to affect. Here are some different ways to massage your dog:

- **Connective.** Medium to full depth and pressure moves that gently push into connective tissue.
- **Effleurage.** Light, gliding strokes target the nervous system. Strokes toward the heart promote blood flow, while strokes away from the heart are calming.
- **Petrissage.** Gently kneading or compressing the tissue, which increases circulation and supplies nutrients and oxygen to the muscle while decreasing overall tension.
- **Skin lifting.** Using fingers and thumb to lift a fold of the skin and release to help increase circulation over sore joints.
- **Stretching.** Gently bending an extremity or joint to improve range of motion in joints and muscles prior to exercise.
- **Tapotement.** Drumming or patting strokes, with fingertips or with cupped hands to tone muscle and tissues and increase blood flow to the area.
- **Vibration.** Used with an electric hand massager that delivers high frequency waves to the deep tissue levels to aid relaxation.

Massage How-To's

If you know how to pet your dog, you can learn how to give him a massage. To begin, choose a quiet room of the house where you won't be disturbed by others, and have your dog lie on a soft, firm surface such as a couch, bed, or rug. Small dogs can fit on your lap. You might want to dim the lights and play some soothing music to relax both of you. Realize that your dog is not going to understand at first what you're trying to do, so take it slow and allow plenty of time so you don't feel rushed.

Sit alongside your dog facing the same way he is positioned so he doesn't feel intimidated by your standing or leaning over him. Be sure to talk to him in a soothing voice. This helps both of you to relax.

Using both of your palms, begin with soft, slow strokes along the length of his muscles from head to tail. Work from the end of the extremities toward the body. Keep your touch light and gentle so your dog will relax. Scratch gently behind his ears and move to his face, chin, muzzle, and top of his head. Gently rub each ear.

With three fingers, progress to slow, small strokes in a circular motion over the neck, shoulders, and chest. Continue with the front and back of the legs, going from top to bottom and then reversing the direction. If at any time your dog wants to run out of the room, it means you're pressing too hard, so ease up on your touch. There should be no question in your mind that your dog is thoroughly enjoying this experience and will probably want more after you're done.

Going to a Massage Therapist

If you prefer to take your dog to a professional canine massage therapist, make sure the therapist has expert massage training and is comfortable around dogs. It helps if the professional is also licensed for human massage because this indicates an understanding that canine massage is a serious matter not to be taken lightly.

To locate a qualified massage therapist, ask your veterinarian, groomer, or other dog owners for people they recommend. The therapist should ask you questions about your dog's condition before beginning any treatment. You should give the therapist information about any recent injuries, past surgeries, and medical treatments. Your veterinarian should provide a written description of your dog's condition to aid the therapist in choosing the appropriate treatment.

When interviewing therapists, ask about their level of experience with massage techniques and with dogs, where they received their training, and how much training they've had. Do some homework and ask your veterinarian what the right answers should be. You want to feel secure with the professional you select, but more importantly, your dog should also like the person you choose.

Tellington Touch

When animal expert Linda Tellington-Jones began working with problem horses in the 1970s, she had no idea that it would spark a whole new natural health movement. Tellington-Jones incorporates physical exercises, body manipulations, and various light touches to improve behavior and health.

E-QUESTION

What undesirable canine behaviors does TTouch help alleviate?
TTouch practitioners claim it discourages dogs from excessive barking and chewing, leash pulling, jumping, and resistance to grooming. It is also an effective treatment for aggressive behavior, extreme fear and shyness, excitability and nervousness, car sickness, and problems associated with aging.

Today there are Tellington TTouch training workshops, seminars, books, and DVDs that teach people how to perform the basic principles of her method. To become certified in TTouch, practitioners must train for two years and work with different companion animals in both shelter and show performance situations, and help animals post-surgery.

Theory of TTouch

TTouch uses a method of circular touches to enhance traditional animal training, healing, and communication. Although TTouch practitioners use their hands to stroke and lift parts of the body, this technique differs from traditional massage methods that relax muscles. Instead, TTouch works at the cellular level to increase a dog's awareness and enhance his ability to learn and focus by only manipulating the skin. Another bonus of this body-work program is that it strengthens the bond between dog and owner.

Different Strokes

Exact but light, TTouch uses specific strokes in a circular pattern to achieve different results, with variations depending upon the stroke speed and the amount of pressure being applied. There are more than twenty different types of TTouches and many have animal names to trigger an image that's easy to learn and remember.

The basic clouded leopard TTouches are named after a clouded leopard in the Los Angeles Zoo. They use the finger pads to develop awareness of the whole body and release fear. The cloud part of the name describes how lightly the hand touches the dog's body, while the leopard explains the variation in finger pressure.

An eleven-foot-long Burmese python at the San Diego Zoo named Joyce was the inspiration for the python lift. Used to relieve and release tension and spasm, this TTouch helps the shoulder, legs, neck, and back. It restores mental and emotional stability and improves balance.

Aromatherapy

Aromatherapy uses essential oils to treat the body, mind, and spirit. These oils are liquids distilled through steam or water from the fragrant parts of a plant—the leaves, stems, flowers, bark, and roots. Highly concentrated, they contain the essence of the original plant. It takes more than a ton of plant material to produce some of these oils. Peppermint leaves yield only 1 percent volatile peppermint oil.

Essential oils are not new. Appearing in hieroglyphs, frankincense and myrrh are also mentioned in the Bible and have been around for 5,000 years. The Egyptians were the first to incorporate them in religion, cosmetics, and medicine, and Hippocrates used aromatherapy massage as a treatment.

How Aromatherapy Helps

Essential oils are antiviral, antibacterial, and antifungal. They work to create balance, and they stimulate and boost the immune system. The aroma provides valuable psychological and physical therapeutic benefits. Dog owners who use aromatherapy claim their dogs remain flea and tick free without the use of chemical insecticides, flea shampoos, or bug bombs. Most say their dogs remain calm under stressful conditions, have sweet-smelling, healthy-looking coats, and rarely become car sick.

How to Use Aromatherapy

Essential oils are diffused in the air and heal through the sinuses. You can orally administer a few oils, namely peppermint, to safely soothe nausea and travel sickness. Others, such as lavender, can be used to treat ringworm, parasites, vomiting, and pain. Eucalyptus treats respiratory symptoms, including pneumonia, and discourages insects and surface parasites. Rosemary is helpful for sprains, arthritis, burns, and cancer. Try tea tree for itching, insect bites and stings, pneumonia, and skin irritations. Other oils can be placed behind the neck or ears to prevent the oils from being ingested.

While practitioners mix multiple drops of a carrier oil such as almond oil to one drop of essential oil, you can buy a quantity that is premixed. You'll find many combinations of oils available through veterinary vendors. Check with your veterinarian to determine which oils are safe for your dog and how much to apply. Be sure to keep the essential oil away from your dog's eyes or mucous membranes.

ALERT!

Use essential oils with caution. Some are very potent and others are toxic to animals. Not all dogs will benefit from every substance and some dogs may have an adverse reaction to an oil. Many practitioners recommend diluting the oil with a carrier oil, which is pressed from seeds, nuts, or kernels and isn't as strong as the essential oil.

Flower Essences and Herbs

Flower power is a natural remedy that deals with your dog's emotional and behavioral issues. Flower essences are dilute extracts of the blossoms of various plants and flowers. When diluted, they are more effective than the flower itself. These essences interact at the dog's cellular level and help balance his emotions and restore a feeling of comfort and calm. Dog owners and holistic veterinarians who use this healing therapy claim that it solves a range of behavioral problems, including insecurity and separation anxiety, and reduces stress.

To commercially prepare flower essences, mature buds or flowers are harvested from the field during the summer, placed in water, and heated either in the sun or by boiling. The flower's intensity dissipates in the liquid and is infused with alcohol (usually brandy) as a preservative. The remedy can be diluted again with water.

Bach Essences

In the early nineteenth century, an English homeopathic physician specializing in bacteriology and pathology named Edward Bach developed the system of using flowers to treat patients. He believed that natural remedies were superior to chemical products and that they could improve specific mental states and emotions.

Experimenting on himself, he tested thirty-eight native English plants to determine their effectiveness. Bach divided these into seven groups based on the emotions they could treat: fear, uncertainty, insufficient interest in present circumstances, loneliness, over-sensitivity to influences and ideas, despondency or despair, and over-care for the welfare of others. For example, aspen helps with vague and unexplained fear, wild oat deals with uncertainty, and walnut gives consistency and protection from outside influences. Today the Bach Flower Essences are found in health food stores and sold worldwide.

Giving Essences

When choosing an essence for your dog, observe his emotions and match them with a description of the essence. You can also consult with a qualified flower essence practitioner to help you select one. When you administer an essence, don't expect an immediate result. It may take six to eight weeks before you'll notice any changes in your dog.

E-QUESTION

What is Rescue Remedy?
A combination of rock rose, star of Bethlehem, impatiens, cherry plum, and clematis, this is a very popular flower combination. It's used to ease stress and can help dogs that fear loud noises or going to the veterinarian. Add four drops in food or rub on the nose, ear, or paw.

To test which remedies work the best, give one essence at a time and observe the difference in your dog's behavior before trying another. It's best to give more frequent doses over a longer period of time. For example, give a few drops three times a day for several weeks. There are several ways to administer a flower essence. You can apply some directly to the mouth, nose, lips, or paw pads. Others must be introduced directly to drinking water. For some, you must prepare a treatment spray bottle. Each essence comes with directions for use.

Besides the Bach Flower Essences, there are other companies that create and market the essences of native plants in Australia, the United Kingdom, and the United States.

Side Effects

Essences are nontoxic and perfectly safe. The only downside to administering flower essences to your dog is the chance that they may not work. You don't need any special training to give your dog flower essences—just love and appreciation for your dog and a desire to help him live a happy and healthy life.

How Herbs Help

Dogs discovered the strong healing power of herbs long before holistic researchers did. When your dog has an upset stomach, she will try to ease the discomfort by finding and eating a bit of greenery.

While you may not want her to vomit the plant matter back up, that's exactly what she's trying to do. The selection practice even has a scientific name. When animals choose to ingest plants, soils, and insects to maintain their health, this is known as zoopharmacognosy.

Herbs in any form, whether dried, fresh, pounded into a cream, or diluted into a tincture, are nature's pharmacy.

Using Herbs

At one time or another you've probably applied some cooling aloe vera to your hands to heal a minor burn. This herb works just as well on canines, especially if your dog has a lick granuloma or an insect bite. A 100% aloe vera gel from a health food store is very effective. The pure aloe vera gel isn't harmful to dogs if they lick it off.

Herbs can remove toxins from the body and improve the immune system. They can often be used instead of drugs. People and animals have used medicinal herbs for healing for thousands of years.

Precautions

While herbs may seem harmless because they're natural, not all are medicinally or nutritionally beneficial. Some can have powerful side effects and others, such as pennyroyal oil and comfrey, may even be toxic.

Herbs may be used alone or to support and complement other treatments. Consult with your veterinarian or a professional herbalist to be sure that you're not giving your dog any herbs that are toxic.

CHAPTER 6

The Right Nutrition

Forget walks, joyrides, and chasing the ball. If you were to ask your dog what his favorite activity is, paws down it would be chowtime. Sure there's the occasional picky eater, but most dogs live for food. When the ingredients are tasty, wholesome, and healthy, you can't much blame them. A good canine diet affects the quality of your dog's life—how he looks, acts, and feels. Whether you feed him a raw, home-cooked, or high-quality commercial diet, he needs six basic components for good health: water, protein, carbohydrates, fats, vitamins, and minerals.

Nutrition Nuts and Bolts

Good nutrition and the appropriate nutritional supplements can add extra years to your dog's life, but choosing the right diet can be confusing. Ask six people what they feed their dogs and you'll hear six different responses. Surely you want to give your dog the healthiest meal possible, but with so many different meal options, making the best choice can be overwhelming. Every food manufacturer and dog owner claims the ingredients they use are natural, organic, and the healthiest way to feed a dog.

FACT

Although there is no single best way to feed your dog, good canine nutrition includes the right quantities of water, protein, carbohydrates, fat, vitamins, and minerals. The holistic approach certainly includes these, but beyond that you should evaluate your dog's overall physical and mental condition to provide a diet that best suits him.

Today, there are more brands and recipes to please every canine age and palate than ever before. Everywhere you look there's a steady stream of television and magazine advertisements, all boasting healthy ingredients. Visit any pet supply store and you'll see bags and cans of food piled high.

Making your own food is another popular option. Far from a fad, feeding a balanced recipe with fresh and unprocessed menu items is the ideal diet, both for people and for dogs. When you use organic, high-quality ingredients without preservatives or artificial colors and flavors, your dog will thrive.

But maybe you don't have the time to cook all of your dog's food. In that case, supplementing a commercial diet with fresh ingredients might be the way to go.

Maybe your dog has health issues and your veterinarian has suggested changing what you feed your dog, but how do you know what's really nutritious? Before you choose a recipe, know what nutrients your dog needs.

Water

Of all the nutrients, water is the most important. It is necessary for everything your dog does, and even a loss of just 10 percent body water can cause serious illness. To remain hydrated, your dog needs to drink approximately ¼ cup of water per 2.2 pounds of his weight per day. If the weather is especially hot or your dog is playing or exercising hard, he needs to drink even more water—at least two or three times more.

E-QUESTION

Do all protein sources provide the same nutrition?
No. Real beef, chicken feathers, and corn are all protein, but the real beef provides the best nutrition. A dog would have to eat a lot of feathers to get the same amount of protein he could take from a small amount of beef.

When it comes to lapping up liquids, dogs aren't fussy. They'll sip from muddy streams or gutters, but this water is far from healthy. Untreated water contains bacteria, viruses, and parasites. Household tap water is a lot safer, although it contains chemical additives such as chlorine and fluoride and has too high a concentration of nitrates, iron, and magnesium.

While there are no published studies about which type of water is preferable, the holistic approach to water for your dog is to give him a clean bowl of fresh bottled spring, distilled, or filtered tap water and to make sure that you change it every day. There are many economical ways to filter your tap water. Remember: If you wouldn't drink your dog's water, don't give it to him.

Protein

When it comes to dog food, it's all about protein. Protein is responsible for your dog's metabolism, growth and development, and digestive and reproductive functions. The main source of energy, protein builds muscle and produces enzymes, hormones, and antibodies. It contains ten essential amino acids that dogs cannot manufacture on their own. These help build structural tissues in the body.

What's really important about protein is not the quantity, but the quality. The quality of the protein is determined by its complement of amino acids and their availability for use by the body. In general, animal proteins are higher quality because of their higher bioavailability when compared to plant proteins. Dogs are omnivores, not vegetarians, and beef, lamb, pork, chicken, turkey, duck, venison, soybeans, and fish are the most popular protein choices in dog diets.

The Association of American Feed Control Officials (AAFCO) sets guidelines for all animal feed products and makes recommendations for how much protein, fat, and vitamins commercial dog food should contain. This governing body advises a diet consisting of a minimum of 18 percent protein for adult dogs, 28 percent for puppies, and 25 percent for performance dogs. When you look at bags of dog food and read the labels, many list different percentages of protein.

ALERT!

Grains should be cooked so the body can utilize them. Quick-cooking oatmeal, millet, and bulgur are high in nutrition and provide protein. Grains are an important source of fiber, iron, minerals, and other nutrients, although fruits and vegetables also supply fiber, minerals, and phytonutrients.

Dogs that expend a lot of energy need more protein. To evaluate whether your dog is getting enough protein, look at his body and overall condition. A thin, dry coat and underdeveloped muscles mean your dog isn't getting enough protein. However, if your dog has liver or kidney problems or produces kidney stones, your veterinarian may recommend limiting the amount and type of protein.

When you're choosing a protein source for your dog's food, consider digestibility also. The protein should be easy to digest, or easily broken down and utilized in the body.

Carbohydrates and Fat

Dogs don't need many carbohydrates because fats and proteins supply all the energy they need. For many animals, sufficient carbs can be obtained by including vegetables, such as sweet potatoes or pumpkin, or complex carbohydrates, such as barley or quinoa. These will help minimize glucose spikes immediately after eating and tend to cause fewer allergies than corn and wheat.

Many commercial brands use grain byproducts such as brewer's rice, corn, and wheat as fillers in the food. They provide as much as 60 percent of the carbohydrate count, but they are lower quality sources of carbohydrates. Processing destroys their nutritional value, and their relatively high sugar content interferes with digestion. Dog food manufacturers favor them because they are inexpensive.

In addition to carbohydrates, your dog needs fat in his diet to absorb vitamins A, E, D, and K, and to help maintain a healthy coat, eyes, and brain. When there's too little fat in the diet a dog may suffer from hair loss, poor coat quality, seborrhea, eczema-like skin eruptions, and wounds that don't heal.

Vitamins and Minerals

Like people, dogs should derive important vitamins from their food rather than through synthetic vitamin supplements. Natural vitamins are absorbed more easily in the body. Your dog should have vitamins A, D, E, K, B, and C in her diet. Some holistic veterinarians will suggest adding a vitamin supplement if a dog is eating a diet that may lack these, but a balanced diet is the best source of all vitamins and minerals.

Special Diets for Special Dogs

Whether you decide to feed your dog a commercial recipe or a raw or home-cooked meal, consider his breed, size, and age.

Large Breed Puppies

Large and giant breed puppies grow fast; however, growing too fast can stress their joints. Therefore, they don't need the high percentages of protein and fat that some pet food manufacturers market specifically for puppies. For this reason, look for a large breed puppy food with reduced calories and calcium/phosphorus ratios compared to conventional puppy formulas. Here are the standard recommendations for dry foods for large breed puppies:

- **Protein content:** 22–27 percent
- **Fat content:** 8 percent or less

- **Calcium content:** 1 percent
- **Phosphorus content:** 0.8 percent

Feeding less than 28 percent protein may reduce the possibility of bone and joint problems, including hip problems these breeds are prone to develop.

Senior Dogs

While veterinarians once believed that senior dogs, or dogs over the age of seven years, should have less protein than mature adults, that is no longer their recommendation.

When deciding how much protein to give your dog, evaluate his activity level, his overall condition, and the environment. Dogs that are exposed to stressful situations or are participating in strenuous exercise require extra protein for tissue repair. In severe cold or hot weather your dog will need a high protein and high-fat diet.

Dogs with Gastric Problems

If your dog has digestion problems, avoid feeding high-fat foods. For dogs with kidney issues, foods lower in phosphorus may be called for.

Lay Down the Rules

Dogs do best when they eat regular meals at specific times every day because they're less likely to eat too much. Consistent meal times also help with potty training. Physiologically, dogs have the urge to go after they eat, so by scheduling meals and taking your dog out immediately afterward, you can accustom him to eliminating at certain times. Finally, dogs are creatures of habit. They like knowing that meals will appear at certain times every day.

Table Scraps a No-No

If you want your dog to eat his regular meals and not hang around and beg at the table, don't give him any tidbits from your plate. Never. Not even once.

This doesn't mean that you can't save some of your salad (without the dressing, of course), baked potato, or leftover baked chicken to give him in his bowl later on or mixed with his regular food, but never give him food while you're eating. If you do, you'll have a permanent mooch on your hands.

No Picky Eaters

There are many reasons why a dog picks at her meal, but sometimes it's not about the food. If your dog walks away from her bowl and doesn't eat after two or three meals, she may be ill. She needs to see the veterinarian for an examination, blood panel, and urinalysis to rule out any problems. If there's no physical reason your dog is rejecting a recipe, continue to offer your dog her food on a regular schedule.

FACT

Feed medium, large, and giant breeds twice a day. Small dogs, especially toy breeds, should eat two or three times a day because they need to maintain their blood sugar and the extra meal gives them energy. Even if they are fussy, they can learn to eat at mealtimes, so don't leave food out all the time for them.

Don't leave food out all day for any dog; fresh food in particular may spoil. Instead, put the bowl down for ten to fifteen minutes. If he hasn't finished the whole thing in that length of time, remove it.

Resist the urge to feed your dog between meals or to hand-feed him. Don't offer him any food again until the next regular meal. This way he'll anticipate his next meal and be hungry at the appropriate time.

If your dog eats only half of his meal before walking away, pick up the bowl after ten to fifteen minutes. At his next meal, give him half his regular portion. Try giving the full portion at the following meal. You may have to repeat this a few times before your dog figures out that it's a better idea to eat everything the first time it's offered.

Healthy Treats

People love giving dog treats, but treats should be just as healthy as regular food. If you're using commercial tidbits, read the labels on the packages. Skip the treats that are high in sugar and fat or contain ingredients you wouldn't use in everyday meals, such as wheat, corn gluten meal, and ground yellow corn. Avoid goodies that contain harmful preservatives and artificial additives.

Not every fruit and vegetable is safe for dogs. Don't feed your dog onions, garlic, grapes, raisins, macadamia nuts, or chocolate. These are toxic to dogs and can cause illness and even death. Other potential dangers include tomato leaves and stems, rhubarb leaves, and potato peelings.

Organic fruit and vegetable pieces are far better and tastier treat options. Cut-up bits of bananas, apples, melons, blueberries, and stone fruits without the pits will be gobbled up. Include raw or lightly steamed chopped greens such as parsley, alfalfa sprouts, and watercress. Be sure to cook corn, peas, green beans, broccoli, cauliflower, and any hard vegetable that you cannot grate. Grated carrots, string beans, and just about all vegetables strengthen the immune system. Their enzymes reduce gastrointestinal upsets by helping the digestion of carbohydrates, proteins, and fats.

Feeding a Fresh Diet

If you wouldn't eat a solid diet of chemically preserved food, you probably wouldn't want to feed it to your dog. Many people make their dogs' meals because they are so dissatisfied with the poor ingredients that commercial dog food recipes contain.

While it takes time to shop and prepare ingredients, there are many benefits to cooking for your dog. Real food is healthier and more appealing than even the best commercial recipe, and you know what ingredients your dog is eating. Fresh, preferably organic, ingredients that are free of chemical preservatives and artificial colors and flavor-enhancers are best. If you have a dog with special dietary needs, you can feed her exactly what she should have and what she prefers to eat. The challenge in preparing your own dog food is setting aside the time to shop for and prepare the ingredients, but it can be done. By planning ahead, you can use the same food you cook for yourself to make for your dog.

Cook your own healthy diet in large batches to last a few days and add a few supplements for your dog's portion. You can freeze or refrigerate meals in single servings so you always have a few bowlfuls ready in minutes. In a pinch, if you run short of a breakfast or a dinner for your dog you can always use a high-quality commercial dog food as a backup.

Ingredients

Making your own meals gives you the flexibility to vary the menu and to modify the ingredients to suit your dog's preferences. It is best to consult with a veterinarian or nutritionist to ensure that your recipe is balanced and appropriate for your dog, especially if you plan to feed this diet for a long period of time. Here are some meal guidelines:

- ❑ **Protein.** 30 to 60 percent of the meal should consist of fresh cooked lean chicken, turkey, duck, beef, lamb, venison, pork, or fish. Other options are eggs, beans, lentils, tofu, or peanut butter.
- ❑ **Carbohydrates.** 30 to 60 percent of the meal should consist of cooked grains, such as rice, millet, and barley. Other options are potatoes, rolled oats, winter squash, and whole grain bread.
- ❑ **Vegetables.** 10 to 30 percent of the meal should consist of vegetables or fruit. Feed raw veggies if they can be finely chopped, or lightly steam green beans, broccoli, summer squash, cauliflower, Brussels sprouts, carrots, and spinach.

❏ **Calcium and phosphorus supplements.** Give puppies that weigh ten to fifteen pounds 1,000 to 1,200 mg of calcium and 500 to 600 mg of phosphorus per day. Adult dogs need half that amount.

❏ **Fats.** Depending on your dog's weight, give him one teaspoon to one tablespoon salmon oil, flax, borage, canola, or olive oil. Fish oil is the best choice for supplementation of an omega-3 fatty acid; flax-seed oil is not as readily converted by dogs.

❏ **Natural multivitamin/mineral supplement.** Use canine supplements. Ask your veterinarian the correct dosage for your dog.

A Raw Diet

Cooking at high temperatures destroys important vitamins, enzymes, and antioxidants, so raw food is an appealing alternative to feeding fresh food. The Biologically Appropriate Raw Foods (BARF) diet, created by Dr. Ian Billinghurst, uses raw bones and meat, some vegetables, and a few carbohydrates. It is meant to resemble a dog's diet in the wild. Recipe ingredients consist of chicken and turkey necks, backs, and wings.

ALERT!

Both raw and cooked bones can cause problems! Never cook bones before giving them to your dog. These are softer than raw uncooked bones and will splinter and cause intestinal obstruction or constipation. Raw bones can fracture teeth and bone shards can lodge in the roof of the mouth or become stuck in the intestinal tract and cause gastrointestinal obstruction.

Many dogs do well on this diet, especially if they suffer from allergies or arthritis, although some dogs cannot tolerate such a pure meal. The first time you serve your dog a raw diet, don't be surprised if he's not overly excited by it. Some dogs are reluctant to try new food that's an unfamiliar texture and temperature.

Gradually incorporate the raw diet into his current food and try serving it at room temperature or slightly warmed up, rather than cold right out of the refrigerator. If you think your dog doesn't like his food in big chunks, try grinding it up.

Bacterial contamination is a concern with raw meat or eggs, although organic certified raw meat raised without antibiotics or hormones is a safer option. Purchase it fresh and keep it refrigerated, and be sure to disinfect all food utensils after handling raw meat. Discuss the pros and cons of feeding raw meat and bones with your holistic veterinarian.

Convenient Commercial Food

When it comes to feeding your dog, nothing could be easier than opening a bag of food and pouring it into her bowl. Unfortunately, this may not be the best diet for your dog's stomach or for her overall health.

Today, veterinarians are seeing more dogs with health issues they attribute to eating an inferior diet. These include skin and ear infections, coat and eye problems, hyperactivity, lethargy, intestinal upset, constipation, arthritis, diabetes, epilepsy, heart disease, and parasites.

When you shop for dog food, read the label listing the contents. Here are nine ingredients found in inferior commercial dog foods that you should avoid:

1. **Butylated hydroxyanisole (BHA) and butylated hydroxytoluene (BHT)** are preservatives that are meant to prevent spoilage and extend shelf life up to one year, although some studies report they are carcinogenic. Natural recipes use healthier choices such as vitamin C (ascorbate) and vitamin E (mixed tocopherols) as preservatives, but these foods have a much shorter shelf life.
2. **Ethoxyquin** is a chemically synthesized preservative; some reports link it to impaired liver and kidney function.
3. **Propylene glycol** is a liquid used in some semi-moist foods to prevent drying out; it may cause central nervous system impairment and changes in kidney function.
4. **Propyl gallate** is a powder antioxidant that prevents fats and oils from spoiling. It is known to cause stomach and skin irritations in people.

5. **Coloring agents** Red 40 and Yellow 5 enhance the appearance of dog foods. Natural brands use natural ingredients, such as carrots, to enhance color.
6. **Phosphoric acid** is a clear liquid. It is an emulsifier and flavoring agent that prevents discoloration. Too much of it irritates skin and mucous membranes.
7. **Sorbitol** is a synthetic sugar substitute that is used as a flavoring agent. It causes diarrhea and intestinal upset in large quantities.
8. **Dl-alpha tocopheryl acetate** is a synthetic form of vitamin E not absorbed as easily as mixed tocopherols. Natural dog food uses vitamin E as a preservative.
9. **Menadione sodium bisulfate vitamin K3** is a synthetic version of vitamin K, also known as menadione dimethyl-pyrimidinol bisulfate. It can irritate mucous membranes.

When selecting a brand and a recipe, look for a nutritionally balanced formula. AAFCO establishes standards of nutritional adequacy for animal foods. Foods that pass their criteria will be labeled "complete and balanced," but these are minimum standards. If a dog food is called complete and balanced it means that it contains all of the nutrients in proportion to one another and is balanced to the diet's energy level. The AAFCO label does not mean that the food has been tested to determine how animals fare on the diet.

FACT

Choose a recipe containing whole meat (chicken, turkey, beef, lamb, fish), rather than meat byproducts. Byproducts, such as lungs, kidneys, brain, and intestines are inferior protein sources. Skip meat "meal" as this is rendered animal tissues, which could include hide trimmings, hair, feathers, or hooves. However, in some foods animal byproducts are used as a filler instead of corn, which provide a better protein source and lower carbs.

AAFCO also sets standards for feeding trials used to test the food on dogs. These trials determine how bioavailable the food is by testing a number of objective variables such as body weight, amount of food consumed, and various blood tests, over a twenty-six-week period. This is a very imperfect method for many reasons, but it is one of the only objective measurements available for determining the nutritional content and proportions of a dog food. While a missing nutrient isn't a problem on a short-term basis, in the long run it will lead to health issues.

AAFCO feeding trials do not guarantee a healthy diet for all animals, but serve as a standard for minimum nutritional requirements. The best test is how your dog fares on the diet. Her coat should be soft and glossy, her eyes should be clear, her skin should be healthy, and her energy level should be normal for her age and breed. She should be able to maintain a healthy weight, and you should be able to see her waist. Her stools should be consistently firm and not watery. No one diet is best for all animals, but there are many very good diets available to choose from. When you shop for a food, decide in advance what ingredients you want to give your dog or ask your veterinarian for recommendations. You will be able to evaluate if a food is good for your dog by looking at her.

Combining Commercial and Home Cooking

If you want to mix a commercial diet with fresh food, reduce the package meal by about 35 percent. Then give your dog an equivalent amount of raw or slightly cooked protein, carbohydrates, veggies, and fruit. Add in one teaspoon of salmon oil for every twenty-five pounds of dog per meal.

Adding Supplements

Supplements are added to food to increase its nutritional value. Whether you're making your own recipe or buying the best commercial brand, you may want to add a supplement to the ingredients you've selected.

No supplement is perfect for every dog, so you may have to try a few different ones to see what works best. Some dogs are reluctant to swallow pills or liquids or anything different in their bowls. If so, try powdered substances; they might be more to your dog's liking and can be disguised with food.

A few supplements include:

- **A good-quality, natural multivitamin/mineral.** For maximum efficiency, the supplement should be made from whole foods rather than a synthetic product and only administered if your dog's diet is known to be vitamin or mineral deficient.
- **A fatty acid, such as chicken fat, or salmon, fish, or safflower oil.** This helps produce a healthy coat and skin.
- **Calcium.** Can be provided in the form of finely ground eggshells, or a calcium lactate supplement. It is important to maintain a 2:1 ratio between calcium and phosphorus for maximum utilization of these minerals. If either is too high or too low, the intestine will absorb from the other.
- **A green food supplement.** Alfalfa, barley grass, blue-green algae, kelp, spirulina, and wheat grass contain phytonutrients and are powerful antioxidants.
- **Digestive enzymes.** These help break down food and increase absorption of vitamins, minerals, and fatty acids.
- **Health blend formulas.** A combination of several essential plant and animal nutrients in powder form provide nutrients that are lost in commercial food during processing. These can be found at natural food companies.

Multivitamins

Some veterinarians believe that even high-quality commercial dog foods lose some vitamins through processing or storage. As a basic supplement, a multivitamin restores daily requirements of the essential nutrients your dog needs for good health. It also helps dogs with a poor appetite that are recuperating from illness and may be missing their daily requirements.

If you're going to give your dog a multivitamin, use one that's made especially for dogs (human-grade vitamins can cause side effects) and ask your veterinarian how much vitamin supplementation your dog needs.

Green Food Supplements

Dogs love to nibble on fresh green grass because it contains vitamins, minerals, and enzymes, which aren't a part of their regular food. Unfortunately, the blades of grass have tiny barbs that irritate your dog's stomach. Powdered green food supplements provide all the benefits of eating grass without the barbs that cause them to vomit.

Digestive Enzymes

Digestive enzymes are involved in every metabolic process and play a vital role in overall health. They help break down the proteins, carbohydrates, and fats in food so the body can use them. A healthy dog may not show any physical changes from taking enzymes, but they will prevent diseases and ward off infections.

There are two types of fatty acids—omega-3 and omega-6. Some quality commercial foods include them. Omega-3s are anti-inflammatory and help ease allergies. They include fish (salmon) body oil. Good Omega-6 is gamma-linolenic acid (GLA), and includes evening primrose oil and borage oil. Avoid foods that contain safflower oil, canola oil, and corn oil as they inflame allergies.

For maximum effectiveness, enzymes should be used with a high-quality food. Signs of enzyme deficiency are gas, diarrhea, and stool-eating. Senior dogs that are picky eaters and often miss getting all the nutrients they need will especially benefit from enzyme supplements.

Antioxidants, Probiotics, and Nutraceuticals

As dogs begin to age, the body begins to deteriorate due to oxidative damage caused by free radicals. Free radicals are toxic, electrically unstable molecules that weaken your dog's immune system. They're responsible for degenerating conditions associated with aging, such as cancer, heart disease, arthritis, diabetes, and cataracts.

Antioxidant supplements neutralize free radicals and decrease the damage. Research shows that giving your puppy antioxidant supplements before free radical damage occurs will help increase your dog's life expectancy. Vitamins A, C, and E, the minerals selenium and zinc, and the nutrients alpha lipoic acid and coenzyme Q10 are antioxidant supplements that protect the body against free radical damage.

E-QUESTION

What is Coenzyme Q10?
Coenzyme Q10, also called ubiquinone, is a powerful, newly discovered antioxidant for people and dogs. Protecting against free radical damage, coenzyme Q10 helps protect senior dogs against heart disease, gum and dental disease, and cancer.

Probiotics

Otherwise known as friendly bacteria, a probiotic helps metabolize food and eliminates harmful viruses, yeasts, and bacteria. Nonpasteurized yogurt or kefir and acidophilus are a few sources, although a probiotic formulated for canines may be more effective. Veterinarians may recommend a probiotic before your dog goes into surgery, if he is ill, or if he is taking an antibiotic that may upset his stomach.

Nutraceuticals

Purified from foods, a nutraceutical provides protection against chronic disease. As natural supplements they can replace or work in conjunction with conventional pharmaceuticals. These include nutrients, dietary supplements, and herbal products.

Glucosamine and chondroitin are combined to provide joint, tendon, and cartilage support. MSM (methyl-sulfonyl-methane), a natural source of sulfur, works with glucosamine as a potent anti-inflammatory and pain reliever.

Yucca root, another anti-inflammatory, helps relieve itching and swelling from minor skin injuries.

Preventing Obesity

Many veterinarians believe that obesity is the biggest canine health problem. Between 25 and 50 percent of all dogs are overweight. This unhealthy condition leads to many health problems, including diabetes, bone and joint diseases, heart and lung diseases, urinary and reproductive disorders, skin conditions, and various types of cancer. Even worse, dogs with extra body weight tend to have shorter life spans.

FACT

Poor quality food is high in fats and carbohydrates. Like human fast food, this inferior diet has refined carbohydrates that add inches to the belly and ribs. When you look down over the top of an overweight dog you'll see a roly-poly outline instead of the shapely hourglass figure that healthy dogs should have.

If your dog is on the pudgy side, the best way to take off a few pounds is to balance his food intake with the amount of energy he expends. He doesn't need any special low-calorie dog food to lose a few pounds. Simply cut down on the amount of food you give him and increase his exercise.

Exercise

For dogs that aren't used to working out, start slowly. Begin with a walk around the block once or twice a day for a few minutes. Gradually add more time until you're able to walk briskly for at least twenty to thirty minutes once or twice a day. Try to schedule your walks when the weather is cool.

With active dogs, increase your walk time or begin slow jogging. Being consistent with exercise helps you achieve the best result. Pain relief should be treated with an anti-inflammatory herbal combination rather than a single herb. The combination causes fewer side effects and has better therapeutic effects. For dogs that show signs of stiffness, the combination of glucosamine, chondroitin, MSM, and fish oil may be enough to limber them up. Consult a veterinarian for the correct doses for your dog.

Nutrition

Increasing the fiber, decreasing the amount of fat, and cutting back on the number of calories you feed your dog will help her lose a few pounds. Aim to reduce 10 percent of her excess body weight at a time. The trick to keeping her in top shape is to reduce slowly and gradually.

To satisfy your dog's hunger while he's on a reducing program, give him more fiber and vegetables. Spinach and broccoli supply vitamins, minerals, and antioxidants. Check with your vet to find out how much spinach and broccoli your dog should get; excessive amounts can cause calcium imbalances that may potentially lead to urinary stones. Green beans may be a safer choice. Cooked oatmeal is a good source of fiber and has a calming effect. Reduce the number of treats you feed your dog; they add too many calories.

Some overweight dogs are anxious and use food to ease their discomfort. Acupuncture is an effective weight loss treatment in these cases, as it reduces anxiety. Flower essences such as aspen, mimulus, impatiens, or Rescue Remedy may also help, as may misting an area with the aroma of lavender.

CHAPTER 7

Grooming and Coat Care

You may think your dog doesn't need to be fussed and mussed with, but underneath that glowing personality is a showy fellow just waiting for a spruce-up. All dogs, no matter what length coat they have, require some grooming. Besides bathing and brushing, your dog needs his nails trimmed, teeth brushed, and eyes and ears cleaned on a routine basis. Paying attention to these areas is one more way to keep your dog healthy. Regular grooming will give you the opportunity to spot any potential skin, eye, and ear problems before they become serious.

Getting Ready

Grooming your dog is first and foremost a bonding experience. It's quality time you set aside once a day or once a week to maintain your dog's overall well-being. To make the procedure as easy as possible, purchase grooming tools especially made for dogs and assemble everything you need to do the job before you begin. Keep all of the grooming tools in a plastic bucket or hang them on a pegboard near the grooming area so you don't have to go hunting for a tool in the middle of a grooming session.

Putting your dog up on a grooming table will make nail trimming, brushing, and combing much easier. Your dog is at eye level and you won't have to bend over him. A grooming arm and noose helps hold him steady. You can also prop him up on a picnic table or on the kitchen counter if he's small enough.

Here's a list of all the grooming tools you'll need:

- **Brush and detangling spray conditioner.** Get a bristle, wire slicker, or rubber glove or brush, depending on your dog's coat type. Invest in a shedding blade or pumice stone for heavy shedding and a spray conditioner for dogs with long hair.
- **Comb.** A steel comb with wide teeth on the bottom and narrow teeth on the top will help remove tangles.
- **Two nonslip mats.** Place one in the bottom of the bathtub and one on the floor next to the tub to provide traction while bathing your dog.
- **Shampoo.** Choose a topical herbal shampoo or a veterinary formula.
- **One or two large cotton towels and a washcloth.** You can also use a high-velocity pet dryer instead of the towels if you wish.
- **Bath restraint.** To help keep wiggly dogs inside the tub, this rubber noose and coated cable slips over your dog's neck and attaches to the wall of the tub with a rubber suction cup.

- **Handheld spray shower attachment.** This helps you control how much water you use on your dog.
- **Nail clippers or electric pet nail grinder.** Styptic gel or powder also comes in handy to immediately stop any bleeding.
- **Canine toothbrush and pet toothpaste.** Both products are specifically designed for a canine mouth.
- **Almond oil and cotton balls.** You'll need the cotton balls to place in your dog's ears before you bathe him and also to wipe out his ears with the oil.

Don't forget a few food treats. It's a good idea to give your dog one or two small tidbits as a reward for standing still during his grooming session. This way he'll look forward to the session instead of dreading it.

Brushing and Combing

Nothing looks and smells better than a freshly bathed and coiffed dog. Your dog feels better too. After all, who doesn't like the way they feel after a scalp massage and a haircut? But caring for your dog's coat isn't just about making him appear more beautiful. It's about taking care of his health.

While most people think that a dog's heart is his most vital organ, the skin or coat is actually larger and requires more attention. Take one look at your dog's coat and you'll have an insight into his physical and mental condition.

When a dog has inflamed, itchy, or flaky skin, it isn't the coat that's the source of the problem. It's usually a sign of an internal issue, such as liver, adrenal, or thyroid disease. Other culprits of skin irritations and abnormal hair loss are allergies, mange, and bacterial and fungal hair follicle infections.

By brushing or combing your dog regularly—daily for dogs with long, curly, or very fine hair, or weekly for short, wiry, or hairless canines, you can check to see if he has any fleas, ticks, cuts, lumps, or tender areas. When you spot a problem early on, you can obtain treatment before the condition worsens.

Dogs love nothing better than to roll around in dust and dirt. As a result, pet fur is a magnet for this grime and debris, trapping it on the skin. While most dogs groom themselves to some extent by using their teeth, tongue, or paws, they can't eliminate all of the toxins. Even if they could, it's not a very healthy way to do it. Combing or running a bristle, wire slicker, or rubber curry brush through the coat rids the hair of the dirt and secretions before they have a chance to accumulate. If left alone, these particles provide the perfect conditions for germs and parasites to thrive.

Introducing a Routine

Begin a grooming routine with your dog the day after you bring her home. Turn off the phone and choose a time when you're not likely to be interrupted. You need to focus your attention on your dog; you increase your chances of hurting her accidentally if you're distracted.

ALERT!

Never leave your dog alone on the grooming table, even if he's secured in place by a grooming noose. He can accidentally fall off or he may decide to take a flying leap off the edge. Either way, he can be seriously injured.

You don't have to perform all of the grooming tasks during the first few sessions, but it's a good idea to introduce her to the new experience so she can become accustomed to being touched or having her nails trimmed. Put her up on the grooming or picnic table and let her sniff the tools. Brush her for a few minutes, trim one or two nails or paws, and let her lick some toothpaste off the toothbrush. After this brief session, tell her she's a good girl and give her a small food treat as a reward.

Repeat the process over the next few days. When you feel comfortable with the procedure, set aside a regular day of the week and a time for grooming so you'll be sure to get the job done.

Brush Training

Taking care of your dog's coat is just as important as feeding your dog a healthy diet and giving him plenty of fresh water, regular exercise, sunlight, fresh air, and a safe environment. Until he becomes accustomed to the pampering, he may not appreciate the effort and you'll need to do some training. You're grooming him for his own health, so be patient and don't give up.

For the first session or two, put him up on the table and spend a few minutes petting and talking to him. Let him sniff the brush and lightly brush his front legs where he can see what you're doing. Even if he wiggles around a little, give him a little food treat as a reward. Having the right type of brush for your dog's coat type will make the job easier. Here are the various types of brushes:

- **Bristle brush.** Short-haired dogs need shorter, tightly packed bristles; long-haired dogs need widely spaced bristles.
- **Pin brush.** A pin brush is best for long, wavy, or wire coats. It is designed to be gentle enough that it doesn't break off the hair; however, if the coat has mats, you will need to demat it with a comb and slicker brush or other dematting tool because a pin brush is designed to brush out hair without mats.
- **Slicker brush.** This brush works for removing mats and tangles and smoothing out the hair after using the bristle brush. This ever-versatile brush is the one to use on long, curly, or silky coats.
- **Undercoat rake.** Use this tool to remove dead hair from the undercoat on double-coated breeds.
- **Rubber nubby brush.** Use this brush on short-haired or hairless dogs.

Shedding

Dog hair has a life cycle. It grows, rests, falls out, and grows again. This is what shedding, or blowing coat, is all about. Dogs shed a little throughout the year, although the hair thickens in the fall to add protection during the cold winter months and drops out during warmer weather after it's no longer needed.

By brushing your dog's coat, you remove the dead hair before it falls on your clothes, carpet, and other parts of your household. Brushing also helps stimulate the natural oils in your dog's skin, giving the coat a healthy, shiny appearance. For heavy shedding, brush and bathe your dog and be sure to dry him thoroughly. This will remove the excess hair and help loosen the hair that's nearly ready to fall out.

Brush heavily shedding dogs with the bristle or rubber brush once a day and use a wire slicker brush, shedding blade, or pumice stone twice a week. This helps remove extra hair. Don't use the sharp slicker or blade more than once a week or with too much pressure or you'll take off too much coat and your dog could wind up looking bald!

How to Brush Your Dog

With shorthaired dogs, use a rubber brush, glove, or mitt with nubby ends. Don't use a bristle brush because it will tear out healthy hair that's not ready to come out yet. If there are tangles, use a steel comb with wide teeth at one end and narrow teeth at the other. Start brushing from your dog's head and continue backward toward his rear. Vigorously brush in the direction the hair grows. If you haven't brushed your dog lately, you will dislodge quite a bit of dirt, debris, and loose hair.

E-QUESTION

Are there any purebred or mixed-breed dogs that don't shed?
No. Every dog has hair that goes through the normal growth, rest, loss, and replacement cycle. A few breeds, such as Poodles, Portuguese Water Dogs, Havanese, and Bichon Frises, don't shed as often because they have a longer growth cycle.

If you have a longhaired dog, use a bristle or slicker brush and begin brushing at the front of your dog and continue toward his tail. Brush in small sections against the direction the hair is growing.

Don't ignore mats. They need to be removed to prevent external parasites from taking up residence inside them. They're also uncomfortable when your dog lies on them. Separate the hair into small sections and use a shedding or dematting comb. To help untangle the mats, spritz the problem areas with a little detangling grooming spray before combing through the hair.

Brush shorthaired dogs once a week and longhaired dogs once a day, especially if the coat mats easily. Dogs with thicker coats can be brushed two to three times a week.

Rub-a-Dub-Dog in the Tub

A clean coat is a healthy coat. Bathing removes the dead skin and hair and gets rid of any odor your dog might have. Once your dog becomes accustomed to the process, he'll actually enjoy the water massage. When you're ready to give your dog a bath, assemble everything you need before you get started—shampoo, towels, brush, rubber mats, and cotton balls.

A rubber brush or grooming glove is an optional—but very useful—bathing accessory. Use it to spread the shampoo thoroughly over your dog's body. It grabs the hard-to-reach dirt and debris and helps loosen the dead hair. The brush also speeds up the rinsing process.

If you have a small dog that weighs less than twenty pounds or so, try bathing him in your kitchen sink. For large dogs, your shower might be just the place for a doggy spa treatment. Otherwise, your bathtub with the sprayer attachment will work just fine. Brush your dog outdoors before bathing him. This dislodges all of the dead hair so it doesn't clog up your tub drain. Before putting your dog into the tub, place a cotton ball in each of his ears to prevent water from dripping inside.

Unless your dog loves water, his first bathing experience may be a challenge. To make your dog feel more comfortable with the process, don't rush him into a full stream of water. Instead, gently place him in the tub with the water off. Then, using the handheld sprayer, add a little warm water to your dog's legs, then his back and shoulders so he can become accustomed to it gradually. Hold off on getting his head and face wet until he relaxes a bit.

Apply some herbal shampoo on his back and shoulders, massaging it in with the rubber brush. Herbal shampoos that contain oatmeal, tea tree oil, calendula, plantain, and aloe are soothing and therapeutic. Continue applying shampoo to his legs and head, but you don't need to work it into a lather. A little shampoo goes a long way. Rinse him off until there's no soap left. Any soap left on the coat will show up as flakes the next day, so be sure to get it all off.

As soon as you turn the water off, place a towel on top of your dog before he begins shaking water all over the bathroom. Begin towel drying him, and be sure to remove the cotton from his ears.

Deskunking Your Dog

It may never happen, but if your dog happens to meet up with a skunk, the experience could really stink. Your dog needs to be bathed as soon as possible, but regular dog shampoo won't do the job—and neither will tomato juice or vinegar.

Shampoo in your dog's eyes can cause corneal ulcers. You can put eye protection drops in a dog's eyes before the bath, but be warned: Some shampoos contain degreasing agents that will break down the mineral oil in those protection drops, and then the shampoo can become trapped under the oil. Use a tearless shampoo for the face, and even then always gently flush the dog's eyes with water after a bath to rinse out any shampoo residue.

Here's a foolproof natural recipe you can make yourself. In a plastic bucket, mix the following ingredients well:

1. Combine 1 quart 3 percent hydrogen peroxide, ¼ cup baking soda, and 1 teaspoon liquid soap. Be sure to wear rubber gloves to protect your skin from the chemicals as well as from the skunk oil.
2. Wet your dog down with water, apply the mixture deep into the fur, and work through the coat.
3. Leave the solution on for at least five minutes, or until the odor is gone; let your nose guide you.
4. Rinse off with tepid water. Repeat if necessary.

Pour the leftover solution down the drain with running water. Never store mixed solution in a closed bottle or sprayer. Pressure can build until the container bursts.

Cleaning Wrinkles

If you have a breed like a Pug or a Chinese Shar-Pei with loose skin on her face, head, or shoulders, you need to clean these folds and wrinkles every day. The deep folds fill with sweat and debris, creating an ideal environment for bacteria and yeast.

ALERT!

If you use a pet dryer, don't leave your dog unattended when the dryer is running. Even on a cool or low setting, the machine dries your dog quickly and your dog can easily overheat. Pet dryers are loud, and your dog may be frightened until he becomes accustomed to the noise. He may also knock the dryer over, which presents another safety concern.

Check the folds for redness, moist sores, rashes, or musty smells. These may indicate infection. If you notice your dog rubbing her head sideways against various objects, she may be trying to rub away the discomfort.

To clean the folds, apply some mild antibacterial soap or hydrogen peroxide to a damp washcloth. Lift the fold and wipe it from one side of the wrinkle to the other. Apply a little baby powder or cornstarch to keep it dry.

Providing Pedicures

Maintaining your dog's feet is an important part of keeping him healthy. A pedicure relieves stress on the feet and prevents nails from breaking and causing pain. When nails are too long they force the toes outward. This offsets your dog's balance and generally makes walking difficult.

Your dog's nails should be cut short and the hair on the underside of the feet and between the toes should be trimmed with blunt scissors or electric clippers. Otherwise, dirt accumulates on the dog's feet and forms mats, which is uncomfortable to walk on.

If your dog has never had his feet touched or his nails trimmed, pedicures can be traumatic. Plan on spending a few sessions conditioning him to relax before you give him a pedicure. To do this, begin handling his feet the day after you bring him home. Pick up each foot and hold it for a few seconds. Reward him with a small food treat when you put the foot down.

While you can take your dog to your veterinarian or to a groomer for nail clipping, it's worth the effort to learn how to do it yourself. To keep his nails short and maintain his feet in good condition, you'll need to trim them once a week. Dogs' nails grow fast and if you wait too long between pedicures it takes longer to trim them.

Tools to Groom

You don't need very much to maintain your dog's nails—a place to clip, a nail trimmer that's easy to use, some styptic gel or powder, and a lot of patience.

It does help to have a grooming table with a grooming arm and noose to hold your dog so he can't move around a lot, but if you don't have one, put your dog up on a picnic or kitchen table. Some dogs don't mind having their nails worked on and are okay lying on the couch or sitting next to you on the floor.

FACT

It's a myth that you don't have to trim your dog's nails if he exercises on cement because these surfaces keep nails short. Like human nails, canine nails naturally grow at different rates and lengths, regardless of what surface their feet are on. The only way to keep your dog's nails short is to trim them back once a week.

There are two basic types of nail trimmers to choose from: the guillotine-style and scissor-style. You can also use an electric nail grinder, which is a rotary sanding tool that many groomers use to file down nails. You can do this at home once you are comfortable clipping nails. The grinder quickly sands away excess nail and allows you to get even closer to the quick than nail trimmers do. Use a pet nail grinder, not a hobby model, as it will shut off automatically if it senses hair around the nail.

How to Trim Nails

If you're going to use an electric nail grinder, turn it on and off a few times before using it on your dog so she can become accustomed to the whirring sound. If you've chosen a nail trimmer, let your dog sniff it so she's more comfortable with it before you put it to work.

To trim your dog's nails, hold the paw firmly, but not too tightly, and examine one of the nails. Look for the darker area in the center; this is the quick. If you're using a nail trimmer, clip off the tip of the nail without nicking the quick, which will bleed if you come too close. If you're using a grinder, start out with a low speed until you're comfortable operating it. The grinder helps smooth over any rough edges and can shape the nails.

During your first session, trim one or two nails. If your dog is okay with the procedure, add a few more nails. Apply some styptic gel or powder if a nail begins to bleed. Be sure to reward your dog with a food treat.

Maintaining Oral Health

Providing regular dental care for your dog is another aspect of proper grooming. Plaque, a composite of saliva, bits of food, and bacteria, sticks to canine teeth. The buildup hardens into tartar and causes swollen and receding gums and spaces for debris to accumulate.

E-QUESTION

Is it okay to use a human toothbrush and toothpaste?
No. Use a dental brush and paste that's made specifically for dogs. A canine brush has two or three sides to reach the upper and lower teeth. For puppies, use a small rubber brush that slides over your finger. The paste doesn't need rinsing.

When you brush your dog's teeth, you brush away the debris that would otherwise cause gum disease. You'll prevent pain, infection, and obnoxious bad breath. Remember, prevention is the cornerstone of holistic veterinary care.

Experts agree that the best defense against periodontal disease is to provide daily oral hygiene. But if you've never brushed your pet's teeth before, take him to your veterinarian for an oral evaluation and professional cleaning before you start brushing his teeth. Brushing alone won't remove a heavy tartar buildup.

Daily Brushing

Teeth need to be brushed once a day. Plaque builds up after every meal and although brushing alone won't remove all of the tartar, it certainly helps. You may need to train your dog to like having her teeth brushed, but once she gets the hang of it she'll actually look excited whenever she sees the brush come out.

If your dog is a chewer, get in the habit of giving her Nylabones, hard rubber toys, or raw bones to chew on throughout her life. Besides giving her something acceptable to chew, these help scrape the tartar off her teeth. Never give your dog cooked bones; these can splinter.

Work slowly to get your dog accustomed to having her teeth brushed. Put some enzyme-based canine toothpaste on your finger and let her lick it off. It's flavored so she'll like the taste of it. Next apply the paste to the brush, and gently lift your dog's lip. Holding the brush to the dog's teeth at a 45-degree angle, insert the brush into your dog's mouth and brush the front teeth. Brush the side teeth and finally the back molars, which are the most important. It's perfectly fine if it takes you a few sessions to work up to brushing your dog's entire mouth.

Professional Cleanings

Despite your best brushing efforts, your dog will still need to have his teeth professionally cleaned by a veterinarian. There are areas of the teeth that brushing simply can't reach. Although a groomer can remove the tartar by hand-scaling, it's difficult to go below the gum line and reach a diseased area without anesthesia.

How often your dog needs a professional cleaning really depends on your dog's age and the size of his teeth. If the teeth are neglected when a dog is young, he's going to need deep-cleaning within a few years. Small dogs usually have small teeth that are crammed together, creating more spaces for food to become trapped and decay to set in. Your veterinarian will examine your dog's mouth and advise you.

During a professional cleaning your veterinarian will anesthetize your dog and use a hand-scraper or an ultrasonic cleaner to reach those areas of your dog's mouth that regular brushing cannot. Many holistic veterinarians acknowledge that new types of anesthesia and improved monitoring devices make this procedure much safer than it once was.

Protecting Eyes and Ears

A dog's eyes and ears need to be properly taken care of to prevent potentially harmful infections down the road.

Eye Care

When you're looking over your dog every day, be sure to notice his eyes. They should not be red or swollen and shouldn't tear excessively. If you notice a discharge, wipe his eyes and eyelids clean with a cotton ball soaked in some warm distilled water. You can also use a warm washcloth to clean the eyes.

ALERT!

Don't let your dog stick his head out of the open window of a moving car. Dirt particles or sharp objects can easily fly into his eyes and scratch the corneas. Even too much wind can irritate a dog's eyes.

For any irritation, take your dog to see the veterinarian. She will examine his eyes to determine what the source of the problem might be.

Bulging, globular eyes need extra protection. They protrude and can easily be scratched by the family cat or from garden plants and bushes that have thorns or sharp leaves. Be on the lookout for and remove anything sharp in your home or garden that's close to your dog's eye level.

Cleaning Ears

Whether your dog has erect or drop ears, they need regular cleaning. Dirt and debris collect inside, which may lead to an infection.

To clean your dog's ears, you'll need cotton balls and some warm almond oil. Pour the oil into a squeeze bottle and drizzle about ½ teaspoon oil into the ear canal. Massage the base of the ear until you hear a swishing sound. Continue for a few minutes so the oil has a chance to loosen the wax inside. Put the cotton inside the opening and wipe out the waxy secretion. Repeat the process until the cotton comes out clean.

It's a good habit to look at your dog's ears every day. If there's a musty odor or a black, waxy secretion, they need cleaning. Some dogs with long ears may need their ears cleaned once a day, while upright ears may only need cleaning once a month.

CHAPTER 8

Banishing Parasites Naturally

Whether internal or external, parasites are troublesome pests that can make your dog's life truly miserable. In order to survive, parasites must sponge off your dog, often robbing her of vital nutrients. As if that's not enough, they can cause major health issues and are even capable of transmitting diseases to people and other animals. Whether it's pesky fleas and ticks, troublesome ear mites, or life-threatening heartworms or tapeworms, your dog doesn't have to suffer. Prevention is the key to avoiding parasites, and there are plenty of safe remedies to keep your dog healthy.

Freeloading Organisms

No one likes a pest of any kind, but especially a creature that feeds off your dog and poses a danger to his health. Once parasites invade the canine system they begin living off their host by feasting on blood meals. Fueled by this plentiful food supply, these dependent organisms quickly multiply and further infect dogs. Symptoms range from mild to fatal.

External parasites, such as fleas, ticks, and mites, live on the skin; internal parasites, such as roundworms, tapeworms, hookworms, and whipworms, take up residence in the intestines. Heartworm is another internal parasite. It lives in the dog's heart and blood vessels. Two protozoal parasites, coccidia and giardia, also infect dogs internally.

To fight parasites there are several chemical preventives that you've probably seen advertised in the media, although these poisonous substances affect the environment and the dog's overall health. Some of these products are effective in controlling fleas and ticks until the parasites begin developing a resistance to them. For this reason, veterinary researchers are always developing new and improved products to control pests.

ALERT!

Check the ingredients of flea and tick products before using them. In 2000, the Natural Resources Defense Council (NRDC, *www.nrdc.org*) linked flea and tick products and serious health problems affecting the nervous system in pets and people. Organophosphate insecticides (OPs) and carbamates are responsible for the danger. OPs are chlorpyrifos, dichlorvos, phosmet, naled, tetrachlorvinphos, diazinon, or malathion. A carbamate includes carbaryl or propoxur. Products containing these chemicals should be avoided.

If you prefer to go chemical-free when treating your dog, there are natural topical alternatives, but these are not always effective for every dog. Some can even be toxic to puppies. Whatever course you decide to take, you must be vigilant about guarding your dog against parasites. Heartworm can be deadly, and medication must be given routinely as a prevention.

Once you know how fleas and ticks wiggle their way into your dog's body and how they survive, you can take steps to prevent parasites from wreaking havoc on your dog's life. By protecting him from pests, you're saving him from discomfort and potentially fatal infestations.

Fleas

Take your dog for a walk in a grassy park and you may spot a flea leaping or crawling along your dog's back or side. If a dog is allergic to flea saliva, one bite can send him into a scratching frenzy, known as *pruritus*, that will last for weeks. This itching is so severe that it may lead to hair loss, inflammation, and secondary skin infections.

FACT

Cold does not harm adult fleas, which can live on your pet through the winter. Female fleas can lay a whopping 2,000 eggs in their lifetime. Flea larvae, which hatch from eggs in one to six days, flourish in carpets and in shaded areas outside.

The bite of a flea can also transmit tapeworm, which can lead to serious anemia and weight loss. Besides, fleas bite people too!

Life in the Flea Lane

The flea has a four-stage life cycle lasting from two weeks to eight months. It needs a warm, humid temperature—70°F–85°F and 70 percent humidity—in order to survive, and thrives in warm, moist winters and spring.

Life begins when the female flea lays eggs on a dog. Some of these eggs may fall on the ground or where the dog sleeps. Two days to two weeks later the eggs hatch into larvae.

The worm-like larvae remain in dark areas and take a week to several months to mature. In the meantime they feast on digested blood from adult flea feces, dead skin, and hair. While maturing, they weave a silken cocoon that sticks to pet hair, carpet, dust, and grass.

They can survive the winter in this stage, but typically adult fleas emerge five to fourteen days later. An adult flea can only live about one week without a blood meal.

Avoiding a Flea Circus

For a healthy dog, an occasional flea shouldn't cause much of a problem, especially if you pick it off quickly. But fleas are especially attracted to weak, sick, or malnourished dogs or puppies whose immune systems aren't functioning well. A poor diet, stress, and unsanitary conditions will worsen the slightest flea reactions.

E-QUESTION

How do you know if your dog has fleas?
To look for fleas, separate the hair on your dog's belly, lower back, and anal region. Fleas have a flattened body, are black to brownish-black, are one-twelfth to one-sixteenth of an inch long, and have six legs. A flea comb can help you look for fleas on a thicker coat or on pigmented skin. If you see or feel dark grit in your dog's coat, take some off and put it on a white paper towel. Add a drop of water. If the grit dissolves and turns red, you know it is flea feces.

While you can fight fleas with insecticides, nematodes, and hormones (discussed later), improving your dog's underlying condition is the best defense. Feeding him a natural diet boosts his immune system to resist all parasites.

In warm weather you can prevent fleas from moving in on your dog by not taking him out to exercise in large grassy areas that may be flea infested. Think twice about going to the dog park because fleas love to hop from one warm dog to another.

Other Remedies

Powders, sprays, and bathing products containing pyrethrin, which is made from chrysanthemums, and vinegar, garlic, citrus, or ginger are good therapies too. Pennyroyal, citronella, and eucalyptus oils are reliable flea repellents for adult dogs, but these topical remedies may be toxic to puppies.

There are a few other things you can do to prevent fleas:

- Groom your dog weekly, especially in warm weather. Look for any fleas while you're bathing and brushing him.
- Comb your dog with a fine-toothed flea comb. This comb is available in pet supply stores and traps any fleas and flea eggs.
- Wash your bedding as well as your dog's bedding weekly in hot water. Cedar-filled dog beds help repel fleas.
- Steam clean carpeting and clean upholstered furniture and draperies before flea season. Once a week, sweep between cracks, crevices, along baseboards, and under rug edges, furniture, or beds to catch any flea eggs, larvae, and adult fleas.
- Keep your lawn mowed and watered. When grass is short, sunlight kills larvae. Tall grass and leaves are favorite nesting areas for fleas.

Getting Rid of Fleas

If your dog already has fleas, they need to be eliminated quickly. Chances are any other animals in the household have fleas too and must also be treated. The fastest way to kill fleas is to use a chemical insecticide or dip and a natural therapy. Today there are new products that safely prevent and sterilize adult fleas. These are less toxic than older remedies and can be administered orally or topically once a month.

Make a homemade flea control spray by mixing two drops of pure lavender essential oil and two drops of pure cedar wood essential oil. Add to a spray bottle filled with warm water. Shake well. Spray over your dog's fur, but don't get any in his eyes or ears! This evaporates quickly, so reapply it often.

But a pill or a liquid isn't enough to kill fleas. Your dog also needs a flea bath. Water destroys the eggs and adult fleas, but new ones from the carpet will hop right back on as soon as she leaves the tub. Spritz her with a flea control spray. To help soothe your dog's itching skin, add a lavender, aloe vera, or calendula herbal rinse after bathing.

FACT

Common conventional flea preventives contain chemicals. While manufacturers insist they are safe, it's important to realize that although most dogs tolerate them well, some dogs may have adverse reactions to the artificial ingredients they contain. If you have a pest invasion, you may decide to use whatever means necessary to ease your dog's suffering, but once the situation is under control, consider natural alternatives.

Wash your dog's bedding and loose rugs in hot water. Vacuum upholstered furniture, all wall-to-wall carpeting and floor areas of your home. Sprinkle flea powder, such as a borate product made specifically for flea control, around the floor edges of every room. Or, hire a commercial flea extermination company to come over and do the job.

Next, rid your outdoor environment of fleas. While dangerous pesticide sprays were once the only way to wipe out fleas in the yard, today you can apply natural diatomaceous earth around the garden. Nematodes are another antidote. These microscopic worms naturally live in soil and consume flea larvae and other garden pests. They are more effective than any chemical. Harmless to people and pets, nematodes eat a few hundred different types of pests that live in the soil. You can purchase nematodes at your veterinarian's office, garden centers, and through organic garden catalogues.

Ticks Are Tough

Far more than just a mere annoyance, ticks can cause serious health issues. After attaching themselves to animals and people, these hard-bodied external parasites feast on blood meals and can transmit Lyme disease, Rocky Mountain spotted fever, and ehrlichiosis. They cause anemia, heart damage, rashes, fevers, and painful joints.

Locating Ticks

The spring and summer months are usually considered tick season. If your dog has returned from an outdoor romp or a walk in a woodsy area, don't be surprised if he comes back with a tick clinging to his chest, neck, or head. Check him over for any ticks before letting him back into the house. At first glance, a tick looks as if a black flattened spider stuck to your dog's coat, but a closer look reveals a head and legs.

These eight-legged insects live in woods, tall grass, weeds, and brush. After climbing onto low hanging plants, they wait to attach themselves to people and pets when they pass by. Ticks cling to a dog anywhere they can grab onto, but they particularly like the head, neck, ears, or feet. It's also not surprising to find a tick stuck to a dog's chest or back.

Fighting Ticks

To prevent ticks from plaguing your dog, follow the same precautions for avoiding fleas by maintaining his health through a good diet and frequent grooming. Also keep your dog out of woodsy areas and trim bushes and cut any low-hanging branches in your yard. Many of the newer oral and topical products that prevent and sterilize adult fleas also work on ticks. Give these seasonally when the chance of flea and tick infestation is high.

Removing a Tick

If you find a tick on your dog, don't panic and don't touch it. Calmly gather some fine-point tweezers, some latex gloves, rubbing alcohol or cooking oil, and a small jar. Use the following steps to safely remove the tick:

1. Using the tweezers, grasp the tick firmly near the head as close to the dog's skin as possible.
2. If the tick is difficult to lift, put a little alcohol or oil on it.
3. Pull the tick gently but steadily to release if from the dog's skin.
4. Drop the tick in the jar and fill it with alcohol or oil to kill the tick.

A month later, take your dog to the veterinarian to check if the tick bite infected your dog. Catching a problem early on and treating it with antibiotics can prevent more serious disease.

Mange

People once believed that mange was a highly contagious and disfiguring skin disease that an affected dog could transmit through contact. This is a myth. Caused by a microscopic mite, mange symptoms often look like flea bite reactions. There are three varieties of mange: demodectic, cheyletiella, and sarcoptic.

FACT

Diagnosing mange can be difficult. The symptoms of mange often look like other skin conditions, including autoimmune diseases, bacterial infections from flea allergies, and contact dermatitis. Despite repeated skin scrapings and examination under a microscope, mites can only be identified in less than 30 percent of cases.

The first signs of mange appear as red cone-shaped bumps on the head, usually on the edges of the ears, or the groin or armpits. Red spots appear as female mites burrow into the skin, which exudes serum. When this dries it crusts and scabs over. Scratching at the infected area spreads it, causing the hair to fall out. A secondary bacterial infection develops and produces a foul odor.

Preventing Mange

Similar to flea and tick infestations, mange needs a weak immune system to thrive. Stressed and undernourished puppies and young dogs are usually the victims. Without any intervention, many mild cases of mange will clear up in time, but more severe infections need some assistance.

Traditional mange treatment applies strong insecticides to the affected skin areas. These toxic chemicals must be repeated, but unless the immune system is strengthened, the mites will return.

Demodectic or Red Mange

Caused by a microscopic mite located in the hair follicles, demodectic or red mange is the most common form of mange.

Demodectic mites are a normal inhabitant of the skin fauna in small numbers. They are passed from the mother to the pup very early in life, and a healthy immune system will keep the parasite in check, preventing any disease. If the immune system is compromised for any reason, the mites can start to proliferate and cause skin disease. It is very uncommon for this mite to be transferred from one dog to another, apart from the mother to pup.

The skin disease presents as either a localized infection or a body-wide systemic infection. Local infection usually appears as a scaly bald patch, often on the face, and usually affects puppies early in life. Generalized demodex is much more severe and can cause hair loss over the entire body with scaly and thickened skin. It can affect either puppies or adults and usually indicates a deeper problem related to the immune system.

Cheyletiella Mange

Known as walking dandruff because it is dry and flaky, these mites usually show up on puppies. They look like a row of dandruff that appears to be traveling down the middle of the back. The motion is caused by mites moving beneath the scaly layer of the skin. This skin disease is highly contagious, can be transmitted to other dogs or people, and can cause intense itching.

Sarcoptic Mange

The sarcoptic mange mite causes intense itching with a red rash on the edges of the ears, elbows, and hocks, or ankles. To diagnose this type of mange, the veterinarian scrapes off a bit of the affected area and examines it under a microscope.

Although the mites may be difficult to locate, many veterinarians suggest treating the condition if the dog is scratching and has scaly skin. In severe cases of sarcoptic mange, your veterinarian may suggest a topical prescription medication, a medicated bath to remove scales, clipping for long-haired dogs, and either a Lime Sulfur dip treatment or an oral drug therapy for very extreme cases. The veterinarian should consider the animal's overall health and look for signs of immune deficiency or hypersensitivity. He may prescribe Chinese herbs and supplements such as fish oil and vitamin E.

Ear Mites

Less than a millimeter in length, ear mites burrow deep in the ear canal of puppies and young dogs with weak immune systems. They feast on the blood and debris in the ear and cause irritation and excessive earwax production. As the wax continues to accumulate, it causes secondary ear infections, pain, and inflammation. Eventually, it causes hearing loss.

FACT

In mild cases, flush the ear with a mixture of essential oils—about ten drops of rosemary, lemon, and eucalyptus oils and four ounces of warm olive oil. You can also use Halo's Natural Herbal Ear Wash, which contains witch hazel, chamomile extract, sage oil, clove oil, horehound extract, southern wood extract, calendula, pennyroyal oil, and St. John's Wort oil.

Dogs with low-hanging ears are especially vulnerable because air cannot reach the inside of the ear and ear mites flourish in the dark canal. If the infection is severe, you can recognize this ear problem by its characteristic strong musty odor. Affected dogs will continuously scratch their ears and rub their heads on the ground to try to ease the discomfort.

Other herbal oils you can use include neem and peppermint. Clean the earwax out by putting some oil inside the ear canal and massaging the outside. Insert a strip of cotton into the ear to wipe out the wax. Never use Q-tips or any other objects because these can injure the ear. Repeat the process twice a day.

If the ears haven't improved after a few days, your dog needs to see the veterinarian. Since ear itching is a common problem, the veterinarian will collect a little of the ear debris and examine it under the microscope to determine if this is a bacterial or yeast infection before prescribing treatment. To treat the ear mites, she may flush the ears. If the problem is severe, she may prescribe a traditional medication, such as a topical insecticide.

Lice

These small and flattened insects are not as common as fleas or ticks, but they are still agonizing annoyances for dogs. Biting and blood-sucking, these external parasites are fast movers but they do not travel back and forth between dogs and people. They limit their residence to either dogs or to people and spread through contact with lice-infested grooming tools or other dogs.

Lice flourish in less-than-hygienic environments, making puppies highly susceptible, especially if their mothers are already lice-infested. These parasites cause tender, intense itching that produces red, scabby areas on the skin. You'll notice nits or eggs stuck on the hair shafts and poor coat condition, but you can use flea shampoo remedies to rid your dog of these parasites.

Heartworms

Mosquitoes are responsible for one of the most deadly internal canine parasites—heartworms. When a mosquito bites a dog, it can infect it with adolescent heartworms. Within six or seven months, the new adult heartworms root themselves in the heart and blood vessels of the lungs and grow as long as eleven inches.

ALERT!

All dogs should be protected from heartworm before mosquito season and until a month or two after the season is over. In some areas, treatment is necessary all year. Indoor dogs that go out in the morning and evening are especially at risk because mosquitoes are most active during these times.

The heart must pump extra blood to handle the extra worm population blocking the blood flow of oxygen to other tissues. There may be no signs of heartworm, but severe cases may present with persistent coughing, lethargy, shortness of breath, weakness, fainting, heart failure, or sudden death.

Early Prevention

Preventing heartworm is the best defense against this deadly disease. Two oral medications—ivermectin and milbemycin—given once a month immediately kill any microscopic heartworm larvae.

As a precaution in regions with high mosquito populations, give your dog coenzyme Q10 as well as antioxidants. These supplements are helpful when there may be damage to the heart, but they are not preventatives for infection. Another way to reduce mosquito bites and your dog's risk of contracting heartworm is to feed him a raw diet. The ingredients may repel mosquitoes.

When your dog goes outside in the early morning or evening, rub a solution of one drop of eucalyptus oil mixed with a cup of water over his face. You can also reduce the risk of mosquito bites by eliminating standing water on your property, maintaining a clean outdoor environment, and by avoiding large bodies of water.

Diagnosing Heartworm

Your veterinarian will use a series of blood tests to check for proteins from heartworms. An ultrasound of the heart and X-rays will reveal the actual worms and the extent of the damage to the heart. Your veterinarian may also run a blood panel to determine if there is any liver or kidney damage.

The veterinarian evaluates the results and determines the level of severity. Sometimes a dog shows no signs of heartworm disease. In minimal cases, dogs may show no symptoms of illness or may cough occasionally or be tired after exercising. Moderately affected dogs have mild anemia and some protein in the urine, while severely affected dogs have difficulty breathing, a persistent cough, weight loss, more severe anemia, and urinary protein loss. In the worst cases, death is imminent and dogs can only be saved by surgically removing the adult heartworms. However, this surgery carries extreme risk because the dog may be too weak to survive the procedure.

Treatment

In serious cases, treating heartworm infection isn't simple or safe. Harsh arsenic-based drugs may be needed to kill adult heartworms. While herbs

THE EVERYTHING NATURAL HEALTH FOR DOGS BOOK

such as rosemary, thyme, mint, sage, clove, garlic, hawthorn berry, milk thistle extract, and dried cranberry have been used to treat heartworms, these may be helpful only in the early stages of the disease.

Other Internal Parasites

There are other internal parasites that live in the intestines and are commonly found in puppies or young dogs. Canine mothers may pass along roundworms and hookworms before or after birth. Adult dogs in poor health can also get roundworms, hookworms, whipworms, and tapeworms. Depending on the health of the dog, the symptoms can range from mild to life-threatening.

Worms

Puppies can become infected with roundworms and hookworms when they are still in the womb. The immature forms of these worms travel through the mother's uterus until they reach the developing fetuses. When puppies begin to nurse, they become infected again through their mother's milk.

E-QUESTION

Can I tell if my pet has intestinal worms?
You may not see any evidence, although roundworms are several inches long, look like spaghetti, and show up in stool or vomit. Hookworms and whipworms are too tiny to see. Tapeworm segments appear in the anal area and look like white rice. Many of these parasites cause digestive upset and diarrhea. Severe weight loss results if they are not treated.

When you take your dog to the veterinarian, your veterinarian will ask you to bring in a small portion of your dog's stool. He will examine it under a microscope to detect any eggs. After this fecal analysis, your veterinarian may prescribe a conventional dewormer and want to perform another fecal exam after treatment to determine its effectiveness.

Natural Remedies

If your dog is receiving treatment for internal parasites, give these natural remedies and supplements to aid healing. Check the dosage listed on the package. These include:

- **Pumpkin seeds.** Give ¼ teaspoon to 1 teaspoon ground seeds for every ten to twenty pounds of your dog's weight once a day. If you buy them raw, grind them in a clean coffee grinder.
- **Coenzyme Q10.** This strengthens the heart.
- **Goldenseal.** This is helpful for mucous membrane infections.

Giardia and Coccidia

Dogs contract giardia from drinking infected water and coccidia from eating contaminated food or fecal matter. These protozoal parasites are the source of gastrointestinal pain, gas, or weight loss. This can be life-threatening in puppies. Coccidian infections cause watery diarrhea, and explosive mucoid diarrhea is common with giardia.

To diagnose either of these single-celled organisms, your veterinarian will want to perform a fresh fecal sample directly from the rectum. If the symptoms are severe, your veterinarian may prescribe medication.

Giardia with grapefruit seed extract may also be an effective treatment. You can give your dog ten to fifteen drops of the liquid grapefruit seed extract for every ten pounds of his body weight up to five times a day for up to fourteen days. Break capsules open and sprinkle the powder onto food or dilute with water. Probiotics and digestive enzymes may also help.

CHAPTER 9

Vaccinations

At one time all dogs went to the veterinarian every year for their booster shots. One syringe filled with five different vaccines kept a dog safe from disease. Unfortunately, vaccines are not always foolproof and can't prevent all life-threatening illnesses. We now know that giving more of them isn't the answer, especially when the effects of overvaccination impair the immune system. Veterinary researchers have different recommendations to protect your dog against diseases.

What's in a Vaccine?

The question of whether or not to vaccinate a dog against a disease is one of the most controversial in holistic veterinary medicine. Every veterinarian seems to have a different opinion on this subject.

Far more than just a needle and some liquid, a vaccine is one of the most important preventive health measures in existence. It is introduced into the body in order to prevent infection or control disease that is caused by a disease-producing organism, such as a virus or bacteria. When your dog receives a vaccine, a tiny amount of antigen, or a disease-causing organism known as a pathogen, is injected into the body. This stimulates the immune system to produce a response by making antibodies to protect it from the invader.

E-QUESTION

Do holistic veterinarians recommend vaccines?
Every doctor has a different opinion. Some give no vaccines at all, some give the core set only to puppies, and some comply with the legal requirements of their state. Other vets administer titers, or blood tests that determine immunity levels, before vaccinating.

When the body is attacked by a real pathogen, the immune system responds quickly by producing antibodies to fight infection or disease. Vaccines are meant to teach the immune system how to respond in case of future exposure to the pathogen. An effective vaccine provides the right amount and the right type of antigen to protect against disease.

The Immune System

Immunizations protect dogs against diseases, viruses, bacteria, and spirochetes by stimulating the immune system. These diseases— such as rabies, canine distemper, canine parvovirus, canine adenovirus, canine parainfluenza, leptospirosis, and Lyme disease— are serious.

While it is ideal to protect dogs from these harmful diseases, administering vaccines becomes counterproductive when dogs experience severe adverse reactions to them. Some dogs have immediate allergic reactions to vaccines. In the mildest forms, these symptoms can include lethargy, fever, loss of appetite, muscle swelling, or permanent hair loss near the point of injection. Moderate reactions include intense itching, hives, and rapid swelling and redness of the lips and around the eyes and neck.

FACT

Rabies is a killer virus. More than 50,000 people and millions of animals contract it every year around the world. Cases occur in all states in the United States except Hawaii. An infected dog can spread rabies when it bites a healthy animal or person. It can be prevented by a series of rabies vaccines.

More serious issues include potentially fatal breathing difficulties, neurological disorders, and autoimmune problems. In cases of autoimmune disease, the body attacks its own cells due to an overactive immune response, possibly triggered by a vaccine or another stimulus.

The stresses a vaccine can place on the immune system can be compounded by poor nutrition, current illness, or emotional and psychological stresses. For females, fluctuating hormones are another stress on the body when she is either coming into estrus, going out of estrus, or is pregnant.

Core Vaccines

Vaccine manufacturers market more than a dozen vaccines for diseases that affect dogs, but this doesn't mean your dog should receive all of them. Maybe you live in an area where one particular disease isn't prevalent or your dog is an indoor dog and is seldom exposed to other dogs that might transmit it.

With all the different types and combinations of vaccines, it's easy to become confused about which vaccine you should give your dog or even how often to vaccinate. For this reason, many people leave it up to their veterinarian to make that decision. Be an informed dog owner and discuss the options with your veterinarian.

In 2006, the American Animal Hospital Association (AAHA) Canine Vaccine Task Force recommended that certain core vaccines should be given to all dogs in the United States. These include the following:

- **Canine adenovirus-2 (CAV-2).** This vaccine protects against infectious canine hepatitis, a disease that affects the liver, eyes, kidneys, and blood vessels. The symptoms include fever, inflammation of the nose or mouth, abdominal pain, diarrhea, loss of appetite, depression, and hemorrhage.
- **Canine distemper virus (CDV).** Distemper is a highly contagious viral infection that affects the nervous system, respiratory system, and gastrointestinal tract with symptoms such as coughing, sneezing, nasal discharge, fever, loss of appetite, vomiting, diarrhea, and seizures. Although it is fatal, this disease is rare today.
- **Canine parvovirus (CPV).** Highly contagious and potentially deadly, parvovirus affects the gastrointestinal tract and white blood cells. The symptoms are bloody diarrhea, vomiting, and lethargy.
- **Rabies virus.** Rabies invades the nervous system and is spread through the saliva of infected animals. It is fatal once symptoms appear. In many states, rabies vaccinations are mandated by law.

The AAHA recommends that these core vaccines be given to puppies starting at six to eight weeks of age and given every three to four weeks until puppies reach fifteen to sixteen weeks of age. A booster should follow at one year and every three years after that. Many holistic and integrative veterinarians suggest the following protocol:

- 9–10 weeks of age: Distemper/Parvo MLV
- 14 weeks: Distemper/Parvo MLV
- 20 weeks or older: Rabies one year killed
- 1 year: Distemper/Parvo MLV
- 1 year: Rabies, three year killed, three to four weeks apart from any other vaccine
- Subsequent vaccines or titers every three years

Non-Core Vaccines

Non-core vaccines are optional. They cover those diseases that are endemic to your particular geographic area, but they are withheld if your dog has a higher risk of an adverse reaction to the vaccine than of contracting the disease itself. All vaccine protocols should be individualized to the dog. Non-core vaccinations include:

- **Bordetella bronchiseptica.** This is referred to as kennel cough because a group of dogs can contract it when they are kept in close quarters. There are several strains and severe cases can progress into pneumonia. The vaccine is most often given nasally. It is short-lived and must be repeated yearly.
- **Canine parainfluenza virus (CPiV).** Highly contagious, this respiratory disease is a strain of kennel cough that can progress into a secondary infection.
- **Leptospirosis.** A spiral-shaped bacteria that thrives in stagnant, warm water such as a pond or a pool. Symptoms are lethargy, muscle pain, fever, and excessive drinking and urinating due to kidney infection.
- **Lyme borreliosis.** Lyme disease. Carried by ticks, it is prevalent only in certain areas of the United States.

Bordetella, coronavirus, and giardia vaccines only provide limited immunity and have variable efficacy. The Lyme vaccine should only be given in areas where the risk of contracting the disease is greater than 50 percent. In areas where the infection rate is less than 10 percent, the AAHA does not recommend the Lyme vaccine. The leptospirosis vaccine only offers limited short-term immunity, and doses must be repeated every six to nine months.

Types of Vaccines

Veterinary researchers are constantly devising new ways to protect dogs through vaccines. Whether or not you believe in introducing antigens into your dog's body to stimulate the immune system to fight diseases, new medical technology is being developed all the time.

Modified Live (MLV)

A modified live vaccine stimulates the immune system by carrying attenuated (weakened) live, disease-causing organisms. The advantages of administering a modified live vaccine include providing a rapid onset of immunity, offering protection in a single dose, and overcoming interference with maternal antibodies. A disadvantage is that it can produce mild signs of the disease, which can be confused with natural infection.

Killed

Killed organisms are used for MLVs. While they cannot cause the infection, protection will not be acquired for one to two weeks from the time a booster vaccine is administered two to three weeks after the initial vaccination. Therefore, dogs without any prior protection will be vulnerable for up to five weeks after their first vaccine.

Recombinant vaccines use bacteria or yeast to produce a bacterial or viral protein that is purified and injected. To provide protection, the immune system creates antibodies to the disease agent's protein. The advantage is that it doesn't need an adjuvant and there's no chance that the dog can become ill from the vaccine.

To help stabilize a killed vaccine and to stimulate the immune system to respond, an adjuvant is added. This is a chemical that may cause inflammation; in many cases, adjuvants have been responsible for producing vaccine side effects.

Vaccine Reactions

Allergic reactions and even serious anaphylactic reactions happen more often with killed vaccines for rabies, canine coronavirus, and leptospirosis. This is because killed vaccines have more virus or bacterial particles per dose and have adjuvants added to them.

Some dogs will have a reaction to a vaccine within minutes or less than twenty-four hours of the vaccination. Common symptoms of anaphylaxis are diarrhea, vomiting, shock, seizures, coma, and even death. The dog's gums will be beige, not pink, and his legs will feel cold to the touch. His heart rate will be fast but the pulse will be weak.

To Vaccinate or Not to Vaccinate

When deciding whether or not your dog should have a particular vaccine, discuss the following considerations with your veterinarian:

- Your dog's overall health. He should be free from any short-term illness, chronic disease, or stress from a lifestyle change in the household. His immune system should be strong and he should be fed a quality diet.
- Your dog's risk of contracting the disease without the vaccination. If your dog never interacts with other dogs he might not need protection from communicable diseases.
- Your dog's age. Dogs over the age of seven years may already have enough protection for certain diseases. There may be a higher risk of a negative reaction at this age.
- Potential risks for your dog's breed. Some breeds have hereditary immune sensitivities. It helps to know your dog's ancestry and health history.
- Legal requirements for your community.

Maintaining your dog's health is your best defense against preventing a bad reaction to a vaccine. Feeding your dog a natural diet and making sure he gets enough exercise goes a long way toward this goal.

Overvaccination

Your dog's vaccinations probably will provide him with immunity for years after the vaccine's manufacturer recommends that you readminister. If your dog is exposed to a disease and is not up to date on his vaccines, he may not contract the disease or might only contract a mild form of it. Of course, he may come down with the disease just as you feared. For this reason, many dog owners tend to repeat a vaccine just to be on the safe side.

FACT

Small dogs, many terriers, and some other breeds may have a higher risk for allergic reactions from vaccination, and this has prompted their national breed clubs to sponsor a grant to learn more. Look up your dog's breed club for more information.

These owners may have relocated and changed veterinarians and don't have a record of when their dog was last vaccinated, or maybe they've acquired a new dog that doesn't have a vaccine record. All dogs should be vaccinated as puppies with the core series to induce immunity. From that point forward, owners and veterinarians should rely on titer testing to signal when a dog should receive additional vaccines. This is the most cautious approach to prevent the possibility of autoimmune reactions to overvaccination.

Puppy Protection

Mother Nature knows how to take care of puppies. When they come into this world and begin to nurse, their mothers' milk contains immunity-producing proteins. These maternal antibodies provide the same protection for the puppy that the mother has. If her immunity level was high, these antibodies may last up to three months. If they were low, the puppy may only have five or six weeks of protection before immunity begins to diminish.

If a puppy receives a vaccine before the antibodies are gone, the vaccine does not take effect and provides no additional immunity. The puppy is protected by whatever immunity the mother has delivered. The vaccine is meant to fill the gap in case maternal antibodies are not sufficient or wane early. Of all the types of disease protection, parvovirus immunity from the mother lasts the longest. In some puppies this can last up to four months.

Some veterinarians recommend that owners keep puppies away from other dogs and places where other dogs usually congregate until about four months of age. This is when the puppy's own immune system takes charge. Many holistic veterinarians recognize that early socializing is important to the behavioral development of puppies and say it's okay to take puppies out to socialize before four months of age. Discuss the pros and cons with your veterinarian before deciding.

E-QUESTION

When should a puppy have his first vaccine?
Between nine and ten weeks of age is ideal. This is in case the maternal antibodies have worn off and before the puppy's own immune system has kicked in. A vaccine booster should be given fourteen weeks after the maternal antibodies are no longer protective and in case the first vaccine was inactivated by the maternal antibodies.

Using Titers

In the past, annual revaccinations were the standard of care after a puppy had been given her initial vaccines. However, research has shown that the duration of immunity is actually longer than one year, and the new standard protocol recommends revaccination every three years. Holistic veterinarians and many integrative veterinarians believe that dogs maintain their immunity even longer than three years for many diseases and don't need vaccination so frequently. Many holistic veterinarians prefer to use a titer before administering another vaccine.

A high titer count reveals a high level of immunity to the disease, while a low titer count indicates that the dog is still susceptible to the disease. Antibody levels can be measured with the distemper virus, parvovirus, adenovirus, and Lyme disease, but they are not available for bordatella, parainfluenza virus, or coronavirus.

If you decide not to vaccinate your dog because you are concerned about an adverse reaction, plan on taking your dog to the veterinarian once every three years for titers. Ask your veterinarian about the expense of having a titer and decide in advance if this fits your budget. Many veterinarians charge the same amount for a titer that they would for a vaccine.

FACT

A titer is a blood test that measures the amount of antibodies that develop after a vaccine is given or after exposure to a disease. It indicates whether the dog has enough protection against the disease. It is expressed by a ratio that represents how many times the blood can be diluted until no antibodies are found. If the dog's blood is diluted a thousand times and no antibodies to the antigen are found, then the titer count is 1:1,000.

Homeopathic Choices

Some holistic veterinarians will routinely give a homeopathic remedy either before or after vaccinating, whether the dog needs it or not. Other doctors choose to treat a dog homeopathically only if he has an adverse reaction to a vaccine.

Another veterinary option is to provide core vaccines only for puppies, or not to administer any vaccinations except for perhaps the rabies vaccine, which is legally required.

Vaccinosis

Many holistic practitioners believe that in addition to the problems in the immune system (hypothyroidism, inflammatory bowel disease, and lupus), overvaccination negatively affects the body's basic life force.

In the nineteenth century, J. Compton-Burnett, a homeopathic doctor in England, coined a term for this effect—*vaccinosis*, which leads to a wide range of diseases ranging from skin allergies and skin diseases to behavior changes. Homeopathic doctors prefer to give their patients homeopathic nosodes, or natural disease products.

Many holistic veterinarians do not agree on whether nosodes offer protection from disease.

Remedies After Vaccines

There are a few good homeopathic remedies that can be used as a preventive after a vaccine is given, such as sulphur, thuja, and silicea. Sulphur can be used for any skin eruptions, indigestion, and seizures.

E-QUESTION

What is a homeopathic nosode?
Given before or after exposure, this remedy is prepared from the disease itself, using a pathological specimen, such as a diseased fragment of tissue, or body secretion like blood or urine. Nosodes stimulate the immune system to react against a disease and can offer protection from kennel cough, parvovirus, and canine distemper.

Thuja is made from the foliage of a red cedar tree. First used by Native Americans and early European explorers to cure scurvy, thuja is rich in vitamin C. Some proponents claim it will aid digestion, ease depression or respiratory disturbances, and help alleviate exhaustion. Other homeopathic veterinarians believe thuja may not be effective because vaccine reactions vary so much.

Silicea stimulates cell metabolism and cell formation and protects the nerves. You can also use it for infections at the injection site, weakness in the rear legs, and chilliness. Other remedies include apis for hot, swollen injection areas, and ledum for cool swelling.

CHAPTER 10

Allergies

When a dog constantly licks and chews at his feet and body and has repeated ear infections, he's most likely suffering from an allergy. Allergies are an abnormal response by the immune system to a normally harmless substance. These seemingly harmless foreign substances such as food, pollens, molds, and dust mites can wreak havoc on a dog's life and are often responsible for repeated visits to the veterinarian's office. Fleas and common household items can be the culprits too.

What's an Allergy?

Allergies affect one out of six people; like their owners, dogs can develop allergies too. But while human allergy sufferers commonly sneeze and wheeze, dogs frequently have skin problems as well as runny eyes, noses, and sneezing. Signs of allergies can include chewing, licking, or scratching; shedding; hair loss; ear infections; vomiting; and diarrhea.

An allergy is an abnormal reaction to an ordinarily harmless substance called an allergen. An allergic reaction occurs when the dog's immune system comes in contact with an allergen and overreacts. An allergen is a foreign material that may come from trees, grass, pollens, food, dust, fleas, wool or nylon fabrics, and rubber and plastics.

Allergens enter the body through inhaling, eating, or flea bites. They can also enter through the skin. Once inside the bloodstream, the immune system mounts a response to the substance by producing antibodies. The antibodies cause certain cells to release histamine, which leads to allergy symptoms.

The most common type of allergy is inhalant, or atopy. This is an allergy to something airborne in the environment and may be seasonal, but it may be year-round if the allergen is always present. Molds, mildew, and house dust mites are common causes of nonseasonal allergies.

E-QUESTION

How old are most dogs when they develop allergies?
It depends on the source of the allergy. Flea allergies can occur at any age, although they are more common in dogs older than six months. Food allergies are highly variable and can occur from four months to fourteen years old, but they begin before one year in up to half of all dogs that develop them. Atopy usually presents between one and a half and three years but is possible as early as four months. As a dog ages, allergies tend to worsen.

Allergy Symptoms

When a dog develops an allergy she may have itchy skin and eruptions and might lick and chew on her feet until they are red and sore. With a white or light-colored dog, the saliva can stain the body coat or feet orange or reddish brown.

If your dog is prone to ear infections, keep the ear clean! By ridding the ear of an abundance of earwax buildup, your dog will have fewer infections. It is imperative to address the food allergy, or the ear infections will recur.

The dog might have a series of ear infections. This is because the glands in the ear responsible for producing wax will overproduce when confronted with an allergen. Bacteria and yeast thrive in the waxy buildup, which leads to infection. In the worst cases the ear can be so severely infected that the anatomy of the ear itself is actually changed. In very extreme cases of chronic ear infections there will be so much swelling in the ear that it will require surgery to correct.

Other signs of allergies include:

- Constantly licking front feet
- Red, swollen toes
- Digestive upsets, including stomach gurgling and gas
- Rubbing the face on the carpet or bed
- Scratching the side and belly
- Dry, crusty, red, or oily skin, depending on the type of coat
- Patchy hair loss
- Secondary bacterial infections from skin lesions
- Irritated anal glands

Allergies can be exacerbated by inappropriate diet, overvaccination, and inappropriate use of steroids, which suppress the symptoms but don't address the cause. Some autoimmune conditions, such as inflammatory bowel disease and hypothyroidism, can compound the symptoms of allergies.

Diagnosing Allergies

Allergies don't crop up overnight. Dogs are exposed to an offending allergen over a period of time. This is called sensitization. Allergy symptoms will often flare up within one to three years after exposure to an allergen. It's important to notice whether the symptoms appear to be seasonal or year round, as this can help identify the trigger.

FACT

To identify an allergy, the veterinarian evaluates the dog and rules out other problems that may produce similar signs. Then the focus shifts to finding the particular allergen. Your dog may be restricted to a hypoallergenic diet or his outdoor time during pollen season may be limited. Then your veterinarian will add one allergen at a time back into your dog's life to test for recurrence of the symptoms and conclusively identify the allergen.

Holistic veterinarians differ in their opinions on the best way to treat an allergy. Some use conventional drugs and allergy injections to relieve serious inflammation and itching, while others believe that the best approach is to strengthen the immune system and identify and eliminate the trigger of the allergy. An allergy will often resolve itself once the dog's overall health improves, but this depends on the dog's immune system's ability to cope with the problem.

Food Allergies

It's easy to blame food for a dog's allergy problems, but food allergies are only responsible for 10 to 15 percent of all allergy problems. Food allergies affect males and females equally, whether or not they are spayed or neutered.

Most dogs are about one year old when they have their first food allergy, although a dietary problem can show up as early as four months of age and as late as fourteen years. While it may seem like a dog suddenly becomes allergic after eating a particular food, it actually takes time for a food allergy to develop. Dogs with food allergies may also have inhalant allergies at the same time.

Common Food Allergens

The top food allergens are corn, wheat, soy, yeast, potato, and beet. Other common offending ingredients include beef, dairy products, chicken and chicken eggs, cheese, nuts, fruits, tomatoes, and carrots. Food additives, colorings, and artificial preservatives also cause hypersensitivity.

Diagnosing a Food Allergy

When a dog has a food allergy, he may have skin irritations and ear infections as well as gastrointestinal signs such as vomiting and diarrhea. To diagnose a food allergy, the veterinarian will recommend a food elimination trial by feeding the dog a diet with only one protein source or with a hydrolyzed hypoallergenic diet.

In a food trial, the dog is fed a simplified diet for sixty to ninety days. This food should be fed exclusively, and all treats, vitamins and supplements, and flavored heartworm or flea medications must be discontinued for this period. This desensitizes the body to troublesome allergens. Following this period, the dog is fed the original diet. If a reaction occurs, one or more of the ingredients is the problem.

Although lamb and rice dog food is often touted as the perfect allergy-free diet, it isn't. Many commercial lamb and rice dog food recipes also contain wheat, egg, corn, or other ingredients that cause food allergies. Lamb is also a common allergen.

Home Cooking

To feed your dog a home-cooked, allergen-free meal, prepare a variety of fresh foods that your dog has not been exposed to in the past. Use a simple stew recipe with one novel protein source, fresh or frozen fruits and vegetables, and whole grains. You can find hypoallergenic recipes in dog cookbooks such as *The Everything® Cooking for Dogs Book*.

Hypoallergenic starches include barley, oatmeal, brown rice, buckwheat, millet, quinoa, tapioca, and sweet potato. To supply essential fatty acids, add ½ teaspoon to 1 tablespoon of raw olive or flaxseed oil to each meal. Give smaller dogs smaller amounts.

Start with a small batch to see how your dog adapts to it before preparing enough for a week or two at a time. Consider freezing some to be used at a later date for convenience. An average portion size is 1 to 1½ cups for every fifteen to twenty pounds of body weight.

Atopy

Atopy is an allergic reaction to an allergen that is inhaled or absorbed through the skin. Most allergies are this type and many are seasonal—at least initially. Over time, these often become year-round allergies. The most common allergens are mold and mildew; grass, tree, and weed pollens; and dust mites and dander. Offending grasses include the following:

- Bluegrass
- Fescue
- Orchard grass
- Redtop/brome grass
- Ryegrass
- Timothy

The weeds that cause the most allergic reactions in dogs include the following:

- Cocklebur
- Dock
- Firebush
- Goldenrod
- Pigweed
- Plantain
- Ragweed
- Russian thistle
- Sage

The following trees are responsible for many inhalant allergies:

- Alder
- Ash
- Birch
- Box elder
- Cottonwood
- Hazelnut
- Hickory
- Juniper
- Mulberry
- Oak mix
- Red maple
- Sycamore
- Walnut
- Willow

When a dog has been exposed to a seasonal allergy, he will chew and scratch only during the time the allergens are prominent. This kind of allergy is easier for the veterinarian to treat than a year-round allergy problem. If she is going to use medication to treat an inhalant seasonal allergy, less medication is needed and the allergen is usually gone by the time the symptoms have disappeared. This treatment will usually be required the following year when the allergen is in season again.

Treating Atopy

To diagnose atopy, the holistic veterinarian may use a blood test to screen for antibodies for common allergens. Two standard blood tests veterinarians use are the ELISA (enzyme-linked immunoabsorbent assay) and the RAST (radioallergosorbent test). Both can produce false positives and false negatives, although more veterinarians rely on the accuracy of the ELISA test.

Intradermal skin testing is considered the gold standard for identifying the allergens that cause atopy because of its accuracy, but it is more invasive. The dog must be sedated and multiple antigens are injected into the dog's skin. Allergic reactions will cause raised red areas. The veterinarian identifies the problem allergens and mixes a small amount of those allergens to create injections for your dog. These allergens will be injected on a specific schedule and will gradually be increased in strength over time. You will often be referred to a veterinary dermatologist for this therapy.

Using natural anti-inflammatory drugs along with fatty acid supplements is another form of allergy treatment. Antihistamines might be effective in controlling allergies as well. When used with other therapies including fatty acids and avoidance techniques, antihistamines can reduce allergic reactions. However, histamine is not the primary cause of allergic inflammation in dogs, so antihistamines have variable results in our itchy canines. About 40 percent of dogs will respond to one of the antihistamines. Therefore, it is commonly recommended that antihistamines be tried one at a time for about two weeks each to see which is most effective. The typical medications used are Benadryl, Tavist, Chlor-trimeton, and Atarax. Because these drugs have side effects, such as drowsiness, careful dosing is essential. It is important to discuss their use with your veterinarian before trying them.

FACT

The American Academy of Allergy Asthma and Immunology (*www.aaaai .org*) provides a pollen and mold count in different areas of the United States. You can use it to determine the pollen and mold concentrations where you live. Levels for trees, grasses, weeds, and molds are given with definitions for low, moderate, high, and very high concentrations.

Many conventional veterinarians will use steroids (such as cortisone, prednisone, dexamethasone, and hydrocortisone) to treat an allergic reaction. Antihistamines and steroids in combination can improve a severe allergic reaction, although many holistic veterinarians are typically reluctant to resort to using steroids if alternative therapies exist. Steroids have serious side effects if used in excess.

Avoiding Allergies

Avoiding offending agents along with other treatments will help manage atopy. First, determine what the allergens are through intradermal skin testing. If your dog is allergic to house dust, vacuum rooms with a HEPA filter vacuum. HEPA filters provide a higher filtration of smaller particles than traditional vacuum cleaner filters and are capable of catching particles invisible to the naked eye. Keep your dog out of the rooms you are vacuuming for a few hours.

Wash your dog's bedding in very hot water and don't let your dog sleep on upholstered furniture, which collects dust and dander. Don't give him stuffed toys, which also fill with dust. Try to keep your dog in rooms that don't have carpeting.

Bathing your dog every day or every other day with a hypoallergenic shampoo will help relieve intense itching. This washes away dirt and offending particles that irritate the skin. Choose shampoos and conditioners with oatmeal and aloe vera and use medicated products containing steroids as a last resort. Use spray-on conditioners between baths for extra itch relief.

To avoid contact with molds, keep your dog out of dark, airless rooms such as basements and restrict access to the yard when the grass is mowed. Use a portable humidifier in your home and clean and disinfect it regularly. If pollen bothers your dog, keep him out of fields and make sure he stays indoors as much as possible during periods of high pollen counts. After an outing in high grass and weeds, give him a bath or at least rinse him off.

Hyposensitization

Another form of allergy treatment is hyposensitization, or specific antigen injections. Holistic veterinarians have different opinions about whether to use these to provide allergy relief in dogs. When symptoms persist despite your best efforts to avoid allergens and to control allergies with appropriate drug and supplement use, many holistic vets will recommend hyposensitization. These allergy shots use the dog's own body to find a solution. Unfortunately, this therapy is very expensive and dogs need to be retested once a year to once every three years because many problems recur.

After intradermal skin testing has identified offending allergens, very small amounts of an antigen are injected once a week. This reprograms the body's immune system to accept the allergen. The goal is to eventually program the immune system not to react to the allergen at all.

If these injections are helpful, the dog will need to have them for several years—sometimes for the rest of his life. There is a 50 to 80 percent success rate with this therapy. However, this does not guarantee complete resolution of the problem—only improvement. Hyposensitization is usually suggested for the adult dog with year-round atopy or for dogs that have an unsatisfactory response to medical treatment.

Conventional Treatments of Skin Issues

When a dog has allergies he also has skin problems. Licking, chewing, and scratching often damages the skin, which leads to bacterial skin infections. Because veterinarians frequently see dogs with this problem, they will usually use antibiotics to treat the infection until it is controlled.

FACT

Autoimmune skin problems occur when the dog's immune system reacts against the skin's cells. A few of these are general immune issues, while others affect only the skin. Pemphigus vulgaris is a severe form of pemphigus, which forms scabs and pustules on the head and feet and spreads over the body.

There is a downside to this method of treatment. Although the dog may improve, the cause of the problem is never really discovered. Later on the same skin problem returns and must be medicated again.

Conventional veterinarians might use steroids and antihistamines to treat skin problems. These stop the itching, but they don't address the cause and there are potentially damaging side effects with these drugs. These include increased appetite and weight gain, constant urination and increased thirst, and hyperactivity or depression. These drugs also compromise the immune system. Other possible side effects include diabetes mellitus, pancreatitis, chronic infections, elevated liver enzymes, obesity, and osteoporosis.

Natural Holistic Therapies for Allergies

Acupuncture helps restore balance and could very well help alleviate allergy symptoms. When applied topically, Western herbs such as chickweed, jewelweed, plantain, tea bags, and witch hazel are useful for providing anti-inflammatory relief.

E-QUESTION

What is the difference between omega-3 and omega-6 fatty acids?
The omega-6 gamma-linolenic acid (evening primrose oil and borage oil) is beneficial in controlling inflammation caused by allergies, but safflower, canola, and corn oil are inflammatory. Omega-3 eicosapentaenoic acid (EPA) and docosahexaenoic acid (DHA) are anti-inflammatory. Flaxseed oil and fish body oil from salmon are also helpful.

Other herbs can be taken internally. German chamomile, yarrow, and yellow dock are soothing options. Consult with your veterinarian before using these as some dogs might be overly sensitive to them. The following herbs can also help restore equilibrium in the body:

- **Alfalfa** provides anti-inflammatory relief, especially in older dogs
- **Aloe vera** helps relieve itching
- **Burdock** helps rid toxins from the dog's system
- **Calendula** applied topically soothes the pain of intense itching
- **Chamomile** provides a cooling effect on irritated skin
- **Dandelion root** rids the body of toxins and supports liver functions
- **Licorice root** is a good alternative to steroids, although dogs with heart and hypertension issues should not use it
- **Nettle** is used mostly for seasonal allergies, although some dogs may experience adverse reactions
- **Red clover** boosts immunity; it contains bioflavonoids
- **Spirulina** supports the immune system and provides an important source of essential fatty acids

Omega fatty acid supplements are very helpful. The omega-6 fatty acids are usually found in commercial dog food, but the omega-3 fatty acids are not because they can't withstand the processing.

Vitamins A and E, quercetin, and bioflavonoids also help control allergy symptoms. Bathing your dog with a hypoallergenic shampoo provides relief from itching. It soothes the skin and reduces the chance that allergens will be absorbed through the skin.

Chinese herbs have been found to be very effective in managing skin disease. These herbs are classically used in formulas that are individualized to the patient according to the symptoms of the disease and the characteristics of the animal. The objective of this approach is to treat the underlying imbalance at the root of the disease. When the appropriate herb is found, most patients can experience complete and lasting relief. As the symptoms change or resolve, many practitioners will adjust the formula accordingly to completely eliminate the symptoms. A veterinarian that is trained in traditional Chinese medicine and herbs will be the best source for this treatment.

CHAPTER 11

Managing Arthritis

Like people, dogs get arthritis. In fact it's one of the oldest diseases in history, and scientists say that even dinosaurs suffered from chronic aches and pains. Fortunately, we now know how to manage this common ailment, so it's important to recognize when your dog is having pain in his limbs. To manage his discomfort and enable him to enjoy life a little more, keep his weight in the normal to lean range and provide homeopathy, herbal support, and acupuncture.

Recognizing Joint Pain

Dogs seldom show you how much pain they're in. From years of living in the wild they've learned how to hide their discomfort from predators who might be ready to pounce on any sign of weakness. Dogs haven't lost this evolutionary adaptation, and they still suffer silently. Often, a dog won't complain unless he is in extreme distress.

For the senior canine set, behaviors normally associated with pain can be misinterpreted as simply growing old, but if you can recognize when your dog is in pain you can obtain treatment and quickly alleviate his aches. In fact, early care and prevention of inflammation helps control the progression of arthritis and gives your dog that much more time to have an active lifestyle.

Arthritis is a mildly inflammatory condition that causes the cartilage between the joints to degenerate. Cartilage acts as a cushion between the bones that form a joint. When there's cartilage loss, bone rubs on bone— a very painful condition. As the condition worsens, movement becomes increasingly more painful and crippling.

E-QUESTION

Is it okay to take a puppy jogging?
No. He'll push to keep up and won't stop when he's tired. Wait until he's at least twelve to eighteen months old when the growth plates in his bones are closed. If you run with him earlier than that, you risk damaging his young joints. It's okay to let a puppy run around on his own because he knows when to quit.

Older dogs are prone to arthritis. It affects one in every five adult dogs and more than 75 percent of all dogs by the time they are ten years of age. Although dogs develop arthritis mostly in one or both hips, it can also affect the back, neck, knees, elbows, carpus (equivalent to the human wrist), shoulders, or ankles.

Signs of Arthritis

If you notice your dog doing any of the following for more than two weeks, he needs to visit the veterinarian for an arthritis evaluation:

- Favoring a limb or limping
- Rising slowly to a sitting or a standing position
- Sleeping more
- Hesitant to jump, run, climb stairs, or leap into the car
- Weight gain
- Less interest in being active or wanting to play
- Depressed attitude or behavior
- Less alert
- Difficulty defecating and/or urinating

In the early stages of arthritis, a dog may move away or flinch when touched if he feels any discomfort. Swollen joints are painful in dogs, just as they are in humans.

Types of Arthritis

Osteoarthritis is the result of damage to the joints. A dog with osteoarthritis will show signs of lameness, which can be brought on by damp or cool weather or exercise. Traumatic injury to bone, cartilage, or ligaments can also trigger osteoarthritis.

To diagnose the cause of pain, the veterinarian will take the dog's health history, perform an examination, and take an X-ray. With rheumatoid arthritis, a special blood test can be done to locate unique antibodies known as the rheumatoid factor. A thorough diagnosis is necessary before treatment begins because bone cancer and other diseases can have similar symptoms.

There are two broad classes of osteoarthritis. Repetitive overuse or misuse of joints causes primary osteoarthritis. Secondary arthritis is more common and is the result of some sort of initiating cause, such as poor conformation, physical injury or trauma, or joint dysplasia. Osteoarthritis is classified as noninflammatory even though there is some mild inflammation that results from the symptoms and progression of disease. Also known as degenerative joint disease, osteoarthritis may be inherited and is usually part of the normal aging process.

FACT

In rare cases, vaccinations can cause immune-based polyarthritis. Symptoms can follow the first injection or a booster vaccination and may spontaneously clear up within a few days. Therefore, it's important for the veterinarian to take a complete vaccination history, including noting previous vaccine reactions, before giving a vaccine.

Inflammatory arthritis includes rheumatoid arthritis and infectious arthritis. Rheumatoid arthritis is an immune-mediated inflammatory condition of the joints. It occurs mainly in small and toy breeds. Dogs are usually between the ages of two and six years when they are diagnosed, although cases in dogs as young as eight months have been reported. Rheumatoid arthritis is caused by an overreaction of the immune system. The body reacts to its own protein sources as if they were foreign protein particles and manufactures antibodies to shut them down. This damages the joint, and the cartilage and the bone in the joint wear away. While the symptoms may be identical to those in other forms of arthritis, the dog may or may not be lame and several joints are usually affected by rheumatoid arthritis. Other groups of inflammatory diseases that cause arthritis include cancer, gastrointestinal disease, infections in the body, and other immune complex diseases. In cases of infectious arthritis, an infectious agent causes joint inflammation.

Spondylosis is a degenerative, noninflammatory condition of the vertebrae. It is the accumulation of new bone (calcium deposits) around one or more joints of the spinal column. This does not usually cause pain, although some dogs do have problems.

Causes of Arthritis

Several conditions contribute to arthritis. The biggest culprit is obesity, which causes inflammation throughout the body. Too much weight also allows pressure on the joints to build up. Other factors include:

- High levels of stress
- Poor nutrition with inadequate protein, vitamins, or minerals
- Faulty genetic bone structure
- Immune system diseases or imbalance
- Lack of exercise
- Too much vigorous exercise before bones are done growing
- Bacterial invasion of joints
- Prior injuries to joints, ligaments, or bones
- Hypersensitivity reactions to antibiotics or vaccinations and boosters

Hip Dysplasia

A common cause of arthritis is hip dysplasia. This genetic condition most often occurs in giant and large breeds of dogs, such as Labrador and Golden Retrievers, Saint Bernards, Great Pyrenees, and German Shepherds, although many medium- and small-sized breeds may also develop the problem.

ALERT!

Medium- and large-breed puppies should not spend the majority of their time indoors on a smooth floor. This causes legs and hips to slide around too much and the muscles to atrophy. Canine feet need traction on a rough surface outdoors. Dogs need to move around freely to build up leg and hip muscle.

Hip dysplasia is a malformation of the hip socket where the femur does not fit tightly into the pelvic socket. The looseness produces pain, and a dog will limp or bunny hop when running.

The problem is usually apparent by the time a dog is eighteen months of age, although a veterinarian can palpate the hip before the puppy is four months of age to determine if there is loose movement in the hip joint. When a dog is two years old, the hip is fully formed and a series of X-rays can diagnose hip dysplasia.

Helping Joints Heal

When a dog is in pain, most owners will do just about anything to provide relief, even if it means giving the dog medications with strong side effects, putting the dog through traumatic and expensive surgery, or laying the dog to rest. While steroids and anti-inflammatory treatments may regulate the pain of arthritis, these don't repair damaged cartilage.

E-QUESTION

What is an NSAID? Does it help heal arthritis?
Nonsteroidal anti-inflammatory medications such as Rimadyl, Metacam, or EtoGesic can be effective. There are potential side effects, including kidney and liver disease and ulceration of the stomach and intestinal tract. Dogs should be screened before commencing NSAID therapy to make sure their kidneys and liver are healthy enough to cope with the medication.

For dogs with arthritis, there are several complementary therapies that ease pain, are less invasive than conventional methods, and offer many long-term benefits. These involve reducing joint inflammation and protecting the cartilage from further damage.

To alleviate pain, keep your dog at a normal weight, make sure he gets enough exercise, and provide physical comfort in the form of therapeutic warm bedding or stairs to the bed, couch, or car.

Steroids

A conventional veterinarian may prescribe steroids such as prednisone, prednisolone, dexamethasone, or triamcinolone to relieve a variety of conditions, such as allergies, inflammation from arthritis, and stomach and intestinal inflammation. Larger doses are prescribed in the beginning, then doses are tapered before the medication is eventually discontinued.

Dogs on these medications need to be closely monitored both by the veterinarian and the owner, as serious consequences can result if they are used incorrectly. Giving too much or too little medication, skipped doses, or abrupt cessation will cause a reaction. Steroids do not cure the problem;

they only suppress the symptoms, and the problem will often recur once the steroid is discontinued.

FACT

A new cutting-edge treatment can help a dysplastic hip joint repair itself. Fatty tissue from the dog's abdomen is removed and placed in a centrifuge that extracts stem cells from the tissue. The cells are injected into the failing hip, where they adapt and develop into healthy cartilage and tendon cells. For more information see *www.vet-stem .com*.

There are unpleasant side effects as well: cartilage damage, diabetes, and increased risk of infections. Other unwanted conditions include mood changes and irritability, increased thirst, panting, weight gain, and suppression of the immune system.

Surgery

If your dog is in intense pain or there is severe joint damage, the veterinarian may recommend performing surgery as a last resort to replace the defective joint. For serious cases of hip dysplasia, the surgeon can perform a hip replacement procedure to improve movement and function by replacing the damaged joint with an artificial one. If hip dysplasia is diagnosed early in life before significant degeneration occurs, a surgical procedure called a triple pelvic osteotomy may be an option to correct the conformation of the joint and prevent later disease and discomfort.

Joint Supplements

Glucosamine and chondroitin work wonders in decreasing inflammation. These supplements produce no side effects and occur naturally in the body.

They relieve pain and inflammation and they also help heal damaged cartilage repair itself by synthesizing new cartilage. Don't expect overnight improvement; it may take four to eight weeks before you see any changes in your dog's condition. Once she begins taking these neutraceu-ticals, however, your dog will need to stay on them for the rest of her life. Once they are discontinued, the cartilage will degenerate in four to six months.

Perna canaliculus is another anti-inflammatory and food supplement that helps heal cartilage and improves joint mobility. A natural source of glu-cosamine, chondroitin, and other nutrients, *perna canaliculus* is an edi-ble green-lipped mussel found off the shores of New Zealand. It contains essential building blocks necessary to rebuild joints and reduces pain, swelling, and inflammation.

Methylsulfonylmethane (MSM) is another effective pain reliever that helps reduce stiffness, swelling, and inflammation in joints. MSM pre-vents pressure buildup in cells, allowing nutrients in and forcing toxins out of the connective tissues as they heal. It insulates the bones from friction and cushions the joints during movement. MSM delivers sulfur to the joint, which, along with glucosamine, makes cartilage stronger and more resilient. This is why it is important to use these two supplements together.

Exercise Management

A moderate amount of exercise keeps your dog's joints lubricated, reduces pain, and strengthens the muscles that align and protect the joint from further damage. Moving around and getting her heart rate up also helps your dog maintain a healthy weight. Not using a sore joint only weak-ens the muscles around it and causes even more pain.

Veterinarians recommend taking your arthritic dog for a walk a few times a day and keeping her as active as possible. Gradually increase the duration of the walk, but never push your dog. If twenty minutes is too much for her to manage, shorten the time and try to build up to longer sessions.

Water Therapy

There are many benefits of swimming and moving around in warm water. People suffering from pain from arthritis and disabilities know the benefits of hydrotherapy, and now dogs are discovering water therapy too. Moving through water helps ease discomfort and aids mobility.

ALERT!

The temperature of the water in the hydrotherapy pool should be 80°F–100°F. This warmth promotes even blood flow to the injured area and increases muscle and joint flexibility. Cold water constricts the blood vessels near the skin and reduces blood flow to muscles, makeing them less efficient.

Veterinarians and water rehabilitation specialists introduce dogs with severe arthritis, hip or elbow dysplasia, and spinal injuries to a heated pool. The buoyancy of the water provides a feeling of weightlessness that enables dogs to use all of their muscles without exerting stress on their damaged or weak muscles. It encourages more movement and supports and lessens the stress on the joints. Swimming helps build muscle mass around the spine, which eases the pain.

Dogs that are not strong swimmers or are nervous in water wear special canine life jackets with handles. The therapist will use these to guide the dog and help him stay calm during the workout.

Dogs can benefit from warm water therapy in many ways. Water therapy has the following effects on dogs:

- Increases range of motion
- Diminishes muscle tension
- Reduces pain
- Reduces stress and anxiety
- Increases body awareness
- Releases emotional stress
- Increases circulation

A veterinarian or a therapist trained in water rehabilitation for dogs should perform hydrotherapy. There are two types of hydrotherapy. In one type, the dog swims in an exercise pool against a current. The other uses an underwater treadmill on which dogs walk against the force of the water. Some therapists prefer using the underwater treadmill for rehabilitating hips and back legs because the therapist can regulate the speed, resistance, and depth of the water.

For dogs that are afraid of water, the treadmill provides a sense of security because their feet can touch the treadmill. The therapist can stand beside the dog to reassure her as she walks.

In the other types of water therapy, dogs have a more thorough body workout and conditioning. Before signing your dog up for water workouts, inspect the facility to make sure the pool is clean and the therapist is licensed according to your state's requirements.

Nutritional Support

Maintaining a healthy lifestyle for your dog by feeding him a natural diet and providing plenty of regular exercise will help keep his joints working effectively. Feeding a raw, grain-free diet reduces joint inflammation in some dogs. Be aware that many commercial dry dog foods contain a large proportion of grains. Here is a suggested anti-arthritic and weight loss diet:

- Eliminate grains
- Avoid peppers, white potatoes, tomatoes, or eggplant
- Do not feed citrus, such as oranges, which aggravates arthritis
- Eliminate most dairy; cottage cheese and raw plain yogurt is okay
- Do not add salt, sugar, flavorings, colorings, preservatives, processed food, or commercial dog food treats
- Feed fresh raw meaty bones
- Add fish body oil
- Add Ester-C (buffered vitamin C, calcium ascorbate, or sodium ascorbate) with bioflavonoids instead of plain ascorbic acid, which may cause an upset stomach

- Limit dietary fat by feeding leaner meat and increasing fiber intake with extra veggies
- Increase fiber by including green beans, psyllium husks, or Metamucil

Incorporate powdered vitamin C into your arthritic dog's daily diet. This helps keep tissues healthy and protects against additional joint deterioration. Begin with 500 mg to 1,000 mg for small dogs, 1,000 mg to 2,000 mg for medium breeds, and 2,000 mg to 4,000 mg for giant breeds. Gradually increase the dose once or twice a year. Cut back slightly if your dog begins having loose stools.

FACT

Water lubricates joints, providing padding, and helps keep them healthy. When joints move, suction pulls whatever water is available from the bone marrow to the joint cavity. When there isn't enough water, the joints can't glide back and forth. Staying hydrated helps the body retain fluid in that area and reduces pain.

Including plenty of raw, grated vegetables in your dog's daily diet reduces inflammation. Beneficial vegetables include green beans, carrots, parsley, beets, celery, broccoli, cilantro, and asparagus. Supplement these with apple, ginger, mango, and papaya. When you steam vegetables, get in the habit of saving the water and giving that to your dog. The steam-distilled water is mineral-free and flushes toxins out of the body.

Fish body oil also helps reduce inflammation in arthritic dogs. Salmon oil and EPA oil provide omega-3 fatty acids that are beneficial no matter what type of diet your dog is on. Cod liver oil does not have the same effect. Omega-3 fatty acids are fragile and break down quickly when exposed to light, heat, or air, so just feeding a commercial dog food that has omega-3 fatty acids added is not usually helpful. Vitamin E supplements are also necessary as fish oil depletes vitamin E.

THE EVERYTHING NATURAL HEALTH FOR DOGS BOOK

Herbal Support

There are several simple herbal remedies that are effective for treating arthritis. Because there are a few types of arthritis, you may need to try a few different herbs or herb combinations to see what works best.

Herbalists who specialize in remedies for arthritis suggest using bitter herbs. Depending upon the case, these may include dandelion, burdock root, yellow dock, and red clover. Try these one at a time or in combination. It's best to work with an herbalist who can custom mix these to help your dog. Aloe is very beneficial as an anti-inflammatory herbal remedy. Also consider marshmallow, prickly ash, slippery elm, Devil's claw, fang-chi, guggval, *Ficus elasta*, and *Dianthus barbatus*.

Other herbs frequently mentioned in combination are turmeric root, yucca, celery seed, meadowsweet, white willow bark, chickweed, cleavers, water, and vegetable glycerine, boswellia, and Chinese herbs. Alfalfa, either ground or dry blended, provides relief without side effects and supplies basic building blocks for the joints. Add ground or dry blended alfalfa or even alfalfa tablets to your dog's regular diet every day.

Homeopathic Arthritic Remedies

Classical homeopathy suggests using one remedy and waiting for the outcome of that remedy before trying another dose or changing the remedy. This works at the most vital level to cure the problem rather than cover up the symptoms.

Providing warmth and massage to joints will help relieve the pain of arthritis. In cold weather, give your dog a warm area or bed to sleep on. There are many heated dog beds on the market that are safe to use. Applying heat and a massage won't cure the problem, but it will provide more flexibility in the joints.

Silicea 30C is used for dogs that have inherited joint and bone disease problems. Stiffness, pain, and distortion of the joints become more severe as a dog ages. It's usually given once.

For pain and inflammation of the bones of the legs, use belladonna 30C and eupatorium perfoliatum 39C. Belladonna is effective when the dog has a fever and sudden painful symptoms. If belladonna doesn't resolve the problem, try eupatorium perfoliatum.

Several other remedies can be used to treat acute arthritic attacks. These include Phytolacca Decandra (Phyt.), Rhododendron (Rhod.), and Agaricus (Agar.). Consult with your veterinarian to determine the best one.

Rhus toxicodendron (Rhus tox.)

Rhus tox is effective for typical arthritic symptoms, especially if a dog is restless and uncomfortable, or has trembling in his limbs, especially after excessive exertion.

Bryonia (Bry.)

This is effective if a dog is sensitive to touch and has pain on her right side, when even the slightest touch or sudden movement makes her uncomfortable. Look for irritability and joints that are tense, red or pale, and swollen.

Ledum (Led.)

Ledum is effective for dogs that have multiple joints affected, Lyme disease symptoms, or tearing or shooting pains.

Ruta Graveolens (Ruta.)

This is especially effective for dogs with lower extremity pain. If the dog's legs suddenly give out or there are signs of weakness, unsteadiness, or trembling, talk to your veterinarian about ruta graveolens.

Adding Acupuncture

While acupuncture cannot prevent arthritis, it can be very effective in relieving pain. Acupuncture provides pain relief in many different ways. Electrical acupuncture can intensify its therapeutic effects.

Acupuncture is gaining favor among conventional veterinarians as well. Many studies have concluded that acupuncture is a reliable form of relief for the arthritic pet. You will usually see the benefits within four to six treatments. Massage techniques help relax and soothe aching joints as well.

CHAPTER 12

Cancer Treatment

Not too long ago it was the rare dog diagnosed with cancer. Today this dreaded disease is the leading cause of death in dogs more than ten years old, and one in three dogs dies of cancer. But take heart! Nearly 50 percent of all forms of canine cancers are completely curable. By understanding prevention and recognizing the early warning signs, a dog with cancer can begin receiving treatment. In some cases conventional veterinary medicine may be the only option, but it's also helpful to explore natural therapies.

What Is Cancer?

Cancer, also called neoplasia, is the uncontrolled replication of undifferentiated cells. Healthy cells in the body have DNA that defines their purpose. For example, a bone cell looks and acts differently than a liver cell. This cellular DNA also helps cells grow and replicate in a normal fashion, only replicating when new cells are needed to replace old or damaged cells. However, when DNA becomes damaged or mutated, the cell's ability to mature into a healthy cell and replicate may be impaired. This can result in cells replicating out of control, forming a mass of immature cells—a tumor.

E-QUESTION

What is a lipoma?
A lipoma is a large benign tumor comprised of fat cells, but it has nothing to do with whether a dog is fat or thin. A soft swelling, lipomas are smooth, round, and movable. They usually grow on the rib cage and body but can be found anywhere, including an eyelid or in the armpit. They seldom cause problems.

Not all tumors are cancerous. Tumors can be benign, meaning they do not invade surrounding tissues and they can usually be removed and will not grow back. Tumors can also be malignant, meaning that they might invade surrounding tissues and can metastasize to distant organs and cause systemic disease. Not all cancers form tumors; for example, leukemia is a cancer of blood and bone.

Types of Cancer

Canine cancers depend on the types of cells in the body. Lymphosarcoma (lymphoma) is a highly malignant cancer of lymphocytes that can affect the lymph nodes, spleen, liver, gastrointestinal tract, and bone marrow. The average dog with lymphosarcoma is between six and nine years of age, although dogs of any age can be affected.

Nearly 85 percent of bone tumors in dogs are osteosarcomas, and 10,000 new cases of osteosarcoma are diagnosed every year in the United States.

Osteosarcomas are highly aggressive tumors that usually affect the limbs of giant and large dogs but can also occur in the skull, ribs, vertebrae, and pelvis of smaller dogs.

FACT

Sarcomas are cancerous tumors formed from connective tissue within the body beneath the skin. Adenoma tumors are noncancerous and form from the cells lining the inside of an organ. They can arise from most of the gland cells in the body. Carcinomas are cancerous tumors arising from skin cells and the cells lining different organs.

Hemangiosarcoma is an aggressive soft tissue cancer of the lining of blood vessels that most commonly affects the spleen, heart, and the tissue under the skin. Using the body's blood vessels and producing its own blood vessel network, it spreads rapidly and produces other tumors throughout the body. This silent killer most commonly affects older, large breed dogs.

Anal sac adenocarcinomas occur mostly in female dogs older than about ten years of age. These tumors arise from the glands on either side of the rectum. Symptoms include straining to have bowel movements and enlarged lymph nodes in the pelvic area.

Mast cell tumors are most often malignant. Dogs of any age may develop them and they occur anywhere on the body as well as internally. They usually appear as raised red areas of hair loss on the skin. These masses may feel soft to solid.

Dogs with dark skin are prone to melanomas. These arise from pigment-producing cells that are responsible for coloring the skin and may be tied to genetics.

Symptoms and Diagnosis

Cancers can cause a wide variety of signs in your dog and may mimic other disease processes. They are often accompanied by other health problems and may have very nonspecific symptoms. There are many changes you may notice in your dog that prompt you to schedule a veterinary visit. Once you arrive at your veterinarian's, there are a wide variety of tests that can help diagnose cancer and guide the treatment plan.

Symptoms

The signs of cancer are very similar to other common problems or other diseases and depend on the type of cancer and where it is located. These include:

- Bleeding or unusual discharge from any body cavity; blood in urine or feces
- Difficulty breathing, eating, swallowing, defecating, or urinating
- Inability to participate in routine activities, loss of energy, reluctance to move, weakness
- Increased thirst and/or urination, vomiting
- Odd lumps or bumps
- Persistent lameness or stiffness
- Sores that do not heal
- Sudden seizures in older dogs
- Unpleasant, pungent odor
- Weight loss

Virtually all types of cancer at later stages will cause some degree of weight loss. Vomiting, diarrhea, and loss of appetite and stamina may account for this.

Laboratory Tests

During a routine physical, the veterinarian examines the dog's body for lumps and bumps. If there's an odd-looking growth, cells from the lump can be tested in order to make a diagnosis.

To diagnose cancer, the veterinarian runs a blood panel and orders X-rays or ultrasound examinations. A chest X-ray will reveal if the cancer has already spread and an ultrasound can pinpoint an odd growth. A conventional veterinarian or a veterinary oncologist can help assess whether or not additional surgery, radiation, or chemotherapy will be necessary.

Causes of Cancer

Dogs can be predisposed to developing cancer if they are born with a genetically weakened immune system. This makes them more vulnerable to emotional, environmental, and nutritional deficiencies that trigger the disease.

E-QUESTION

Can a veterinarian accurately diagnose a tumor by its appearance?
No. Simply looking at a tumor and feeling is not enough to reveal its cause. A microscopic analysis is one of the ways to ascertain if the cells are cancerous or not. Microscopic analysis will reveal whether there are any abnormalities in the growth.

Commercial dog food with inferior ingredients such as animal and grain byproducts, chemical additives, and preservatives is often blamed for causing cancer. Manufactured diets made from organ meats and meat meal have high amounts of growth hormones that are used to fatten cattle. It is speculated that growth hormones and artificial colors cause cancer. There is no scientific evidence proving the link between these additives and cancer, however.

Exposure to too many vaccinations, antibiotics, steroids, environmental toxins, and pesticides impact the immune system. Some of these stimulate the immune system and some of them depress it.

Preventing Cancer

Today more dogs are surviving cancer. This is due to their owners' diligence in learning about the causes of this disease and obtaining treatment as early as possible.

While you may not be able to change the way a dog was born, particularly if he has a genetic predisposition to developing certain types of cancer, it helps to be aware of ways you may be able to decrease your dog's chances of developing this dreaded illness. There are a few preventive strategies you can take to help protect your dog against some types of cancer.

Avoiding Environmental Toxins

Limit repeated exposure to toxic environmental agents that pose a risk of cell mutations, such as house and garden pesticides and herbicides that can lead to cancer. Cocoa mulch is toxic and studies show that dogs exposed to weed-killing products containing 2,4-D (2,4-dichlorophenoxyzcetic acid) have twice the risk of contracting lymphoma as unexposed dogs.

ALERT!

Don't let your dog hang his head out of an open car window or ride in the back of a pickup truck. Aside from the possibility that your dog can be catapulted out of the vehicle if there's an accident, he can inhale toxic fumes and smog.

Prevent a parasite invasion and the need to use chemical pesticides by keeping your dog, home, dog's bedding, and outdoor area pest-free from the start. Use natural flea shampoo on your dog, vacuum floors and carpets frequently, and put borates, salt, or diatomaceous earth on floorboards and around the edges of rooms.

Avoid indoor pollution as much as possible. Cigarette and secondhand smoke contains toxic chemicals that cause lung cancer in people and nasal sinus cancer, lung carcinoma, and lymphoma in dogs as well as other respiratory illnesses such as asthma. Your dog will be affected if there are several people in your home who smoke.

Keep the windows in your home open as much as possible or make sure it is well ventilated with an electronic air cleaner or automatic air filter to reduce indoor pollutants. Many common houseplants and blooming potted plants help filter pollution inside the home. They absorb carbon dioxide, benzene, formaldehyde, and trichloroethylene, which are harmful to people and pets, and release beneficial oxygen. Golden pothos, Chinese evergreen, bamboo or reed palm, philodendron, and peace lily can help you filter the air in your house.

Avoid Repeated Vaccinations

Because too many vaccines can stress your dog's immune system, you should know exactly what vaccines your dog has had before revaccinating her. If your dog already has cancer, avoid giving vaccines during this time because they may interfere with the treatment process. Discuss this with your veterinarian.

Spaying and Neutering

To greatly reduce the risk of mammary cancer, spay your female before her first heat cycle. After she is spayed, there is still a chance that this cancer may attack her system later in life. There are many cases of spayed females developing breast cancer when they are seniors. Once a month, feel each mammary gland for lumps and examine each nipple for any discharge.

A cancer-fighting diet is moderate in fat and protein and low in carbohydrates. It contains about 50 percent protein (fish or poultry, preferably organic) and 50 percent mixed frozen or fresh vegetables. Olive oil should be used as a source of fat calories. Feed your dog a daily vitamin-mineral supplement with a calcium carbonate source—about 250 mg per fifteen pounds of body weight.

Neutering a male dog will prevent testicular cancer. Veterinarians report that one in ten males who are not neutered will develop this disease. Almost all testicular cancer is benign and just requires castration as treatment. Intact males should have their testicles palpated once a year to make sure they do not have any tumors. In older males this should be done once a month.

Manage Stress

It may be hard to imagine, but dogs suffer from stress too. Neglect, loud arguments, or anxiety can trigger stressful emotions in your dog. While studies fail to confirm that stress alone can be responsible for producing cancer, researchers know that stress does compromise the immune system.

One way to reduce your dog's anxiety is to give him plenty of regular exercise. Being fit strengthens the immune system and helps ward off chronic diseases such as cancer. Sustained, vigorous exercise stimulates tissues and increases blood circulation. This helps cleanse toxins from the cells.

Optimizing Nutrition

Feeding your dog a fresh, natural diet without any preservatives or chemical additives is the best tool for protecting her against cancer. Once cancer invades, certain nutritional changes may be helpful. Tumors need carbohydrates for their energy, so reducing carbohydrate content in your dog's diet may slow tumor growth.

Dark green cruciferous vegetables, such as broccoli and Brussels sprouts, strengthen the immune system. Choose fruits and vegetables grown without pesticides and fertilizers. Just be sure to wash all fruits and vegetables to remove any residue of pesticides.

Maintaining a healthy appetite can be a problem because dogs with cancer often don't feel like eating. To encourage your dog to eat more at each meal, sprinkle on a little turmeric, both for its anticancer effects and to enhance the flavor of the food.

Add in whole grains, such as brown rice and millet, and include salmon body oil to provide a source of omega-3 fatty acids. If you feed a commercial diet, add fish oil, fresh meat and vegetables, and extra vitamins. Sprouts and grasses are good sources of vitamin B and trace minerals. The tempting aroma and taste of these additives will encourage your dog to eat. Veterinarians can supply a prescription diet canned food that contains extra omega-3 fatty acids, amino acids, and nutrients.

Cancer-Fighting Supplements

Recently, many commercial cancer cure supplements have been introduced to the market. Before giving any of these to your dog, ask your veterinarian for a recommendation of what to add to your dog's diet. Generally it's best not to add more than four or five supplements in a single serving; more than that may increase the risk that the supplements will counteract one another.

FACT

Coenzyme Q10 is a strong antioxidant with many benefits for cancer patients. Although coenzyme Q10 is mostly credited with the positive treatment of heart disease and dental issues, it also helps the immune system work more efficiently and enables the body to resist certain infections and cancers.

Beneficial vitamins and antioxidants are the same for healthy dogs and those with cancer. These vitamins and antioxidants include:

- Beta carotene
- Bioflavonoids and plant extracts
- Coenzyme Q10
- Ginkgo biloba
- Gammalinolenic acid
- Green tea and grape seed extract
- Omega-3 fatty acids
- Selenium
- Vitamins A, C, and E

Chinese herbs are also beneficial. Try echinacea, astragalus, licorice (on a short-term basis), ginseng, and yunnan pai yao, which is helpful in bleeding tumors such as hemangiosarcoma. Cat's claw, medicinal mushrooms, or mushroom extracts such as reishi, cordyceps, tremella, maitake, and pau d'arco are touted as anti-cancer herbs. Other beneficial complementary therapies are milk thistle, goldenseal, dandelion leaf and dandelion root, ginseng, and red clover.

Weight Management

Excess weight places a dog at a higher risk for cancer. Besides the extra stress on all systems of the body, the additional fat cells secrete a substance called adiponectin. In a dog at normal weight, adiponectin has a protective effect. When the body is already storing fat, adiponectin is only released in very small amounts and provides little or no protection against cancer. Therefore, maintaining your dog at a healthy lean weight might decrease your dog's risks for some types of cancer. Fat cells are metabolically active cells that release many different chemical mediators that alter immune activity. This is why obesity is considered a low-grade inflammatory condition. This condition sets the body up for the potential of various forms of chronic disease, including cancer.

Water Helps

Providing only pure water helps protect your dog against cancer because it rids the body of toxins. However, some tap water contains dangerous chemicals such as lead, arsenic, and nitrates.

E-QUESTION

What conventional cancer research is being done?
Veterinary researchers are conducting clinical trials of a vaccine to treat melanoma and other tumors. The vaccine uses human DNA and is available from veterinary oncologists at referral clinics and veterinary schools with teaching hospitals. Researchers hope the vaccine may someday have human applications.

Consider filtering your tap water with a good-quality water purifier or use bottled or distilled water. Make sure bottled water is not chlorinated or fluoridated. While a water filtration system is more expensive to purchase in the beginning, it's more economical than bottled water in the long run.

Don't let your dog drink water from public areas, creeks, or ponds as they may be contaminated. Street puddles often contain cancer-producing toxins, such as auto hydrocarbons and asbestos dust.

Clean your dog's water bowl every day and refill with fresh water. Keep it protected from dust and debris so he's not ingesting toxins.

FACT

Willard's water is a nontoxic, altered form of water made by a patented catalyst. A blend of minerals with water in a concentrate, it helps detoxify the body during cancer therapy. Adding one ounce per gallon of drinking water helps remove heavy metals from the body, reduces swelling, and increases absorption of nutrients.

Natural and Conventional Treatments

When a dog is diagnosed with cancer, there are three treatment possibilities: maintaining a quality life for your dog until the end, adding more quality time, or treating the tumors and ridding the body of cancer. With good nutritional and homeopathic treatment, your dog can have more good days than you might expect. The following are a few herbal and homeopathic treatments:

- **Arsenicum.** Good for relieving the pain of stomach cancer.
- **Conium.** For cancerous hard tumors and weakness in hindquarters.
- **Hydrastis.** For painful cancers, mammary tumors, and cancer of the stomach or liver.
- **Natrum.** Helpful when stimulating appetite.
- **Phosphorus.** Effective with tumors that bleed.
- **Scirrhinum and carcinosin.** Nosodes for mammary, uterine, and other cancers.
- **Silicea.** For dogs with solid tumors or lymphosarcoma.
- **Symphytum.** Effective for bone cancer.
- **Thuya.** If possible, administer this when you begin cancer treatment; it lessens the effects of prior vaccinations that may encourage the tumor expansion.

It's important to plan a treatment program as soon as a veterinarian diagnoses cancer. While these options for treating dogs with cancer seemed extreme just a few years ago, they are now commonly accepted approaches. Veterinary oncology is an accepted specialty, just like canine ophthalmology and orthopedics.

Depending upon the prognosis and the type of cancer, conventional treatments include surgery, chemotherapy, or radiation. Variations within these programs include surgery with follow-up chemotherapy; radiation and surgery; or chemotherapy and radiation.

Cancer can be a deadly disease and sometimes combining both conventional and complementary therapies may bring the best results. Discuss all of the options with your holistic veterinarian. Your dog is depending on you to make the best decision for him.

Managing the Pain

When it comes to the day-to-day care of a dog with cancer, pain management is everything. Whether the pain comes from the growth of the cancer or from treatments such as surgery or radiation therapy, pain relief medication may be necessary to hasten recovery. A complete diagnostic workup, a treatment plan with a board-certified veterinary oncologist, and a consult with a holistic veterinarian trained in acupuncture and herbs is the best approach.

Types of Pain

The pain your dog experiences depends on the type of cancer he is fighting. Dull, throbbing pain accompanies bone cancer, while severe pain in the abdomen occurs with bleeding hemangiosarcomas (spleen tumors). Mast cell tumors can sometimes produce burning pain in the skin, and nasal tumors like fibrosarcomas produce pressure-associated pain. Burning and irritation leading to urgency to urinate arise from bladder tumors like transitional cell carcinomas. Frequently, the brain and spinal cord's reaction increases the pain.

Pain Relief

Different kinds of treatments or combinations of treatments warrant different kinds of pain relief. It is often more effective to combine medications and modalities to achieve the best pain relief. Modalities of pain relief include surgery, conventional medications (oral, injectable, and transdermal), palliative radiation, herbs, acupuncture, chiropractic, physical therapy, massage, and heat/cold application. The following tumors often require aggressive pain management:

- Bone tumors
- Central nervous system tumors, such as brain tumors
- Gastrointestinal tumors, such as esophagus, stomach, colon, and rectal tumors
- Mammary tumors
- Genitourinary tract tumors, such as kidney and bladder tumors
- Prostate tumors
- Oral cavity tumors
- Intranasal tumors
- Invasive skin tumors

A dog may experience short-term pain after surgery or consistent irritation from chemotherapy or therapeutic radation. Because dogs do not want to show pain, it may be difficult to recognize, but it should be assumed. Dogs show pain in different ways. Some indicators that your dog may be uncomfortable include loss of appetite, lethargy, disinterest in normal activities, limping, hiding, aggression, and anxiety. If your dog just seems "off," it is worth trying a pain medication to see if he seems more himself with treatment.

Other pain management strategies include good general nursing care, warm and comfortable bedding, and massages and physical therapy to ease aching joints. Acupuncture is very effective in pain relief.

There's no question that pain weakens an already compromised immune system. To provide relief for your dog and to make his days as comfortable as possible, consult with your veterinarian for effective pain management.

CHAPTER 13

Seizures

Although many seizures are idiopathic, meaning the cause is unknown, some seizures are caused by vaccines, encephalitis, food allergies, and other factors. Seizures are generally a symptom of disease and not the disease itself. A thorough diagnostic work-up is essential to determine the cause. Fortunately there are a few precautions that can be taken to prevent or reduce the frequency of seizures depending on the root cause of the symptom.

Seizures Are Scary

Seizures take many forms, but it is always terrifying to watch a beloved canine lose physical and mental control. Most people who have never witnessed a dog convulse before have a hard time understanding what is happening. Owners feel helpless and don't know how to comfort their dog or what to do.

FACT

Seizures and epilepsy are not the same thing. Epilepsy is but one cause of seizures; it is a brain disorder that results in recurrent seizures without an identifiable brain lesion. Not all dogs that have seizures are epileptic.

Seizures are unpredictable. A dog may have one seizure and then never experience another episode again. Other dogs suffer repeated seizures. Although a dog may act completely normal before a seizure and then again after, it's entirely possible that serious and progressive disease is the underlying cause.

The Anatomy of a Seizure

Seizures are uncoordinated surges of the neurons or electrical activity within the part of the brain called the cerebrum. Because the nerves are not coordinated, they will affect how a dog will feel and act for a few minutes. Seizures are not a disease but a symptom of many different disorders that can affect the brain. These include cancer, metabolic diseases, genetic predispositions to environmental toxins, and trauma.

Types of Seizures

Seizures can be partial or generalized. Partial seizures happen when only one portion of the brain is discharging abnormally. This brain damage happens after trauma, infection, circulatory disorders, or cancer. They are known as focal seizures; the movements are limited to only one area of the body, such as turning the head or body to one side. These can progress into a generalized seizure, which affects the entire body.

Complex partial seizures are linked with bizarre behavior during the seizure, such as chewing, fly biting, aggression, or hysterical running. The dog may not lose consciousness, but she may not be aware of her surroundings.

Generalized seizures are either petit mal or grand mal. A petite mal seizure is barely noticeable. The dog may click his teeth or blink repeatedly. Petite mal seizures typically last ten to twenty-five seconds. A grand mal seizure is a series of serious convulsions. The dog may fall, grind his teeth, salivate excessively, lose control of his bladder and bowels, and experience violent jerking and uncontrollable leg kicks. The dog may also lose consciousness. Sometimes it can take as long as a day or two for dogs to recover.

E-QUESTION

What should I do if my dog has a seizure?
Remain calm. Lay the dog down to minimize injury. Don't put your hand in your dog's mouth. Dogs don't swallow their tongues, but they could bite. Try to time the seizure. Even a rough estimate will help your veterinarian get a sense of the episode. If your dog experiences more than one seizure or if one seizure lasts longer than ten minutes, call your veterinarian.

Dogs can have multiple seizures within twenty-four hours. When the dog has enough time to return to consciousness and begin to recover between seizures, these are known as cluster seizures. When a dog has one or more grand mal seizures in quick succession without recovery from the previous seizure, this cycle, known as status epilepticus or status, can continue for hours. Dogs that experience cluster seizures or status epilepticus must be taken to a veterinarian immediately because these conditions can be fatal. In the worst case scenario, the seizure cannot be controlled and the veterinarian may advise euthanasia, but a veterinarian may be able to stabilize the dog's condition long enough to determine the problem and begin treatment.

Signs

No two seizures are alike, but a dog that is about to experience a seizure often exhibits warning signs a few hours or days before he begins seizing. These signs are often so subtle that owners never notice them. They include slight changes in mood or behavior.

The pre-seizure phrase is called the prodromal state. The dog may seem nervous, apprehensive, or agitated, perhaps sensing that something unusual is going to happen. He may seek affection or try to hide.

In the ictus stage, which is the actual seizure, the dog will often become stiff first and then start convulsing or paddling. He may lose consciousness and may not be able to respond to his owner's voice. He might lose control of bodily functions and urinate, defecate, and/or salivate. This can last seconds to minutes.

Some young dogs and even seniors will noisily yip and paddle their legs wildly while asleep. This normal activity usually means that the dog is experiencing deep sleep. Some people think that the dog is dreaming about chasing after rabbits or running through an open field, but he is not having a seizure.

The post-ictal phase begins when the seizure ends. During this period of recovery, the dog is exhausted and may pant and seem disoriented. Some dogs experience temporary blindness or deafness. This phase may last for minutes, hours, or sometimes days.

Most seizures occur at night or early in the morning, although they can come on when you least expect them. Dogs rarely become vicious during an episode, but you'll want to protect him and yourself. It's best to move any furniture or objects that could hurt him if he falls, or put a blanket around him to cushion his fall. Keep the lights low and minimize noise.

While a dog is not aware of his surroundings during a seizure, you can comfort him in a calm, reassuring voice and gently stroke his hip or side. Stay away from his feet because muscle spasms might cause him to kick.

Remain beside your dog throughout the seizure so you can comfort him when it ends.

What's Not a Seizure

Sometimes a dog will have an episode that an owner mistakes for a seizure. One example is disease of the middle ear. The nucleus of the brain causes an abnormal head position and the dog loses balance. This is not a seizure, but it's still important to contact your veterinarian for an evaluation if this occurs.

A dog's seizure threshold is the level at which a seizure will occur. Epileptic dogs have a very low seizure threshold, and every dog inherits a predisposition to seizures. The threshold can be altered by certain types of tranquilizers, such as acepromazine, which can actually induce seizures in dogs with a low threshold.

Fainting is often mistaken for a seizure. Dogs with cardiac and respiratory disease may become weak and fall. They may pant to compensate for a loss of oxygenation, so they may appear to be suffering from seizures. It could signal a medical problem, so schedule a physical examination with your veterinarian.

Reverse sneezing is characterized by a series of violent and noisy sneezes. The chest and abdominal muscles contract spasmodically and an owner may think the dog is having a seizure. This is not a medical emergency, but a dog that continually experiences reverse sneezing should be taken to a veterinarian for a checkup.

What Causes Seizures

Seizures have many causes, and the aim of both holistic and conventional veterinarians is to determine and treat the root cause. Some causes are metabolic, such as hypoglycemia (low blood sugar), especially in toy breed puppies, and hypocalcemia (low calcium levels), which is common in females who are nursing puppies. Hypocalcemia and hypoglycemia can also be responsible for seizures in young puppies with intestinal parasites.

Brain Tumors

Brain tumors in dogs older than five or six years of age are often responsible for seizures. The seizures may range from partial to grand mal. Cluster seizures may also develop. Onset of seizures or neurologic changes will often be gradual. A dog with a brain tumor may experience some of the following symptoms:

- **Appetite.** The dog may be ravenous or entirely uninterested in food.
- **Difficulty breathing.** Breathing seems labored and stops and starts while the dog is asleep.
- **Fatigue.** The dog lacks energy and tires quickly during exercise.
- **Gait is unsteady, stumbling, or staggering.** The dog may have difficulty climbing stairs or walking on uneven ground.
- **Geriatric separation disorder.** A dog awakens at night for no reason and may whine, pace, or seem restless.
- **Loss of bladder or bowel control.** This is apparent in dogs that were previously housetrained.
- **Mental confusion.** The dog may forget familiar commands, fail to recognize family members or familiar people, become disoriented in familiar places, and have a glazed expression.
- **Pain.** The dog may whine and whimper seemingly without reason.
- **Personality change.** The dog may have obsessive behaviors and may be less affectionate or very docile.
- **Sensory problems.** The dog may experience loss of sight, hearing, or even sense of smell.

Lead Poisoning

Lead poisoning is the most common toxic cause of seizures. Dogs can ingest lead if they lick or eat oil-based paint chips, batteries, linoleum, roofing materials, champagne bottle foil, golf ball coverings, and pie, fishing, or drapery weights. The amount of lead necessary to instigate a seizure depends on the dog's seizure threshold.

Encephalitis

Encephalitis, or inflammation of the central nervous system, will also cause seizures. Some seizures are triggered by immune-mediated encephalitis, a low-grade inflammation of the brain that is caused by a reaction to proteins and organisms in a vaccine. Noninfectious causes of encephalitis include granulomatous meningoencephalitis (GME) and chronic encephalitis that mostly affects Pugs and a few other flat-faced breeds.

Other Causes

The following conditions can also be responsible for causing seizures:

- Blood glucose levels too high or too low
- Congenital defects
- Fevers and heat stroke
- Head trauma
- Infections such as distemper
- Liver disease and hypothyroidism
- Low oxygen levels in the blood
- Toxins, such as insecticide, rat poison, antifreeze, or chocolate
- Various forms of cancer

Congenital causes of seizures include hydrocephalus and lissencephaly. Hydrocephalus, the most common congenital brain malformation, involves the increased accumulation of fluid (cerebral spinal fluid) in the ventricles of the brain. Seizures are one symptom of this disease. Puppies with hydrocephalus will often seem dull and be slow to learn. They may have gait abnormalities as well. Another congenital defect that causes seizures in Lhasa Apsos, wire-haired Fox Terriers, and Irish Setters is lissencephaly, a brain malformation. This neurologic abnormality may show up during the first year of life and includes behavioral, visual, and convulsive disorders. In Lhasa Apsos, signs of alternating depression and excitability, aggression toward owners, and seizures may be apparent.

Setting Off a Seizure

Dogs with low seizure thresholds are prone to them. Stress or prolonged excitement can instigate a convulsion. A dog could have a seizure during a game of chase, when the family returns home, or if he receives a really tasty treat. Other triggers include any sudden, subtle, or radical changes in food or environment.

FACT

Use caution when vaccinating breeds that are prone to epilepsy, and with any dog that has a history of seizures. Monovalent vaccines should be used for the puppy series, and adults should be vaccinated with only the core vaccines and vaccines that are appropriate to the risk of disease. Titers can be used to measure a dog's immunity to disease after vaccination.

Some dogs react so violently to thunderstorms, changes in barometric pressure, or extreme cold weather that they will seize. For other dogs, separation anxiety, car rides, visits to the veterinarian, or extreme fatigue or nervousness will bring on a seizure.

Diagnosis

After your dog has a seizure, he should visit the veterinarian for a complete physical and neurological evaluation. If your dog had only one mild seizure, the doctor may suggest that you keep a log of any future episodes and take notes of the details of the convulsions and report back.

For dogs that have more than one seizure, the veterinarian will thoroughly review the dog's history. This will include information about all vaccinations the dog has received, his potential exposure to toxins, his diet, any illnesses or injuries, and all behavioral changes. The veterinarian will also record the dog's breed, age, and sex and the results of complete examinations and basic tests.

Diagnostics rule out various intracranial and extracranial causes. These typically include a thorough history, a physical and neurological exam, complete blood chemistry and CBC, and, if indicated, toxicology screening, radiographs, ultrasounds, and brain imaging (CT or MRI).

A glucose test will check for hypoglycemia, and a thyroid panel checks for low thyroid function or hypothyroidism. The veterinarian will also run a blood test to check for lead poisoning and a complete blood count to determine if there is infection or inflammation. The chemistry profile reveals metabolic causes of seizures by testing for markers of liver, kidney, glucose, and electrolyte disturbances. A urinalysis examines changes in the urine that will reflect kidney or other metabolic irregularities. A cerebrospinal fluid analysis will check for encephalitis, distemper, or another infection.

E-QUESTION

What medical test diagnoses epilepsy?
There is no laboratory test that diagnoses epilepsy. To confirm this condition, the veterinarian must rule out other causes of seizures. She will do a thorough physical and neurological examination along with bloodwork and X-rays or other diagnostic imaging.

After the results have been analyzed, the veterinarian will have one of three outcomes: a definitive diagnosis, a potential cause that requires further tests, or no explanation. Do not be disheartened if the tests do not turn up a conclusive diagnosis. The majority of seizure disorders are classified as having an unknown cause. This is referred to as idiopathic or primary epilepsy. As odd as it may seem, a large percentage of seizures are diagnosed as idiopathic. This is an inherited disorder in some breeds.

Providing a Health History

To help your veterinarian determine the circumstances that may have triggered a seizure, give him as much information about the seizures and your dog's health as possible. It's helpful if you can provide the following information:

- Length of the seizure
- Number of seizures

- What your dog looks like during a seizure
- Any unusual signs before or after a seizure
- Possible exposure to toxins
- High fever or signs of any other illnesses
- Vaccination history
- Exposure to unfamiliar dogs, including boarding
- Diet and meal schedule
- Any behavior changes

It also helps to keep a log of your dog's daily activities. This doesn't have to be elaborate—just some notes about what your dog comes in contact with throughout the day that might be out of the ordinary. Spending a few minutes each day compiling this information may go a long way toward saving your dog's life.

Medications

If a dog has only had one seizure or her convulsions are few and far between, most veterinarians will not rush to prescribe anticonvulsant medications. These medications are serious drugs that should be considered carefully. Once medical treatment is initiated, it will likely need to be continued for life. Depending on your dog's case, it may be better to start with treatments that have fewer side effects, such as diet changes, herbal treatments, and acupuncture. If these are not sufficient, drug therapy can be initiated.

If a dog has cluster seizures, violent seizures, or frequent seizures, medication may be warranted. Frequent seizures will interfere with your dog's quality of life and can lower her seizure threshold further, resulting in even more seizures. Therefore, it is important to be proactive about a seizure disorder. Medications will have variable results depending on the cause of the seizures. When using drugs, here are some helpful tips:

- Use the lowest effective dose of the safest drug that will produce the fewest side effects.
- If your veterinarian prescribes phenobarbital, be sure to consistently monitor the amount of the drug in the body through serum drug testing.

- Ask your veterinarian if you can give valium to your dog at home if she has a seizure. Valium, also called diazepam, can interrupt cluster seizures.

Consult with your veterinarian to make sure your dog is receiving the correct dosage and combination of drugs to achieve the most control with the fewest side effects. If, for example, a dog does not respond to a combination of phenobarbital and potassium bromide (KBr) or has severe side effects, another drug might be added. This may help control the seizures and allow the dog to be given a reduced amount of phenobarbital or potassium bromide.

Veterinary researchers are always testing new drugs and trying to find safer alternatives to the standard anticonvulsants, which can cause undesirable side effects. There are a number of new anticonvulsants, and some can be used as sole medications to control seizures with a reduced risk of side effects. The most studied option is a drug called Zonisamide, which is also available in generic form. Discuss alternatives with your veterinarian.

The Diet Connection

Nutritional deficiencies can cause seizures. Correcting them will reduce or control seizures and may even eliminate them completely. Some dogs have a food hypersensitivity that will cause seizures. Chemical flavorings or other additives contained in commercial dog foods can be responsible, as can artificially colored dental and chew toys. Dairy and eggs can also be a source of convulsive episodes if your dog has an allergy to these foods.

Preventing Hypoglycemia

Hypoglycemia occurs when there is a low level of glucose, or sugar, in the blood. The brain relies on glucose in order to function, but this organ can't store it. A drop in blood glucose level causes seizures. Puppies and many toy breeds are predisposed to developing hypoglycemia because they're too small to metabolize as much glucose as bigger dogs.

Once the veterinarian determines that seizures are due to hypoglycemia, feeding frequent small meals of food that is high in protein, fat, and complex carbohydrates is recommended to manage the condition and control seizures.

Using Nutrition

Changing a dog's food from a low-quality recipe to either a superior grade commercial diet with premium ingredients or a natural home cooked diet with added vitamins, minerals, and supplements may help control seizures. Nonessential amino acids, such as carnitine, have been found to reduce the incidence of seizures and can be an appropriate supplement for the epileptic dog. Discuss your options with your veterinarian.

Taurine is an amino acid that appears to be released from the brain during seizure activity. Some studies have suggested that taurine might exert a protective effect on the brain. This is a matter of debate, but taurine supplementation can be tried for dogs with seizure disorders. It has been reported as effective in decreasing the frequency of seizures.

Metabolic and digestive enzymes are important catalysts that speed up biochemical reactions in the body. They are responsible for the smooth operation of organs and tissues and assist in supporting the body by utilizing proteins, carbohydrates, and fats.

A quality commercial diet needs to be free of artificial colors and flavors, sweeteners, preservatives, and additives, including chemical preservatives BHA, BHT, ethoxyquin, and propylene glycol.

For some dogs, feeding a BARF raw diet with added vitamins, minerals, and nutritional supplements is the best option, but it's best to limit the portions of liver and kidney meat to once a week. These organ meats can be contaminated by environmental toxins, such as pesticides, hormones, and antibiotics and may trigger a convulsion. For some dogs, a meat-free diet may also help reduce seizures.

Strengthening the Nervous System

Although diet is instrumental in controlling seizures, nutritional supplements, vitamins, essential fatty acids (EFAs), and alternative treatments also have healing powers.

Homeopathy and Herbs

If you are administering drug treatment to your dog, Bach flower essences, including Rescue Remedy and dimethyl gycine (DMG or vitamin B_{15}), can be helpful.

Ask your homeopathic veterinarian about giving your dog belladonna 30C and silicea 30C. These have been known to be effective in reducing seizures. Arnica Montana 30C is helpful for dogs that develop seizures after a head injury.

Herbs can be a very effective way to control seizure disorders. Western herbs that are reportedly successful in managing seizure disorders include skullcap, passionflower, and hops. A combination of these herbs seems to be most effective. Chinese herbalists have been treating epilepsy successfully for thousands of years. The herbalist considers both the type of seizure and the characteristics of the dog to create a formula. Depending on the underlying imbalance, herbs such as gastrodia and uncaria (tian ma gou teng yin) or pinellia, atractylodes, and gastrodia (ban xia bai zhu tian ma tang) might be very effective treatment options. Always consult with your veterinarian before using herbal supplements.

Megavitamin Therapy

Adding vitamins and minerals to your dog's daily diet helps improve a range of medical conditions, but increasing levels of antioxidants is especially beneficial. This is referred to as orthomolecular medicine.

Some forms of epilepsy respond well to vitamins and other natural treatments, especially when given in conjunction with conventional treatments. These include supplementation of crystalline ascorbic acid and vitamins A, E, and B_6. The antioxidant minerals selenium, magnesium, and manganese are especially beneficial.

Acupuncture

Many dogs with seizures respond well to acupuncture. There are different ways of understanding how acupuncture helps. In traditional Chinese medicine, the metaphor for seizures is the "internal invasion of wind." Various imbalances can lead to this condition and acupuncture points are selected based upon the diagnosis. Acupuncture points are selected to either strengthen the problem or calm the system in an effort to rebalance the body.

Western medicine has come to embrace acupuncture but understands its mechanism differently. In the case of seizures, acupuncture has been proven to alter peripheral and central nervous system input to the brain and to cause the release of various neurotransmitters that alter the chemistry of the brain. This has been found to be an effective method of reducing the frequency, intensity, and progression of seizures in many cases. These treatments must be repeated, but gold bead implants may prevent the need for repeated acupuncture treatments.

E-QUESTION

What are gold bead implants and are they helpful?
Gold-plated beads about the size of poppy seeds can alleviate pain. They carry a slight magnetic charge and neutralize negative conditions in the joint or meridian. They may alter the pH of the nerve receptor sites. After the dog is anesthetized or sedated, the beads are injected at specific acupuncture points.

Gold-plated bead implants do have possible side effects including infection and migration, but they are also used for hip dysplasia, osteochondritis, arthritis, and spondylosis of the back. They have a weak positive charge that may encourage the growth of tumors, cancer, or bone infections so they should not be used if these conditions are present.

CHAPTER 14

Gastrointestinal Problems

All day, your dog is busy eating, digesting, extracting nutrients from his food, and getting rid of waste. The gastrointestinal (GI) system processes these activities. It includes the mouth, esophagus, stomach, small and large intestines, colon, and anus. Many of the problems that crop up in a dog's life involve these areas. It helps to recognize important medical issues such as stomach trouble, vomiting and diarrhea, inflammatory bowel disease, and deadly bloat in the early stages so you can give your dog some relief.

Your Dog's Stomach

Dogs eat the strangest things. But while some canines appear to have stomachs of steel where nothing they eat irritates them, others only have to look at certain foods to have their tummies turn queasy. Like people, some dogs just seem to have stomachs that are more sensitive than others.

It's not unusual for a canine tummy to gurgle and grumble from time to time, and a few stomach rumblings here and there are nothing to worry about. Besides, it's the rare dog that doesn't vomit at least once in his lifetime. But you should be concerned if your dog has repeated episodes of vomiting.

E-QUESTION

Why do dogs eat grass and then throw it up?
Many reasons are suspected. Maybe dogs just like the taste of grass, or perhaps eating grass helps them rid their stomachs of an irritation. They could also be trying to supplement commercial or unbalanced home-cooked diets lacking essential nutrients and fiber.

There's often no apparent reason for this discomfort, but in some cases there are a few good explanations. Sometimes, the problem is caused by overeating. At other times, ingesting rotten or tainted food or food that's difficult to digest will cause tummy upsets. But your dog does not have to suffer from digestion problems. Preventing him from rooting through garbage cans and compost piles helps avoid stomach issues. It's also a good idea to keep all toxic substances, such as antifreeze, human prescription medications, cleaning products, fertilizers, and pesticides out of paw's reach. Dogs can suffer from a range of afflictions that affect their gastrointestinal well-being, including the following:

- Bacterial infections
- Cancer
- Food allergies
- Foreign substances in the digestive tract
- Infectious diseases

- Inflammatory bowel disease
- Kidney or liver failure
- Metabolic diseases
- Pancreatic disease
- Viral infections

All About Digestion

When a dog's digestive system is working properly, the typical meal takes between seven and ten hours to pass through the digestive system. Digestive problems can begin anywhere along the GI tract. Sharp, specially shaped molars break down the food by gripping, tearing, and shredding it. This aids the digestive process by helping to digest animal flesh and fat. Saliva lubricates the food as it makes its way down the esophagus.

ALERT!

If your dog has severe or frequent vomiting and diarrhea that persists for more than two days, she may become dehydrated and malnourished. Call the veterinarian immediately. He may ask you to bring in a fecal sample. If your dog has watery diarrhea without blood or mucus and shows no sign of straining when defecating, it may indicate inflammation of the small intestine.

The stomach produces hydrochloric acid. This is necessary to help break down animal proteins, bones, and fat. A fluid known as chyme migrates into the small intestine to combine with other digestive enzymes produced by the pancreas and liver. These enzymes add carbohydrate and fat digestion—converting carbohydrates to simple sugars, fats to fatty acids, and proteins to amino acids. When the food reaches the large intestine, the nutrients have been absorbed into the system and whatever remains is disposed of as stool.

Common Gastrointestinal Problems

Different breeds are prone to different problems, and your dog's age may also contribute to his gastrointestinal distress.

Acute Gastritis

Acute gastritis is a sudden onset of inflammation of the inner lining of the stomach. Dogs with gastric irritation will first vomit their stomach contents and later vomit clear or yellow fluid, which is mucus or bile. This will usually last less than seven days.

ALERT!

Eating large bone fragments that are indigestible may cause acute gastritis. This happens to dogs that are not accustomed to eating bones. Only give your dog large raw bones with extra B vitamins. This adds adequate stomach acid to aid digestion. Always supervise; if your dog persists in swallowing large bone segments, he probably shouldn't have them.

Dogs that are homeless or who are allowed to roam free are likely to suffer from acute gastritis at one time or another. They dig through the trash or compost piles or ingest dead animals. Young dogs are more apt to suffer from gastritis than senior dogs because they are often fond of checking out the trash. Gastritis can also be brought on by ingesting foreign bodies, plant material, hair, or by overeating. Chemical irritants or toxins, such as fertilizers, cleaning agents, or lead, will also cause acute gastritis, as will food allergies or dietary intolerance. Inflammatory bowel disease and stomach cancer can also cause this problem, although the symptoms will usually persist.

Swallowing foreign objects such as small toys may be a serious problem because they can cause an obstruction of the intestines and cause gastritis.

Chronic Gastritis

The signs of chronic gastritis are intermittent vomiting for at least one to two weeks. Be on the lookout for excessive vomiting with digested blood that resembles coffee grounds, lack of appetite, weakness, weight loss, diarrhea, and black tarry stool, which also signifies digested blood. To treat this condition your veterinarian will want to determine the cause of the illness, restore and maintain fluid and electrolyte balance in the dog's GI system, and rest the gastrointestinal tract.

Megaesophagus

When a puppy or adult dog repeatedly regurgitates immediately after eating or a few hours later, megaesophagus may be the culprit and should be ruled out by a veterinarian.

Megaesophagus is a common congenital problem in puppies that causes weakening and enlargement of part of or the entire esophagus. Miniature Schnauzers, Great Danes, and Dalmatians are at increased risk of the congenital form of megaesophagus, whereas German Shepherds, Golden Retrievers, and Irish Setters may be at increased risk for the acquired form.

It is not known why some dogs are born with megaesophagus. When a dog develops megaesophagus later in life it may be due to myasthenia gravis, Addison's disease, hypothyroidism, generalized neuropathy, or myopathies. Feeding the dog on an elevated platform is the only treatment for the congenital form. Prognosis is poor due to the risk of pneumonia from inhaling food into the lungs. Sadly, pups are often euthanized.

Vomiting and Diarrhea

Many first-time dog owners panic the first time their dog vomits, but it may be normal—even if it happens once or twice a month. Vomiting or diarrhea that occurs with greater frequency is a problem that should be treated. With vomiting and diarrhea comes dehydration—an excessive loss of bodily fluids and electrolytes.

Dehydration is serious. When left untreated, it can cause many health problems and even death. If a dog is dehydrated, his fluids need to be replenished by drinking small amounts of water rather than gulping large amounts. If he refuses to drink he needs to see the veterinarian immediately.

Serious signs of vomiting and diarrhea that you should bring to the attention of your veterinarian include:

- **Blood in vomit or stool.** The dog could have an obstruction, bleeding ulcers, a toxin, or a bacterial infection.
- **Protracted vomiting or diarrhea for more than a few hours.** If the dog continues to vomit despite withholding his food and water for twenty-four hours, it is important to see the vet. If the vomiting and diarrhea are profuse and the animal seems otherwise ill (lethargic, in pain, or weak), it is considered an emergency. Dogs in these situations may become dehydrated.
- **Dry heaves, distended abdomen, or restlessness because of discomfort.** Bloat may be a possibility and your dog needs to see the veterinarian immediately; bloat is life-threatening within hours.
- **Mucus in the stools.** This signals an imbalance in the colon.
- **Panting, shaking, or whining.** May signal exposure to a toxin or possibly an intestinal obstruction.
- **Straining to defecate.** May signal a possible obstruction in the colon.
- **Unusual color changes in the stools.** Gray stools signal trouble in the liver or intestines (inflammatory bowel disease) or pancreas (pancreatic enzyme insufficiency), while black or tar-like stools indicate bleeding in the upper intestinal tract. Bright yellow or green usually indicates that food is moving through too quickly to be absorbed, and orange might indicate blood abnormality or gallbladder disease.
- **Vomiting or regurgitating water.** If this lasts for more than twelve hours, notify your veterinarian.
- **Weight loss.** Any weight loss due to vomiting or diarrhea indicates either severe or chronic disease and should be discussed with your veterinarian.

Vomiting is a symptom, not a disease. When there are problems with digestion, severe stomach irritation or spasms will cause vomiting. This is how the body rids itself of the offending substance.

Treatment for Vomiting

When a dog vomits, withhold all food and water for twelve to twenty-four hours. This gives the stomach a chance to rest. After twelve to twenty-four hours, begin giving your dog a small amount of water. If she does not vomit again, add a little food a few hours later.

FACT

Vomiting is not the same thing as regurgitation. Vomiting is the forceful expulsion of stomach contents. It is characterized by heaving or retching, and dogs shows signs of nausea with drooling, pacing, or whining. Regurgitating is the passive expulsion of esophageal contents, similar to spitting up. Dogs do not heave or retch and there are no other signs prior to the episode.

Feed small amounts of a bland diet, consisting of two-thirds rice, sweet potato, and oatmeal and one-third cooked fish, cottage cheese, or boiled chicken. Feed only half the amount of a typical meal a few times a day, rather than one or two large meals a day. Add herbal products to soothe the stomach. Contact your veterinarian if your dog begins vomiting again.

The veterinarian should take a complete medical history, including information about the dog's regular diet, any recent medications she has been taking, if she's had any exposure to toxins or has eaten anything unusual, recent vaccinations, and a description of her symptoms. He'll also want to know what the expelled matter consisted of.

To identify the underlying cause the veterinarian can perform routine blood work and fecal analysis to rule out problems such as kidney disease, Addison's disease, or parasites. If a second visit to the veterinarian is necessary he may recommend a second round of laboratory tests to include abdominal X-rays and/or ultrasound.

Diarrhea

A healthy stool is the sign of a healthy dog. Diarrhea clears the body of unwanted toxins and often indicates disease. An attack of acute diarrhea comes on suddenly and usually lasts for a few days to a week or two. Technically, the definition of diarrhea includes bowel symptoms ranging from a watery stool, to any abnormal stool that is softer than normal, or very soft stools with an abnormal color or odor. Straining to defecate but only passing gas is also a symptom of diarrhea.

E-QUESTION

Should a dog with diarrhea go to the veterinarian?
There's no need to take your dog to the vet if he seems strong, happy, and active. Do go if he is lethargic, acts sick, or has a rectal temperature above 103.5ºF. Rush if he looks bloated or has persistent vomiting, is passing large amounts of blood in the stool, or is dehydrated.

If your dog seems okay, treat him at home by reducing the amount of food you are feeding him by half. Instead of a commercial bland diet, give him one-third cooked meat low in fat, such as chicken or boiled hamburger without the fat, and two-thirds white rice or cooked oatmeal. Add one to three tablespoons of yogurt, a probiotic, and two to four tablespoons of boiled sweet potato. Slippery elm will heal and soothe the intestines. Add one to three capsules of this herb to some broth twice a day, or just sprinkle onto the bland diet.

Long-standing chronic diarrhea can be debilitating. The body becomes malnourished, which affects the immune system and the body's ability to repair itself. A visit to the veterinarian will be necessary to alleviate the problem.

Diagnosing Inflammatory Bowel Disease (IBD)

For dogs and their owners, IBD is one of the most frustrating conditions. IBD is a group of disorders that result in chronic inflammation in the gastrointestinal tract. The inflammation causes frequent episodes of vomiting and diarrhea, but diagnosing it is difficult.

Chronic diarrhea and vomiting are hard on a dog's system and upsetting to the family. In severe cases, dogs can become depressed, refuse to eat, develop fever, and lose weight. And just when you think you've found the solution to the problem, it flares up again.

FACT

IBD is not an actual disease; it is a group of gastrointestinal diseases, all of which involve inflammation of the intestinal wall. There are many causes, including serious food allergies and over-vaccination. Some veterinary researchers believe IBD is an autoimmune response that causes the body to react inappropriately to antigens or proteins in food.

The reason why some dogs develop IBD is unknown, although genetics, nutrition, infection, parasitic infestation, hypersensitivity or intolerance to dietary ingredients, and an impaired immune system may all be responsible.

Symptoms

Chronic and intermittent diarrhea and vomiting are the most common signs of IBD. When the stomach and upper portion of the small intestine are involved, vomiting is more common. When the colon is involved, the dog is more apt to have diarrhea. Weight loss, increased mucus in the stool, blood in the stool, abdominal pain, rumbling stomach, and flatulence are additional hints.

Diagnosis

To diagnose IBD, the veterinarian will do blood work to rule out other problems, such as pancreatitis, Addison's disease, kidney disease, or a malignancy. She will examine a fecal sample for parasites or giardia and bacteria. Ultrasound and X-rays will check for obstructions. An intestinal biopsy will reveal the amount of white blood cells found in the intestinal lining. This is obtained through an endoscopy of the stomach or a colonoscopy of the lower gastrointestinal tract.

Dietary Changes

The first step in treatment for IBD is an elimination diet. All foods and treats are discontinued and a new diet is given, composed of novel and simple ingredients: one protein, one fat, one carbohydrate source with appropriate vitamin supplementation, or a commercial hypoallergenic diet with hydrolyzed proteins. If symptoms resolve, a diagnosis of dietary allergy or intolerance is likely and no further treatment is necessary.

Some supplements have been found to help in some cases. Probiotics have been proven to help reduce inflammation in the intestines by providing a source of "good" bacteria. If your dog is on a hypoallergenic diet, be sure to find a probiotic that contains no wheat, dairy, corn, or animal products.

E-QUESTION

Why do dogs eat their own poop?
There are many reasons for coprophagia that involve behavior and/or nutrition. Puppies investigate and play with feces if it's around. Stress or inadequate nutrition or nutrient absorption are other factors. Some dogs will stop as they age, but adding digestive enzymes to your dog's food and cleaning up stools promptly are the best deterrents.

Fish oil has also been recommended for treatment, but it should be avoided if any fish allergy might exist. N-acetylglucosamine seems to help by altering inflammatory pathways in the cells. And adding yams or sweet potatoes to the diet can help solidify the stools.

Some holistic veterinarians might recommend the use of western herbs or Chinese herbs to calm the intestines. Peppermint has been shown to relax the intestines and reduce intestinal motility. Boswellia is an herb that seems to reduce clinical signs in some cases. And some vets might suggest trying chamomile, slippery elm, or licorice to reduce the symptoms. There are a number of Chinese herbal formulations that might be appropriate for your dog. It is best to consult with a vet versed in TCM for this therapy. Add antioxidants such as vitamin E, vitamin A, and selenium. Add vitamin B complex, zinc, and some trace minerals, as well as fish oil, a probiotic and N-acetyglucosamine to heal inflammation in the bowels. The goal is to control IBD through the right diet, although a permanent cure might not be possible.

Nutritional Support

Regardless of what breed or mixed breed you have, a healthy dog doesn't produce a lot of gas, his stools are well-formed without an excessively strong odor, he has plenty of energy, and his appetite is hearty. A fresh natural diet that is free of artificial flavors and colors, additives, and chemical toxins and contains plenty of high-quality, digestible ingredients is a good way to maintain optimum health in your dog's gastrointestinal tract.

For routine gastrointestinal problems, many conventional veterinarians will recommend over-the-counter medications such as Tagamet or Pepcid to stop the production of acid in the stomach. While this might help the immediate symptoms, these aren't beneficial in the long run because the stomach acid actually helps with digestion. Liquid or tablet Kaopectate or Imodium is frequently recommended to treat diarrhea. If you and your dog are on vacation or you are unable to get to a veterinarian for a few hours, these may be beneficial for a short time. But while these take care of the symptoms fairly quickly, they fail to deal with the cause and your dog will still need to see the doctor.

FACT

Slippery elm works well for dogs with sensitive stomachs. It helps ease the symptoms of diarrhea, colitis, and other simple inflammations of the intestinal tract. This tree bark eases mucous membranes of the intestines and respiratory and urinary tracts.

Decreasing the amount of stomach acid may lead to bacterial infections and yeast overgrowth. Herbs and nutraceuticals will enhance digestion, soothe the stomach, and calm the intestinal lining to return the body to natural health. Many dogs' symptoms can be well controlled with hypoallergenic commercial diets. These diets contain proteins that have been broken down to a form that does not cause immune stimulation in the intestines.

Alternative Therapies

In addition to providing nutritional support for gastrointestinal problems, several homeopathic remedies can be soothing to the system. These include:

- **Aloe vera juice.** Calms muscular contractions of the colon.
- **Arsenicum.** For dark, bloody diarrhea.
- **Ipecac.** Helpful to reduce persistent nausea and vomiting.
- **Ginger root.** Stimulates the colon with smooth contractions to propel food through the esophagus and intestines.
- **Licorice root.** Helps soothe intestinal tissues against inflammation.
- **Marshmallow root herb.** Calms the lining of the intestinal tract.
- **Nux vomica.** Soothes nausea and vomiting.
- **Phosphorus.** Provides help if a dog vomits water or undigested food.
- **Rosemary leaf.** A gentle stimulant.

Herbal remedies such as chamomile tea will also help calm an upset stomach.

Dealing with Carsickness

If you have a puppy that gets carsick, try to put him in the car when his stomach is empty and after he's had a chance to potty. Most pups outgrow this uncomfortable feeling, but until then he needs to become accustomed to it. Try giving him a few drops of Rescue Remedy, tincture of peppermint, or a teaspoon of honey about 30 minutes before departure. Powdered ginger root capsules will also help calm the stomach.

At first, just spend a few sessions sitting in the car with your dog without turning on the car's engine. A few sessions later turn on the motor but don't go anywhere. Build up to just driving down the driveway before progressing to around the block and making very short trips.

Life-Threatening Bloat

Bloat, or gastric dilation-volvulus (GDV), requires emergency treatment to save the affected dog's life. The stomach fills with air, food, or fluid and twists and traps the stomach contents inside the abdominal cavity, blocking off blood circulation. This can cause death within hours.

Giant and large breed dogs between the ages of two and ten years are most often affected and are highly predisposed to developing bloat. Nervous, anxious dogs and dogs with some aggressive characteristics have a higher risk than easygoing, calm dogs.

The signs of bloat are restlessness, excessive salivation, drooling, and repeated attempts to vomit. Some dogs will try to hide in a far corner of the house or yard so as not to call attention to their weakened condition. Look for overall discomfort and a distended, swollen abdomen that continues to swell.

Reducing the Risk

To prevent bloat, feed a natural, home-prepared diet of multiple smaller meals and do not allow a dog to guzzle large amounts of water at one time. Provide regular exercise but restrict the amount of exercise your dog has just before he eats and for two hours after a meal. This reduces the amount of air the dog swallows and the chances of twisting the stomach. Minimize the stress your dog may experience close to feeding time as much as possible. Choose a quiet location to feed him and let him rest for two hours afterward.

Any deep-chested dog can suffer from bloat, although Great Danes have the highest incidence. Nearly half will bloat before the age of seven years. Swallowing abnormalities interfere with the dog's esophagus. This causes a dog to swallow more air and become less able to expel the trapped stomach gas.

Try to slow down your dog's eating; that may reduce the chance of bloat. Special dog bowls have raised areas inside or have a heavy chain with large links in the bowl with the food. This forces the dog to slow down and eat around the obstacles. It is now believed that placing your dog's dish on a raised platform is counterproductive, and increases the risk of bloat.

Surgery

For giant and large breeds with a family history of bloat, veterinarians can perform a surgical procedure called a gastropexy that will prevent the stomach from twisting. The stomach is sutured to the abdominal wall, which prevents it from twisting. In giant and large breeds this procedure is frequently performed as a preventive measure at the same time as a spay or neuter surgery.

CHAPTER 15

Issues of the Heart

Stories are told and songs are written about the strength of the human heart, the most important organ in the body. The heart is no less vital for dogs. It is responsible for pumping blood through the body and for keeping everything in good working order. But when the heart's own needs are not met, poor circulation and inflammation weaken the circulatory system and lead to heart disease. No cardiac irregularity in your dog should go unnoticed. By paying attention to early warning signs, taking preventative steps, and using natural treatments, it's possible to avert disease.

Discovering Irregular Heart Sounds

Like people, dogs can have heart problems. In fact, heart disease is one of the most commonly diagnosed problems in dogs, especially in older canines.

Some canine heart diseases are congenital, or present at birth. These may or may not be genetically passed through from one or more generations. Other heart irregularities are acquired and develop gradually over time.

FACT

A dog's heart is 0.6 to 0.9 percent of total body weight. Located in the chest cavity, the base of the heart is closer to the spinal column and the highest point is closer to the breastbone between the dog's front legs. This muscular pump is divided into four chambers, two on the left and two on the right.

Dogs suffer from heart problems such as heart base tumors, cardiomyopathy, heart murmurs, and irregular heart rhythms. There are two common types of heart disease that develop gradually over time and result in heart failure.

Dilated cardiomyopathy occurs mostly in large and giant breeds and causes the stretching of the heart muscle, producing swelling. The heart muscle becomes so weak that it cannot pump blood around the body.

Valvular heart disease can occur in any breed. As a dog ages the heart valves begin to wear out and degenerate. They cannot close properly and this allows blood to flow back and forth through the heart chambers. This reduces the blood supply to the body.

The Circulatory System

The heart, blood, and blood vessels—which include the arteries, arterioles, capillaries, and veins—comprise the circulatory system. It supplies all of the dog's tissues and vital organs with the oxygen and nutrients he needs for survival. The canine heart is very much like the human heart. Both have four chambers that include a right and left atrium and a right and left ventricle. The chambers on the right side receive blood from the body and send it to the lungs, where oxygen is added. The blood returns to the heart on the left side, where the left ventricle pumps the blood to the body.

Dogs have blood vessels just like people do. These include large arteries that connect to the abdomen, head, and heart, as well as smaller capillaries connecting to the arteries and veins. The arteries are large muscular blood vessels that carry oxygen and nutrients from the heart to the entire body. The system of blood cells is also the same in dogs as it is in humans. Red blood cells carry oxygen, while white blood cells fight off infection. Platelets and plasma assist in blood clotting. The blood carries hormones, nutrients, and waste products to and from the cells.

FACT

Von Willebrand's disease (VWD) is a common inherited bleeding disorder. It is a blood clotting defect that is prevalent in more than fifty breeds. Dobermans are the most frequently affected, but it is also found in Corgis, Doberman Pinschers, German Shepherds, German Shorthaired Pointers, Golden Retrievers, Miniature Schnauzers, Shetland Sheepdogs, and Standard Poodles, among others. A test checks for the clotting factor in the blood.

During a routine checkup, your veterinarian will examine your dog's heart by listening to the heart and lungs. She will observe the quality of the dog's pulse, check the color and nature of the mucous membranes, and look at the blood vessels in the eyes. The doctor will use her hands to feel for abnormalities in the abdomen and chest to determine if the heart is beating harder than normal. She can tell if there is pain and whether the organs are enlarged or if there's a mass or fluid inside. If she suspects an abnormality, chest X-rays will reveal the size and shape of the heart, the condition of the lungs, and the blood vessels. The electrocardiogram (ECG) assists in evaluating the rate and regularity of the heartbeat, while a blood sample checks the hydration status and functioning of other organs for signs of other underlying diseases.

Sometimes puppies are born with circulatory system problems. The chambers of the heart may not be fully formed or may be malformed. Blood vessels may have holes, may be too small, or may be situated in the wrong place. Heart valves may be defective and may not close properly. As puppies grow, they may develop infections, heart failure, or genetic predispositions to heart ailments.

Signs of Problems

During the early stages of heart disease there are few signs that most breeders could easily recognize. Many precursors to heart failure can be diagnosed only by a veterinarian's examination.

Heart problems are often discovered when a dog needs to have surgery or a dental cleaning. Veterinarians usually perform laboratory blood work and an electrocardiogram to screen for any problems before the procedure. An ECG will help rule out cardiac blockages, arrhythmia (irregular heart beats), and cardiac enlargement.

Heart disease and heart failure are different. Heart failure is caused by heart disease, although many types of heart disease don't result in heart failure. Symptoms of heart failure include the accumulation of fluid in the lungs, chest cavity, or abdomen; and low peripheral perfusion, or blood flow to the extremities. The signs of mild to moderate heart failure may include heart enlargement, coughing or hacking, wheezing, swelling in limbs, abdominal bloat, and poor circulation. Also be aware of decreasing energy or stamina, especially after exercise or exertion.

Severe heart disease symptoms include difficulty breathing, fainting, inability to exercise, loss of appetite, and weight loss. Sometimes owners do not recognize the early signs of heart failure until it is too late. One cause of potential heart failure is heartworm disease. Before dispensing heartworm preventative, the veterinarian will take a blood panel to test for the presence of heartworms. Heartworm disease is frequently detected through the blood test long before routine symptoms of the disease become apparent.

Diagnosing Heart Disease

Heart disease is frequently diagnosed in both small and large breed dogs. Genetics play a role in whether a dog will develop heart disease, but there are other risk factors as well. If a dog has a condition that increases the demand for cardiac output, such as anemia or pregnancy, there is an increased risk of heart disease. Dogs that are not given heartworm preventatives are at a higher risk for contracting heartworms, a devastating but avoidable condition.

FACT

Heart failure is a major canine health problem. According to the American Veterinary Medical Association, approximately 3.2 million dogs in the United States acquire some form of heart disease and may be in heart failure. Heart disease can be present at birth or acquired later.

All conditions need to be diagnosed by a veterinarian, and may involve laboratory tests. If heart disease is suspected, the veterinarian will want to rule out heartworm disease with a heartworm test, chemistry blood panel, and X-rays. X-rays will also help determine the presence of any tumors, lung congestion, or fluid surrounding the heart.

Once a thorough medical assessment has been made, a natural approach can help prevent a minor problem from progressing. At the very least, natural remedies may help slow the disease. Natural approaches are available to complement conventional medications.

Valvular Heart Disease

Valvular heart disease, also known as endocardiosis, is the leading cause of acquired heart disease in dogs. Senior dogs, particularly small breeds, are prone to developing it; a third of all dogs that are affected by it are over the age of twelve.

Stated simply, the heart valves become inflamed, thickened, and scarred. This causes the valves to leak and wear out over time, preventing them from closing as tightly as they should. Instead of pumping blood forward, the blood leaks backward into the atria of the heart. A veterinarian can detect this in a routine examination. He can hear a heart murmur—the sound of the blood flow moving backward from the ventricle to the atrium—when he listens to the dog's chest with a stethoscope. When the blood backs up on the left side of the heart, it leads to lung congestion and coughing. When the blood backs up on the right side, fluid builds up in the abdomen, making breathing difficult.

E-QUESTION

Can the heart valves be repaired?
A few specialized canine heart centers perform open-heart surgery to repair some types of congenital heart defects of the valves. This surgery is very expensive and there are many restrictions on which patients are acceptable candidates. New surgical techniques are in trials and may one day be available to canine patients with valve disease.

The disturbance in forward blood flow causes compensatory changes to the structure of the heart. Because blood backs up into the atrium, the atrium will overfill. In response, it will become enlarged to accommodate the excess blood. Eventually the atrium will not be able to expand any further and pressure will build, causing blood to back up into the lungs or abdomen. This is called congestive heart failure.

No dietary changes have been found to reliably affect the outcome of valve disease, although salt restriction is recommended once congestive heart failure begins. Potassium supplementation must be recommended with caution because some heart medications cause potassium retention and hyperkalemia is potentially life threatening.

Dilated Cardiomyopathy (DCM)

Many large breeds of dogs may develop dilated cardiomyopathy as young as four years of age, although some smaller breeds are affected by it as well. The cause is unknown but is likely genetic in most cases.

In this common genetic heart problem, which encompasses several different diseases, the heart muscle is diseased and gradually becomes dysfunctional. The heart enlarges as the muscle itself thins out and becomes too loose to contract properly. When the diseased heart muscle no longer pumps enough blood throughout the heart, the dog will develop congestive heart failure.

Warning Signs

If you happen to notice that your dog is slowing down and is not his usual peppy self, it's wise to look for other signs of cardiomyopathy. Early detection will help obtain treatment for your dog. The signs include:

- Depression and lethargy
- Fainting, stumbling, or collapse
- Little interest in food or eating
- More time sleeping
- Overall weakness
- Reluctance to get up and down or to climb stairs
- Shortness of breath, coughing, and wheezing
- Swelling in limbs
- Pale gums
- Increased heart rate

Dry, hacking coughing at night may be due to pulmonary congestion (fluid in the lungs and chest cavity) and/or due to enlargement of the atrium.

Treatment

Conventional treatment for heart disease includes medications. When drugs are used, dogs need to be closely monitored for serious side effects, such as kidney disease.

Veterinarians may prescribe heart medications, along with diet recommendations, herbs, supplements, and acupuncture. Diuretics may be prescribed to remove excess water from the body. ACE (angiotensin-converting enzyme) inhibitors are used to lower blood pressure. Calcium channel blockers decrease the contraction of the heart and widen the arteries to make it easier for the heart to pump blood. Digoxin increases the ability of the heart to contract and reduces heart rate. A new drug called Pimobendan is becoming the drug of choice for many cases of DCM that have resulted in congestive heart failure. It opens up the blood vessels and returns blood to the heart, which reduces pressure on the muscle. Discuss this option with your veterinarian.

Any deep-chested dog can suffer from bloat, although Great Danes have the highest incidence. Nearly half will bloat before the age of seven years. Swallowing abnormalities interfere with the dog's esophagus. This causes a dog to swallow more air and become less able to expel the trapped stomach gas.

The side effects of these medications should be seriously considered before giving them to your dog. Diuretics require monitoring to avoid electrolyte imbalances. ACE inhibitors may reduce appetite, cause diarrhea and vomiting, or lead to kidney insufficiency. Digoxin and Pimobendan may cause loss of appetite, vomiting, diarrhea, lack of coordination, depression, and abnormal heart rhythms.

These medications are frequently and routinely combined by cardiologists, but blood parameters must be followed to ensure proper kidney function at the start of treatment. An overdose of calcium channel blockers will cause an abnormal drop in blood pressure, heart failure, and an overall slowing of the heart.

Adding Taurine and Carnitine

In some breeds, nutritional deficiencies in the amino acid taurine have been linked to the development of DCM. Some Boxers with cardiomyopathy have responded to treatment with supplemental L-carnitine. Not all dogs respond to supplementation; successful treatment largely depends on the underlying cause of disease.

Several giant and large breeds are genetically predisposed to DCM. These include Boxers, Doberman Pinschers, Newfoundlands, Portuguese

Water Dogs, and Great Danes. If you have one of these breeds consider supplementing your dog's diet with carnitine and taurine under a veterinarian's supervision. If there is a deficiency, providing extra carnitine improves heart rate and protects against heart muscle weakness. Extra carnitine won't have any impact if there is no deficiency. Dogs often show improvement in heart muscle function with the added amino acid.

Dogs with valvular disease have a high enough level of taurine and wouldn't benefit from the additional amino acid. A supplement of carnitine may or may not help valvular disease, although the combination of taurine and carnitine has been shown to improve life expectancy in some dogs with DCM.

Congenital Heart Disease

Congenital heart disease is present at birth, and there are a variety of conditions that fall into this category.

Patent Ductus Arteriosus

Patent ductus arteriosus (PDA) is a common heart defect that is present at birth. The ductus arteriosus is a short blood vessel that normally allows blood to bypass the lungs, which are nonfunctional in an unborn dog. The ductus closes shortly after birth, but when it remains open, the blood leaks back into the other side of the heart. The heart must pump more blood to maintain a normal blood flow. PDA is detected by a continuous heart murmur.

Certain breeds, including the Miniature Poodle, German Shepherd, and Cocker Spaniel, are more prone to the condition. It is also more common in females than males. The signs of PDA include the following:

- Collapse
- Coughing
- Exercise intolerance
- Heart murmur
- Labored breathing

- Seizures
- Fainting spells

Heart failure ultimately results and surgery is required as early as possible to close the patent ductus.

Pulmonic Stenosis

Smaller dogs are more prone to pulmonic stenosis. This common congenital heart defect is the third most common canine congenital heart defect. Pulmonic stenosis is a narrowing of the right ventricle and the pulmonary artery of the heart. The narrowing causes an overload in the right ventricle and ultimately produces thickening of the heart muscle.

A revolutionary new method of treating PDA is interventional catheterization. Catheters are used to close the PDA. The surgeon inserts a stainless steel fiber–embedded coil into a catheter to close off the hole. This procedure is less invasive than traditional surgery and the recovery time for the dog is minimal. However, not all dogs are suitable for this type of closure.

Severe cases of pulmonic stenosis require treatment. Valvuloplasty is more successful if conducted early before extensive remodeling of the heart has occurred. In this procedure, a catheter with a balloon is inserted into the heart through a blood vessel. The balloon is inflated to widen the stenosis. Balloon valvuloplasty is less invasive for the dog than traditional surgery and is 70 percent more successful.

Early Prevention

Sometimes there isn't much you can do to save a dog that is born with life-threatening heart disease. But you can help your dog maintain a quality life and add extra years.

Limiting environmental toxins such as pesticides helps alleviate many symptoms of heart disease. Appropriate medical management, supplements and herbs, diet and exercise, and control of environmental factors also go a long way to helping your dog. Keep your dog away from cigarette smoke; secondhand smoke can cause irregular pulse, difficulty breathing, and coughing.

Cut the Calories

Preventing your dog from becoming overweight or even obese helps keep his heart healthy. Too much weight places an enormous strain on his heart and makes breathing far more difficult for him.

Heartworm Prevention

If you live in an area with a high mosquito infestation rate during certain times of the year, discuss heartworm prevention with your veterinarian. Mosquitoes transmit larvae to healthy dogs; the larvae penetrate the skin and migrate to the heart through the circulatory system. Eventually they reach the dog's heart and pulmonary vein. Once inside the heart, heartworms can grow as long as eleven inches and cause a tremendous amount of damage to the heart and lungs. When left untreated, heartworm disease is fatal.

Avoid Dental Disease

Keeping your dog's teeth clean and free from dental disease helps prevent heart problems. When bacteria is allowed to remain on a dog's teeth and gums it eventually enters the bloodstream and settles on the heart valves.

Brush your dog's teeth regularly by wrapping gauze or a washcloth around your finger and use it like a toothbrush. You can gradually progress to a soft doggy toothbrush and water. Later on you can use enzymatic toothpaste or a paste of baking soda and water.

If you have a small or toy breed, her teeth should be professionally cleaned by the veterinary hygenist every three months. This helps to clean those places in the teeth and gums that you just can't reach.

Natural Heart Health Treatments

Besides keeping your dog at a healthy weight and providing plenty of regular exercise, reducing her chances of developing heartworm, and maintaining regular dental health, other therapies can help you treat your dog's heart disease.

Coenzyme Q10 (CoQ10)

The body naturally manufactures Coenzyme Q10, an antioxidant, to promote cell growth and repair. As your dog ages, her body produces less CoQ10. Supplemental CoQ10 increases oxygen flow to cells and has been shown to be helpful for dogs with heart disease. It can slow the progression of heart disease as well as aging. Available in capsule form in health food stores, this potent antioxidant increases energy, improves circulation, and promotes weight loss.

Hawthorn

As a heart supplement, this herb helps support dogs with mild heart failure. Holistic veterinarians recommend it as an alternative to digitalis, a powerful cardiac stimulant made from foxglove, because it strengthens the contractions of the heart muscle and blood vessels, improves coronary artery blood flow, and reduces blood pressure. It takes six to eight weeks to reach maximum effectiveness.

FACT

Hawthorn is a flowering shrub or small tree found mostly in Europe. Its leaves and flowers were once used as a sore throat remedy and as a diuretic for kidney problems. Today its fruit is used to relieve many cardiac problems in people, including angina, cardiac arrhythmia, hypertension, and atherosclerosis.

Hawthorn contains antioxidant properties from its variety of bioflavonoids. It may also improve circulation to the extremities. It is synergistic with most heart medications and in some cases allows lower doses to be effective.

Omega-3 Fatty Acids

The fatty acids docosahexaenoic acid (DHA) and eicosapentaenoic acid (EPA) are important to heart health. Frequently found in fish oil, flaxseed, grains, and legumes, fatty acids cannot be manufactured by the body and must be obtained from food. They contain anti-inflammatory properties that benefit dogs at high risk of heart disease—especially those with muscle-wasting conditions—and they aid in the preservation of normal heart rhythm.

Other supplements that may have cardiovascular effects include the following herbs:

- Barberry
- Bugleweed
- Burdock
- Coleus
- Dandelion leaves
- Devil's claw
- Evodia
- Garlic
- Ginger
- Ginkgo
- Goldenseal
- Motherwort
- Oregon grape
- Salvia
- Stephania

Remember to consult with a veterinary herbalist before using herbs, especially in combinations. Some may cause side effects or interactions with any medications your dog is taking. Be careful of feeding your dog too much garlic; it can be poisonous to dogs in high doses.

Acupuncture may also be effective in treating your dog's heart condition. It helps to rebalance the body and remove blockages.

Food and Exercise Matter

Providing a fresh, natural diet that is designed to regulate sodium and giving your dog plenty of regular exercise are the best ways to keep his heart and lungs healthy.

A Natural Heart Diet

A low-sodium, high potassium diet with extra omega-3 fatty acids is recommended for dogs with heart disease. Fresh, raw, or slightly steamed vegetables should be added for supplementary nutrition. Bone-meal tables or bonemeal powder should be given for calcium and phosphorus. Be sure to include a multivitamin mineral supplement, omega-3 fatty acids, plant enzymes, and green food or health blend without additional salt.

FACT

Dogs with heart failure must be fed low-sodium diets because they retain sodium instead of filtering it through the kidneys. Talk to your veterinarian about starting your dog on a low-sodium diet if your dog has been diagnosed with heart failure. Remember that the low-sodium diet applies to snacks as well as regular meals.

Most dogs with heart problems have little or no appetites and suffer from low potassium levels due to decreased food intake. Ask your veterinarian about adding potassium and magnesium supplements to your dog's food to prevent deficiencies.

Move for Heart Health

An exercise regimen is important in preventing heart disease. If a dog already has clinical disease, depending on its severity, restricted exercise might be necessary. To start a preventive routine, gauge your dog's activity level. For dogs that aren't accustomed to working out, start off slowly. Do something you both enjoy. Walking is the best exercise for both of you. If you don't feel comfortable going for a stroll in your own neighborhood, then pack your dog in the car and drive to another location. You don't have to pick an exotic locale; a local park is a good place to start.

If you're a city dweller, many shopping centers have dedicated walking paths around their perimeters. Dedicated dog walkers have even taken their dogs strolling in parking garages.

If you prefer a more active workout, consider signing up your dog for agility training. In agility, dogs run through an obstacle course that includes climbing an A-frame, going through a tunnel, jumping through a suspended tire, and weaving through poles. This is a fast and fun way for you and your dog to exercise her heart muscle.

CHAPTER 16

Kidney Disease

The urinary tract is the one system that all owners pay very close attention to when they're trying to housetrain their puppy. The two bean-shaped kidneys are responsible for the excretory system. They are located—one on each side—in front of your dog's rear legs close to the spinal column. They have an important job—filtering waste from the blood and processing extra water and waste products. Sometimes the kidneys don't function properly and kidney failure results. There are two kinds of kidney failure—acute and chronic.

What Is Kidney Failure?

Kidney failure, also known as renal failure, happens when the kidneys are unable to work properly. It affects an estimated 25 percent of dogs and is not to be taken lightly.

E-QUESTION

What is the prognosis if my dog is diagnosed with kidney failure?
In acute cases, the prognosis often depends on the root cause of the kidney failure. Blood and urine tests are performed to evaluate kidney function. In acute cases, the prognosis is significantly better if azotemia, the buildup of toxins in the bloodstream, begins to resolve within the first forty-eight to seventy-two hours of therapy, although kidney regeneration and compensation may take several weeks or months. Dogs can live with chronic kidney failure for a long time, depending on how well therapy preserves their quality of life.

The kidneys have multiple tasks, including helping to regulate blood pressure, activating vitamin D, and producing erythropoiten, a hormone that stimulates red-blood cell production. The kidney's primary job is conserving water and filtering out waste and toxins.

Acute Kidney Failure

Acute kidney failure is a sudden loss of kidney function. Sometimes this is reversible—but not always. Acute renal failure can be the result of other diseases such as uncontrolled diabetes, leptospirosis, and cancer, as well as the result of these serious conditions:

- Adverse effects to medications such as chemotherapeutics or non-steroidal anti-inflammatory drugs
- Antifreeze or rat poison ingestion
- Circulatory disorders
- Heart failure
- Heavy metal poisoning
- Kidney or bladder stones

- Reaction to anesthetics
- Reaction to blood transfusion
- Reaction to vaccines
- Shock

Chronic Renal Failure (CRF)

Chronic renal failure is an irreversible loss of function, and often veterinarians do not know what causes it. CRF can occur over months or years and comes on gradually. The most common form of kidney disease in dogs, it is the most common cause of death in dogs older than ten years of age. All dogs older than seven should have annual bloodwork and urinalysis performed to watch for early indicators of renal insufficiency and other diseases. Early detection, the appropriate diet, supplements, and even fluid therapy can prevent or forestall the onset of kidney failure.

Unfortunately, if bloodwork isn't monitored, the signs may go unnoticed. By the time symptoms become apparent, kidney disease is far advanced. The signs of kidney insufficiency include:

- Anemia
- Appetite loss
- Bad breath
- Dehydration
- Dull coat, hair loss, and heavy shedding
- Excessive thirst and urination
- High blood levels of metabolic waste
- Lethargy and depression
- Mouth and tongue ulcers
- Vomiting and diarrhea

With chronic kidney disease, there's a shortage of healthy nephrons to adequately filter and reabsorb excess water back into the bloodstream. Dogs with this condition drink copious amounts of water just to maintain an adequate volume of fluids in the body, and produce large amounts of dilute urine.

Why Kidneys Fail

Nephrons are microscopic funnel-shaped tubes that perform filtering and reabsorbing operations. Poisons, aging, infection, trauma, cancer, autoimmune diseases, and genetic predisposition can damage them. When this happens, nephron activity ceases. The kidneys will continue to operate, but they will have lost their ability to concentrate the urine. When damage occurs gradually, the remaining nephrons can grow larger and the body will attempt to compensate by stimulating thirst and altering blood pressure; if more water passes through the kidneys, toxins can still be removed despite lower nephron efficiency. Ultimately, the animal cannot drink enough and toxins begin to build up. This is called uremia. Due to the body's ability to compensate, many dogs won't begin to show obvious signs of kidney insufficiency until after approximately 75 percent of the kidney function has been lost. At this point, toxins will start to build up and the symptoms of kidney failure will become evident.

Results of Kidney Failure

If the kidneys fail to perform, they cannot clear the blood of the toxic waste products, including urea and creatinine. Urea is a nitrogen-containing byproduct of protein metabolism. Creatinine is a chemical byproduct of muscle contractions and metabolism.

As kidney function is lost, toxins will build up in the bloodstream. This is called azotemia. Blood tests can measure the amount of blood urea nitrogen and creatinine to determine the degree of kidney damage. Different animals can tolerate different degrees of azotemia, so not all azotemic animals will seem sick. However, as these values increase, dogs will feel sicker and will show signs of uremia or poisoning from these increased levels of toxins.

Loss of kidney function will also create imbalances in the calcium/phosphorus ratio and losses of potassium and blood proteins in the urine.

Kidneys in Balance

The key to avoiding kidney disease is prevention. When kidneys fail to function, all the organs in the body are affected. The holistic approach views the body as a whole, rather than concentrating on only one organ, whether diseased or healthy. Therefore, it's important to strengthen and balance all organs in the body. This takes pressure off the weakened kidneys and allows them to work at their optimum level.

Water Is Important

Your dog should always have access to fresh water. Giving your dog plenty of grated fresh or lightly steamed vegetables, which contain high water content, is another healthy addition to his diet.

E-QUESTION

Does the type of water a dog drinks really matter?
Yes. Filtered water is recommended, although steam-distilled water or reverse osmosis is better for dogs with lower urinary tract disease, as it moves inorganic minerals. Always add plenty of fresh water to your dog's food, and adding some organic apple cider vinegar to the water dish helps clear up any yeast infections and prevent any future ones from forming.

Getting Rid of Toxins

In dogs with normal kidney function, food with lower protein levels results in fewer byproducts being created. For dogs with kidney problems, these byproducts are not eliminated easily. And, the fewer number of toxins ingested, the easier the excretion process. So, to prevent protein malnutrition, the best diet for a dog with compromised kidneys is a food with reduced but high quality and highly digestible protein.

Causes of Kidney Failure

A wide variety of diseases and conditions contribute to kidney disease. This section outlines some of the most common.

Bacterial Kidney Disease

Bacteria can cause kidney infections. The bacteria can ascend to the kidneys from the bladder or can descend to the kidneys through the bloodstream or from other organs.

Leptospirosis is a contagious bacterial disease that affects dogs and humans. It impairs kidney function and may result in kidney failure. It is spread by infection by a bacterial pathogen called leptospira. Signs of leptospirosis include vomiting, impaired vision, and convulsions. The disease is transmitted by contact with the urine of infected animals or objects contaminated with the urine of infected animals.

Although a vaccination for leptospirosis is available, some dogs experience allergic reactions to this vaccine. While the risks of not vaccinating for leptospirosis were once thought to outweigh the risks of vaccine reaction, the type of leptospirosis that is protected against in the vaccine is often not the type that dogs come in contact with, frequently rendering the vaccine ineffective. For this reason, many veterinarians do not use this vaccine unless the risk for infection is substantial.

Antifreeze and Rat Poisoning Danger

Ingesting even a small amount of ethylene glycol–based antifreeze that may have accidentally spilled on your driveway can impair your dog's kidney function.

ALERT!

Antifreeze has a sweet taste that attracts dogs, but it is deadly. About 10,000 pets every year die from antifreeze poisoning. It immediately forms crystals inside the dog's nephrons. A better alternative to protect your car and dog is to use propylene glycol–based antifreeze. Decorative snow globes can also be dangerous if broken; about 2 percent of a snow globe is antifreeze.

Rat poison containing calciferol (a form of vitamin D) is also lethal to dogs. When it is ingested, the calciferol increases the dog's calcium level, which causes mineral deposits, inflammation, and additional damage inside the kidneys.

Antibiotics

While most antibiotics will not harm the kidneys, a few can damage the nephrons. One of these is gentamicin, which inhibits bacteria by suppressing protein synthesis and growth. The anticancer drug cisplatin and amphotericin B, a drug for serious fungal infections, can also cause acute kidney damage.

If a conventional antibiotic is prescribed for your dog, always ask your veterinarian about the benefits and risks and discuss other options.

Diagnosis and Treatment

The veterinarian will take a complete medical history. He will ask about exposure to antifreeze, recent surgery or anesthesia, exposure to toxic drugs, and any previous illnesses. If kidney disease is suspected, tests may include a urinalysis, a complete blood count, X-rays of the abdomen, urine culture, ultrasound, kidney biopsy, and serum biochemistry tests.

Chronic kidney disease can leave dogs more susceptible to acute kidney failure, due to their weakened state. Proper treatment and regular monitoring will go a long way toward helping dogs with chronic kidney failure to have a quality life for many years after first detection. The conventional treatment may include:

- Antibiotics if the cause is bacterial
- Inducement, then control of vomiting
- Intravenous or subcutaneous fluid therapy
- Management of blood electrolyte abnormalities
- Monitoring urinary output and urine concentration
- Management of anemia
- Peritoneal dialysis or hemodialysis
- Surgical removal of any blockages or obstructions

This is a life-threatening condition and dogs with acute kidney disease must be continuously monitored. Despite intensive therapy, some dogs will die anyway.

The Bladder and Urethra

Think of the canine bladder as a pouch. It receives urine from the kidneys via the ureters and collects and holds it until it is so large that it stimulates urination. Urine stored in the bladder passes through the urethra before leaving the body.

Depending upon his size, a puppy's bladder is so small that it usually fills up every thirty to sixty minutes when he is active. As dogs age, they can hold their urine longer, although some seniors lose muscle tone and they must urinate more frequently.

All systems need to be in good working order in order for the urinary tract to function properly. Any imbalance in one system will affect the kidneys' ability to perform their task.

To maintain a healthy urinary tract and to prevent kidney damage, avoid dehydration by making sure your dog always has access to plenty of fresh water. The bowl should be emptied, cleaned, and refilled daily. In some households, you may need to check it a few times throughout the day. Dogs will drink heartily if the bowl is deep and the water is cold, which is why many of them will drink out of the toilet!

ALERT!

Your dog should have ready access to the outdoors where she can urinate when the urge arises. Middle- to large-sized dogs need to empty their bladders about once every three to four hours. Longer than that and the bladder has to stretch to hold the urine, which eventually can lead to loss of muscle tone and chronic problems.

Senior dogs should have their kidney function evaluated by having their blood and urine checked with a blood test every six to twelve months.

Undetected urinary infections crop up more frequently with older dogs, and problems can be treated if they are caught in time.

A fresh, balanced diet supplemented with omega-3 fatty acids and plenty of regular exercise also helps maintain good health. If there is any physical or emotional stress in your dog's life, strengthen his immune system by supplementing his diet with vitamin B-complex and antioxidants.

Bladder Stones

Like humans, dogs can suffer from bladder stones. This is known as canine urolithiasis. In this condition, the urine can be either too acidic or too alkaline, which causes excessive amounts of tiny crystals to form in the urinary tract. Urolith formation can also occur when there is a high urine concentration of salts or urine retention; it can also be the focus of infection on which crystallization can occur. When left untreated, these crystals become enlarged and can form stones.

Stones are usually formed in the dog's bladder, but they can also form in the kidney or the urethra. Crystals cause urinary tract irritation and pain during urination. When too many crystals or a small stone becomes lodged in the dog's penis, they can painfully block the stream of urine and prevent the dog from urinating. While females may form crystals too, they easily pass because of their anatomy and do not cause a problem.

There are several types of stones, but the only way to determine what kind your dog suffers from is to retrieve a stone and have a laboratory analyze it. If the stones are very small they can be flushed from the bladder and forcefully expressed. The only other way to obtain a sample is to surgically open the bladder and remove the stones. Surgery is invasive but quickly removes the stones, while catheterization is less invasive but often less effective or not possible.

Struvite Stones

Struvite stones can form when there is a bladder infection or if the pH of the urine is consistently alkaline. The crystal form is composed of magnesium, ammonium, and phosphate. Struvite crystals can be found in normal urine and are not a problem unless they are present in very large amounts, cause discomfort, or form stones.

FACT

Some Dalmatians are prone to developing uric acid stones in the kidneys or bladder because of their unique uric acid metabolism. These dogs should eat a well-balanced, low-protein diet. They should avoid stress and purines (organic compounds contained in meat and especially organs), drink plenty of fresh water, and be taken outside to urinate once every three hours during waking hours.

Nearly 85 percent of patients with struvite bladder stones are females. Bichon Frises, Cocker Spaniels, Beagles, Miniature Schnauzers, Miniature Poodles, and English Cocker Spaniels are prone to forming these stones. Most dogs first develop them when they are around three years of age.

Oxalate Stones

Oxalate stones need an acidic pH to form. Calcium oxalate stones cannot dissolve over time; diet change does not work as it does with struvite or uric acid bladder stones. After stones are removed either through surgery or catheterization, the focus is on lifelong prevention by maintaining a balanced pH and minimizing the amount of protein in the diet.

The breeds that are prone to developing calcium oxalate stones are Miniature Schnauzers, Lhasa Apsos, Yorkshire Terriers, Miniature Poodles, Shih Tzus, and Bichon Frises. Most cases of these stones develop in dogs between the ages of five and twelve years of age.

Treatment

Attempting to dissolve existing stones is risky because they can become lodged in the urethra and cause a life-threatening urinary blockage. This is especially true in male dogs due to their anatomy. If you notice signs of a blockage, immediately contact your vet. Be on the lookout for increased frequency of urination, straining to urinate without producing any urine, reduced volume of urine, or blood in the urine.

ALERT!

Dogs with kidney disease need a diet that restricts the amount of protein, phosphorus, and sodium. A diet low in phosphorus may help slow the progression of kidney failure by reducing mineral deposits. Dogs with stones should not have additional vitamin C or excess salt in their diets.

Dietary management and prevention of urinary tract infections is key to helping your dog avoid urinary stones.

Urinary Tract Infection (UTI)

Bacterial urinary tract infections are common in dogs and cause much pain and discomfort. Signs of UTI include painful or difficult urination, increased frequency of urination, increased volume of urination, excessive thirst, pus in the urine, blood in the urine, crystals in the urine, and lower back pain. After an examination, a conventional veterinarian may prescribe antibiotics to treat the infection. A holistic veterinarian may recommend the homeopathic remedies uva ursi, berberis, cantharis, and staphysagris to heal the infection. These soothe the infection and minimize the pain.

Home Cooking

To help your dog avoid forming struvite stones, use a high-quality protein, low-carbohydrate diet that is low in magnesium. Avoid high-magnesium foods such as spinach, beans, and barley.

Supportive Care

Several natural remedies combined with the right nutrition can help the kidneys and fortify other organs. Commercial kidney diets maintain low protein, fat, and sodium, but they might also contain harmful chemical additives, preservatives, and byproducts, which put a strain on the already overburdened renal system. Consult your veterinarian to find the best treatment for your dog.

Herbal Therapy

Several herbs are known to help detoxify the kidneys. Use astragalus, burdock, dandelion leaf, echinacea, garlic, ginkgo, gotu kola, hawthorn, and marshmallow. Chinese herbs, especially one called rehmannia, is highly reputed and can reverse azotemia in some cases, especially when used early in the course of disease. Acupuncture is used to enhance the effectiveness of the herbs to increase the renal blood flow. This combination is highly recommended.

Homeopathic Help

Homeopathic remedies are helpful for urinary tract problems. Aconite is useful if a dog is straining to urinate, especially if the weather is particularly cold or damp. Arsenicum helps incontinence, a minimal urine flow, straining, or blood in the urine. Belladonna can be administered if there's sudden onset of straining or incontinence.

Berberis will help alleviate painful urination or tenderness and is useful for frequent urination or mucus in the urine. If there is blood in the urine, give cantharis, which will also help alleviate straining or discomfort during urination. Equisetum is particularly beneficial for puppies and senior females and if there's incontinence, a slight urine flow, or pain or discomfort after urinating.

CHAPTER 17

Emergencies Happen

In a perfect world, you and your dog would grow old together and you would never have a medical emergency. Unfortunately, that's not always the case. Despite your best care, sometimes bad things happen to good dogs. There may come a time when your dog runs into a glass door, gets stung by a bee, or gets hit by a car. Knowing when you can treat him yourself at home and when you should rush him to your veterinarian could mean the difference between life and death.

When Is It Serious?

If your dog ever has a medical issue and you're unsure whether he needs to see the veterinarian, it doesn't hurt to call. Your veterinarian will be able to tell you whether you should come in for an emergency appointment or what you should do to handle the situation yourself.

FACT

Like people, every dog has a slightly different body temperature. Find out what your dog's baseline temperature is so that you can measure any changes. The average normal temperature ranges from 100°F (approximately 37.8°C) to 102.5°F (slightly over 39°C).

Get into the habit of observing your dog every day for changes that may signal distress. Look closely at his posture, gait, and coat, and notice any irregularities in his behavior, activity level, eliminations, or appetite. You'll be surprised at the changes you might see from day to day.

This information will enable you to spot a potential health issue in the early stages and to know when it is something serious that needs a veterinarian's attention rather than something you can tend to on your own. In natural medicine, good health begins with prevention and the balance of body systems—mental, emotional, physical, and spiritual. Anything out of the ordinary is a sign of a bigger problem.

Taking Your Dog's Temperature

Knowing your dog's temperature is the first step in determining if your dog has a serious illness. To take his temperature you'll need a rectal thermometer. Shake it a few times until the reading is below 99°F (approximately 37.3°C); if you have a digital thermometer, you won't need to shake it. Lubricate the bulb end with lubricating jelly and hold your dog's tail while you gently slide the thermometer into your dog's rectum. Remove the thermometer after 1 minute or when the digital thermometer beeps.

Measuring Pain

Unlike people, dogs don't usually moan or complain if they are in pain. They suffer quietly and keep to themselves. In the wild this was necessary to prevent predators from detecting any weakness. Today it's up to you to identify the source of your dog's discomfort. That's why it's so important to notice changes in your dog's behavior, body language, and temperature. These signs may indicate that your dog is in pain:

- Arching the back or holding the front legs out away from the body
- Constantly biting or licking at one place on his body
- Dilated pupils
- Hiding in the yard or a corner of the house
- Limping longer than a day
- No interest in food or water
- Pacing and restlessness
- Panting excessively
- Unwillingness to move or lethargy
- Whimpering or growling

Vomiting and Regurgitating

At some point in your dog's life, he will vomit, regurgitate, gag, or let food and water drop out of his mouth. The first time that any of these occur can be alarming, but once you can tell the difference between a one-time event and a serious problem, you'll be able to treat your dog without panicking.

E-QUESTION

How do you know when vomiting is serious?
Contact your veterinarian if your dog has diarrhea, no appetite, vomits several times within a few hours, or if the vomit is bloody. Also notify your veterinarian if your dog's abdomen or sides look bloated, he seems uncomfortable, or he vomits every time after eating, drinking, or waking.

If you're thinking of contacting your veterinarian, correctly describing your dog's stomach upset symptoms will help her arrive at a diagnosis.

Before your dog vomits you may notice drooling and heaving abdominal muscles. When he regurgitates there's no drooling or heaving, but a little chewed up solid food or liquid will bounce back. If he gags or hacks up mucus, fluids, or foamy liquid, it's probably just a cough. Dropping food or water or continually trying to swallow may look like regurgitation, but the dropped food is usually whole pieces. Perhaps he doesn't like what he's eating or his throat, mouth, or teeth are bothering him.

Broken Bones and Limping

If your dog runs into a solid surface, is hit by a car, or falls from a high location, it's possible he has a fracture and needs medical attention. More than likely he won't be able to walk on a broken leg and may yelp if you touch the injured leg. While some fractures are more serious than others, your dog needs to see the veterinarian right away for any broken bone.

A compound, or open, fracture occurs when a broken bone tears through the flesh and punctures the skin. There's possible infection and loss of blood. If the bone doesn't poke through the skin it's a closed fracture with little risk of infection. When the bone is broken in more than one place, it is a multifragmentary fracture that is either open or compound (closed).

Chances are his leg isn't broken when your dog limps. But if he won't let you touch the leg or if the limping persists for most of the day, your dog needs to see a veterinarian. These could be signs of ligament damage or a broken leg.

Environmental Dangers

Going green is all the rage these days, and there's a very good reason for this natural phenomenon. The contaminants in air, water, soil, and food are affecting not only the environment, but human and canine health as well. Indoors and outdoors, there are toxic gases and pollutants that cause a host of medical problems.

Household Toxins

While there are some dangerous substances in the environment that are difficult to avoid, you can remove others from your own home, including asbestos, automotive and paint products, cleaning supplies, poisonous plants, dust, and mold. In addition, some common household items and foods should be kept out of your dog's reach. These include mothballs, fabric softener sheets, onions, chocolate, raisins, and products sweetened with xylitol, such as sugar-free gum. Prevention is the first natural defense in safeguarding your dog's health.

ALERT!

Contact the ASPCA Animal Poison Control Center (*www.aspca.org*) at (888) 426-4435 if you think that your dog has eaten anything poisonous. The website has a list of dangerous household items and toxic plants, and you can speak to an expert if you have a question. There is a $60 consultation fee applied to your credit card.

Avoid using hazardous household cleaners by using natural methods to clean your home. Baking soda is a great scouring powder that doesn't scratch delicate household surfaces, and lemon juice fights odors, helps remove stains, and works as a glass cleaner.

Garden Pesticides

Pesticides don't remain in one location for very long, and they can travel from outside to inside the home without your realizing it. In one study, the Environmental Protection Agency (EPA) found that twenty-three types of pesticides in dust and air were tracked into homes on the soles of shoes.

Since your dog goes outside a few times a day, the pads of her feet also pick up dangerous chemicals. Not only does she track them into your home, she ingests them when she licks her feet.

To avoid the chance that your dog will come in contact with pesticides, try cutting the lawn before weeds go to seed, which will prevent them from spreading. To create a healthy ecosystem, avoid using any synthetic fertilizer or pesticides in your organic garden and learn what plants grow best alongside one another and what plants may help repel pests. For example, basil encourages tomato growth and repels flies and mosquitoes.

E-QUESTION

Are pesticides safe for dogs to be around?
A study by the National Cancer Institute found that dogs from homes that used the common pesticide known as 2,4-D had double the chance of developing malignant cancer; in yards treated by lawn care companies, dogs were 30 percent more likely to have canine malignant lymphoma.

Be sure to dispose of pesticides and chemicals you no longer use by contacting local waste-management facilities about their hazardous waste collection programs. Talk to your neighbors and discuss your concerns with the pesticides they may be using. Maybe they're not even aware of the effect these dangerous substances have on their pets.

Blue-Green Algae

It may look like great fun to let your dog dash through a refreshing pond or lake for a healthy dose of exercise. Many spaniels and retrievers love nothing better than fetching a stick from a shallow watering hole—but this activity can be deadly if they ingest the blue-green algae that lurks in the water.

Algae are a natural part of any watery environment, but when the bacteria bloom they produce deadly toxins that turn the water green or blue-green and produce a musty or earthy smell. Resembling pea soup or pond scum, the toxic algae may even look foamy or appear bright green, brown, or red. If you don't know whether a pond or stream is safe, it's best to avoid it completely.

If your dog comes in contact with blue-green algae, she will suffer a toxic response within minutes to hours. Neurological symptoms include stumbling and falling, elevated heart rate, foaming at the mouth, and seizures. Wash her off immediately to prevent self-cleaning contamination and transport her to the veterinarian as quickly as possible.

Insect Bites and Stings

Chances are you won't know when an insect bites your dog until after it's happened. You may see him furiously scratching or biting at his skin, but some dogs have no reaction at all other than several big bumps on the top or sides of the head or along the body. On short-haired dogs, these eruptions will be very noticeable, while long-haired coats tend to disguise them.

Relief

If possible, try to identify the offending insect so you know what you're dealing with. If you see a stinger, remove it by rubbing the skin with the edge of a dull knife.

There are several natural ways to relieve painful itching. First, cleanse the area with mild soap and water. Next, make a paste by combining baking soda and a few drops of water and apply it to the sting or bite. Ice will relieve your dog's pain.

ALERT!

Take your dog to the veterinarian immediately if she becomes lethargic, develops an abscess or hives, or begins thrashing around biting herself. Many dogs are highly allergic to bee stings and mosquito bites and could die if they don't receive emergency treatment.

If bee stings are a problem in your yard, consider cutting back blooming plants or trees that naturally attract bees. Make sure weeds and standing water are eliminated from your property to reduce the chance of a mosquito infestation.

Natural Support

You can also provide relief to your dog through nutritional support, homeopathy, herbs, and antihistamines. Nutritionally, bromelain (pineapple extract) helps reduce edema and inflammation, while the bioflavonoid quercetin inhibits histamine. For painful, red swelling, give your dog apis or ledum as an alternative.

Some herbs, such as aloe vera gel, slippery elm, calendula, or chamomile, are effective for mild insect irritations. To be on the safe side, it's always a good idea to have quercetin or human antihistamine (Benadryl) in any form on hand if you have a highly allergic dog.

Cuts, Bruises, and Bleeding

After a romp outdoors, it's not unusual for your dog to come inside with a cut on her face or paw. Clean the area with soap and water.

There Will Be Blood

If there is only a slight trickle of blood from a cut, you don't have to do much. Clean the cut and check it later in the day or the next day to make sure there isn't more bleeding. If there's a lot of bleeding, apply pressure to the wound and administer phosphorus or yunnan pai yao. This should stop the flow; if it doesn't, you'll need to take your dog to the veterinarian. A dose of Rescue Remedy along the way is a good idea.

Colorful Boo-Boos

You may never see a bruise on your dog. It doesn't mean that dogs don't bruise after a nasty bump or fall; it just means you won't see it because their hair covers their skin. Like people, dogs do feel tenderness and soreness from a bruise.

Administer ice within the first twelve to twenty-four hours after your dog's mishap. This will help any bleeding below the tissue to subside. You can also give your dog arnica and bellis for painful bruises. After twenty-four hours, alternate between applying hot and cold compresses to create circulation in the tissue.

Nail Trouble

A broken or bleeding nail is a fact of life. If there's a slight amount of bleeding that stops fairly quickly, you don't have to do anything. However, if the bleeding doesn't stop, you'll need to take your dog to the veterinarian to have the torn nail removed. Although it may be sore for a few days and your dog may limp, it will heal and in time the nail will grow back completely.

Respiratory Distress

It's frightening to see your dog lying listless or suddenly go limp due to choking, electric shock, trauma, or drowning. He may not be breathing and his heart may have stopped, but before you panic, realize there is something you can do to help him.

Mouth-to-Snout Resuscitation

If your dog has stopped breathing, you can perform mouth-to-snout resuscitation. This life-saving technique was adapted from mouth-to-mouth resuscitation between humans. With dogs, the person performing the procedure will breathe into the dog's nose, not his mouth.

To begin, open your dog's mouth and look inside to make sure there is no blood or mucus that may be blocking his throat. If there is, remove it. Gently pull your dog's tongue out of the way to clear the airway, and place a few pellets of *Carbo vegetabilis* (vegetable charcoal) 30C on his tongue. Add a few drops of water on the tongue to dissolve the pellets.

Close and hold your dog's muzzle and make sure the upper lips completely cover the lower lips. Place your mouth over his nose and exhale five or six quick breaths into his nose in 1 minute. If this doesn't jump-start his breathing, increase the number of breaths into his nose to twenty per minute. Continue until he's breathing normally on his own.

After you have been performing mouth-to-snout resuscitation for a few minutes, place two drops of Rescue Remedy on your dog's tongue. Place two more drops on his tongue every five minutes until the dog is breathing on his own.

CPR for Canines

If your think your dog's heart has also stopped, you'll need to perform cardiopulmonary resuscitation, or CPR, to try to keep your dog alive until his heart and lungs can begin to function on their own again. The technique for dogs is similar to traditional CPR used for people.

FACT

According to the American Red Cross, choking is the number one hazard for puppies. The organization teaches classes in pet CPR and first aid. Participants practice on animal mannequins with compressible chests and stomachs. There is also a Red Cross pet first aid book and an instructional video.

Before beginning chest compressions, check for a heartbeat. To find your dog's heartbeat, feel the area where his left elbow touches the chest. If you don't feel pulsing there you will need to perform chest compressions. You can probably do the job yourself if you have a small dog, but a large dog may require two people. Begin by rolling your dog onto his back, and placing your hands on either side of his chest. Quickly squeeze and depress the chest one to three inches ten times. If there's no response, you'll need to increase the number of compressions until you see the chest rise.

Your Holistic Emergency Kit

Emergencies always happen when you least expect them, but if you know what to do and have the right supplies on hand you can provide temporary relief for your dog until you can transport her to your veterinarian. Keep a first-aid kit in your house and one in your car and you'll be covered for emergencies both at home and on the road.

There are ready-made kits you can buy from online services or from your holistic veterinarian, or you can put one together yourself. Use a hard plastic tub with a tight-fitting lid, and make sure everyone in the household remembers where you store this. Put the ASPCA Animal Poison Control Center's (*www.aspca.org*) phone number, (888) 426-4435, in the kit. Contact them if you think your dog has ingested anything poisonous. There may be a $60 consultation fee.

The following items will come in handy for all dogs:

- **Activated charcoal.** For use in cases of accidental poisoning. The charcoal helps absorb the poison and remove it from the body. Before using it, contact your veterinarian and/or the National Animal Poison Control Center (NAPCC) because it may interact with other medications your dog is taking.
- **Aloe vera gel.** This is invaluable for soothing burns, cuts, and abrasions.
- **Arnica.** This is ideal for sprains, trauma, and wounds.
- **Arsenicum album.** This helps treat allergies.
- **Bandages or Vetwrap.** Include different shapes and sizes of gauze rolls or pads or Vetwrap, which clings to itself and doesn't shift off the wound.
- **Bandage scissors.** You'll need these to cut bandage material to fit the wound.
- **Bulb syringe.** This is indispensable for irrigating wounds.
- **Clean towels.** One or two bath or hand towels will come in handy to absorb blood, wipe down your dog, or cleanse a wound.
- **Cold packs.** Use these to reduce swelling or pain. Wrap one in a towel before using it so it's not too shocking on the skin.
- **Diphenhydramine (Benadryl).** Use this antihistamine for allergic reactions, such as spider bites or bee stings. Contact your veterinarian for the correct dosage for your dog.
- **Disposable gloves.** Use these to protect your hands and prevent contamination if your dog is bleeding or has an open wound.
- **Emergency blanket.** If your dog has been injured, this will keep her warm and help prevent shock. It also comes in handy if she is bleeding and you need a clean place for her to lie while you transport her to the veterinarian.
- **Eyewash.** If your dog has dust or particles in her eyes, you'll need this to flush out the material.
- **Goldenseal.** An antimicrobial and anti-inflammatory herb, it has a soothing effect on open sores.
- **Heating pad.** If your dog goes into shock or her temperature is very low, this will help keep your dog warm until you transport her to the

veterinarian. Cover the heating pad with a towel so that it isn't too hot on the skin or fur.

- **Hydrogen peroxide.** Used topically, this is useful for cleansing wounds.
- **Kaopectate or slippery elm.** This is effective for diarrhea.
- **Lubricating jelly.** Apply this liberally to a thermometer before inserting it.
- **Muzzle.** This is for your protection. Any dog—even yours—who is injured and in extreme pain may bite. If you don't have a muzzle, you can make one from a roll of gauze in a pinch.
- **Pedialyte.** A fluid of water and electrolytes, this prevents dehydration.
- **Rescue Remedy.** This will help your dog re-establish balance and harmony.
- **Slip leash.** If you can't reach your dog's regular leash, this quickly slips on your dog without a collar.
- **Thermometer.** If your dog refuses to eat or has diarrhea, use a digital or rectal thermometer to register her body temperature. This is helpful information for your veterinarian.
- **Tea tree oil soap.** This helps cleanse wounds.
- **Tweezers.** These are useful for removing foreign objects from your dog's paw or skin.

To make sure these items stay in good condition, put a note on your calendar to check your first-aid kit once every few months. Be sure to add anything specific that your dog needs. Keeping a pet carrier in your car or someplace where you can easily access it is invaluable in a disaster situation. If your dog must be confined for any length of time, or if you or someone else has to transport her to the emergency clinic, the carrier is the safest place for your dog.

You should also have your veterinarian's current phone number and the name, address, directions, and phone number of the emergency clinic in your first-aid kit. In an emergency you may not remember this information. If you become separated from your dog or are unable to care for her, write down the name and phone number of someone you authorize to care for your dog in your absence.

If You Are Forced to Evacuate

Unfortunately, fires, floods, hurricanes, and earthquakes are devastating facts of nature. When people have to evacuate their homes during a disaster they don't usually have time to look around the house for the things their dogs will need. If you can assemble an evacuation kit for your dog long before you actually need it, your evacuation will be a little less stressful.

In addition to the first-aid kit, put the following items into a separate waterproof container with a tight-fitting lid:

- Bottled water. You'll need at least a two-week supply. Replace it every two months.
- Blanket for your dog's comfort
- Commercial quality dog food. Place a two-week supply in a sealed container and replace it every three months.
- Dental cleaning supplies
- Dog life preserver
- Grooming supplies
- Leash and collar with an identification tag. Although you probably have a leash you use every day, you may not have time to go looking for it.
- Medical records and any medication your dog is taking
- Plastic bags for waste cleanup
- Recent photograph of your dog with his name, description, age, and medical information, and your name, phone number, and address. Include the name and phone of a contact person who will know your location if you become separated from your dog.
- Toys

Disaster Preparedness Kit

If there's ever a disaster in your community and you cannot leave your home, having a few emergency supplies on hand for your dog will keep him safe and healthy until normal conditions are restored. Plan ahead with the items on the following page:

- A sealed bag of treats. Your dog will appreciate these reassuring tidbits if your home is dark and cold.
- Bottled drinking water. Keep a two-week supply or about a quart a day per dog. Store in a dark place and replace it every two months to guarantee freshness.
- Cooked dog food in the freezer. Keep a two-week supply, but keep alternatives ready in case you lose power. This may mean stocking a food your dog does not normally eat.
- Commercial dry food in a sealed bag in case you cannot heat the frozen food. Keep a two-week supply.
- Medication. If your dog is on medication, keep an extra two-week supply on hand at all times.
- Rescue Remedy. This will calm your dog if he becomes fearful.

Don't forget to keep a few special toys in reserve and a dog sweater or an extra blanket for your dog's warmth.

CHAPTER 18

Communicating with Your Dog

Fortunately, there are many ways to understand your dog without using words. Her own body language speaks volumes. Your job is to listen and learn to interpret what she's trying to tell you. How you communicate with your dog directly affects her overall health. She'll feel stressed if she doesn't understand you or if you don't understand her. For effective training, use positive reinforcement, clicker training, and treats.

The Mind-Body Connection

Have you ever wondered why your dog begins salivating the minute you pick up his food bowl? The answer lies in your dog's memory. When a circumstance arises that reminds your canine companion of the past, his mind automatically replays that experience, and he fully expects that it will happen again. Your dog doesn't forget a thing.

His mind is his most powerful asset and it feeds directly into his body. He anticipates that he's going to eat (yum!) the minute you approach his dish. His mind and his body are working together on the same level, and the link between them is very strong.

To maintain your dog's health, take the mind-body connection into consideration. When you interact with your dog and care for his body, you're also nourishing his inner canine. You can't do one without affecting the other.

How you communicate with your dog—and this also includes how you train him—will either strengthen or weaken his physical response to emotional and environmental stress. If your messages are loving and positive, you can enhance his body's response to almost any health challenge.

E-QUESTION

What's a timeout?
If your dog becomes too excited to pay attention or is being destructive, he needs time by himself. Don't yell or say anything. Instead, calmly pick him up or tell him to go into his crate. Once he's calmed down, let him out.

Using effective communication has many health benefits. It will help your dog heal from injuries and recover from surgery more quickly, fight infection more effectively, and reduce or eliminate his symptoms of depression. If you yell or scream at your dog, use physical punishment, or train him with harsh methods, his emotional state will deteriorate and his health will suffer.

Training Pure and Simple

Sometimes training your dog to do something new can be frustrating. It takes a lot of effort before the new behavior finally clicks into place. Throughout the training process, your dog makes every attempt to connect with what it is you're asking her to do. Until that happens, she will be stressed, which is physically harmful to her body.

FACT

Colonel Konrad Most is recognized as the father of traditional dog training. He trained military dogs in Germany and his book, *Training Dogs, A Manual,* was considered the bible of dog training when it was published in 1910. Many military programs still use his methods, which rely on collar corrections and discipline and reflect the same discipline that soldiers receive.

It helps to recognize when your dog feels stressed. That way you can tweak your training method and routine to reduce your dog's apprehension. The goal is to create a happy, positive work ethic for your dog so she can act and feel her best. Carefully look at your dog's body, head, and facial features for these signs of stress:

- Muscle tremors or body shaking
- Excessive panting and drooling
- Sweaty or very warm pads of the feet
- Extreme shedding
- Dilated pupils
- Diarrhea or frequent urination
- Repeated chewing or scratching at feet or body
- Head and tail down
- Skittish behavior
- Withdrawn or pacing activity

Training Fundamentals

There are many ways to train a dog. People even invest in trendy gadgets, such as harness leashes, electric shock collars, and invisible fences, to do the training for them. Some training methods are better than others, but the one you select has to be right for you and your dog.

E-QUESTION

How do they train dogs for movies and television?
Many trainers use a clicker. Once the cameras start rolling, the dog is expected to act with the trainer close by but out of sight. If the dog does a good job, she hears the clicker. No click means the dog will have to repeat the behavior until she gets it right.

When you choose a training program, the first step is to decide what it is you want your dog to do. Find out as much as you can about your dog's breed and the job it was originally developed to perform. If you have a mixed breed dog, study her body type and features and estimate what breeds might be in her ancestry. This evaluation may help you decide what job strengths she may possess.

If you've always wanted to volunteer with your dog in search and rescue work and you have a Chihuahua, you'll have quite a training job on your hands, and you'll need a lot of time and patience to get the job done. If you have a Bloodhound who was born to sniff out and find people, your training will be comparatively easier. Working with your dog's natural gifts will make the process much easier for both of you.

Every dog can be trained to do almost anything, including the basic obedience commands: sit, stay, stand, down, and come. All methods rely on trial and error—trying new techniques to see how they work, then refining the directions, language, and rewards to achieve the result you want.

Using New Techniques

Training methods are always improving. A trainer will use a technique as long as the dog is learning quickly. But if a routine is difficult and the dog just isn't getting it, the trainer will test new techniques. The trick of training is to keep trying different things until something works.

So much of effective training depends on the dog. This has nothing to do with how smart a dog is, but rather how willing she is to please you. Many trainers say that they would rather have a dog of medium intelligence and a great amount of heart than a dog that's smart enough to perform brain surgery but couldn't care less about the patient. Training a dog like this is a real challenge, making some breeds easier to train than others.

Border Collies, Labrador Retrievers, Golden Retrievers, and German Shepherds have reputations for being smart service and working dogs. In reality, they are skilled at deciphering hand signals, facial expressions, and body language. This makes it easy for them to understand exactly what people want them to do. They will do anything to please their owners, while dogs that have been bred to work independently from their trainers are trickier to manage.

Keeping It Positive

If you worked hard and successfully completed a project, wouldn't you appreciate a bonus? And once you received the bonus, wouldn't you try really hard the next time so that you could earn another bonus? Of course you would. The same is true for your dog.

Keep the treats in your pocket or in an open fanny pack so you can give one to your dog the minute she does what you want her to do. You don't have time to walk to the kitchen and fetch a piece of food. If you wait too long to reward her, she will miss the connection.

The reward for a job well done is the basis of positive reinforcement. Using positive reinforcement to train your dog means giving him a reward immediately after he does what you've asked him to do. The reward is the most powerful tool you have in shaping his behavior.

Food Treats

When you're just beginning to train your dog, use the tastiest food treats you possibly can as extra incentive. Something small and soft works better than something crunchy. Your dog can gulp them down quickly, and immediately refocus his attention on you for more. Crunchy treats take longer to eat and your dog will be more concerned with the crumbs than paying attention to you.

Chicken and small pieces of leftover roast beef cooked with garlic, cheese, or apple slices work well. These are easy to use, but you can also motivate your dog to work well for you with his favorite toys or a special, loving pat on his chest coupled with a few upbeat "attaboys."

Every time you give your dog a treat, back it up with verbal praise in a happy tone of voice. This gives your dog a double reward, and the praise can be used instead of a treat if one isn't available.

Shaping Behavior

When you first start training your dog, give him a treat every time he does what you want. If you want to reinforce something close to the behavior you're training, such as shaking hands, make him do a little more before you give him the treat. At first, give him a treat for just lifting his paw. Once he has that behavior mastered, only treat him for lifting his paw higher. And once that behavior is established, treat him only when he touches your hand.

ALERT!

Ignore undesirable behavior. If your dog knows the command and doesn't perform it when you ask, don't give him the treat. Try another behavior or repeat the command and place him in the right position. When he complies, be sure to reward him either with food or lavish praise.

Once your dog knows a behavior, taper off on the treats. Reward him with a treat three out of four times, and then two out of four times. Eventually, you'll be rewarding him only occasionally, but always give plenty of verbal praise. Dogs are smart, so vary the times you hand out the reward so that he repeats the behavior, thinking that he'll eventually get what he wants.

Clicker Training

Clicker training has become one of the most popular ways to train dogs. It is also used with whales and dolphins.

What's a Clicker?

The clicker is a small plastic box with a button that emits a distinct clicking sound when you push and release it. This device gives the dog immediate feedback that she's done a good job. Follow the click with a yummy treat and your dog will do her very best to make that sound (and the treat) happen.

FACT

Clicker training was invented and developed by Keller and Marian Breland and Bob Bailey to help train dogs in the mid-1940s. It became a training movement in the early 1990s when Karen Pryor and Gary Wilkes popularized it with seminars.

Clickers are entirely positive and don't involve any physical compulsion or intervention. While the clicker doesn't work for every dog and every behavior, it is very effective in many situations.

Training your dog with a clicker has instant rewards both for you and your dog. It gives you something to do (click the clicker) when your dog does what you want her to do, and it gives her a fast and fun way to receive instant approval. The payoff is being able to follow up the click with a reward—either through praise or a treat.

Getting Started

To start training your dog with a clicker, make sure you have plenty of really yummy treats on hand. The first and most important step is to teach your dog to recognize the sound of the clicker. Choose a room that is free from distractions and interruptions.

Press the button on the clicker and give your dog a small treat. Repeat this a few times. It won't take long for your dog to connect the click with a treat. Once your dog understands what the clicker is all about, you can progress to teaching her simple behaviors. Use the clicker and give your dog a treat every time she repeats the behavior you want.

Using Hand Signals

If you want to train your dog with hand or verbal signals as well as clicks, you can use the clicker to speed the learning. As she learns these signs, she will be able to respond to the clicker or the signals whether she receives a bonus or not. Eventually you can phase out the clicker and just give your dog a hand or a verbal signal.

Understanding Dogspeak

Your dog expresses the way he is feeling with hundreds of different body positions. As animals that once lived in packs, dogs have developed these variations in order to protect themselves from other animals. In the wild, they must know who is in charge and where they stand in the social pecking order. They also have to defend their territory and what belongs to them.

Your dog uses his body language to communicate with other dogs. As soon as they meet each other, dogs show how they're feeling. They also know how to size up other dogs in order to establish rank.

Reading the Signals

If you watch your dog very closely, you'll be able to learn how to recognize more than feelings of happiness or sadness. You'll be able to notice when your dog is feeling nervous, annoyed, or affectionate.

As odd as it sounds, leaning is another form of communication. No doubt your dog loves to lean against your legs. You return the favor by reaching down and rubbing his head, but that may not be what your dog wanted. It may be his way of saying, "I'm in charge and I'll choose where I put my body, not you." It's also the reason why some dogs will put their foot on top of yours. Here are a few more signs of canine body language:

- **Body.** Pawing you or another dog signals appeasement. Play-bowing (front legs extended, rump up, tail wagging) shows happiness and invites play. Freezing in place signals fear.
- **Eyes.** Direct eye contact means confidence. Casual eye contact signals contentment. Averted eyes signal deference. Dilated pupils signal fear. Narrowing eyes mean anger or readiness to defend.
- **Ears.** Relaxed ears indicate a calm dog. Erect ears mean an alert dog. Up and forward ears mean the dog is challenging you or another dog. Ears laid back mean the dog is worried.
- **Hair.** Raised hair indicates a dog is afraid or is challenging another dog. Smooth hair reveals calmness.
- **Head.** Laying the head over another dog signals boldness. Dropping the head indicates submission. High carriage means superiority.
- **Lips.** Licking another dog's face is submission or an invitation to play. Tightly closed lips signal uncertainty. Lips pulled back are a warning sign.
- **Mouth.** Panting means a dog is nervous, excited, playful, or hot. A relaxed mouth signals calmness. Smiling may mean he wants something from you; dogs never show this sign to other dogs.
- **Tail.** Tail between the legs shows fear. Tail held high and wagging signals excitement. An erect tail signals alertness. A relaxed tail signals calmness. A tail held straight out and wagging shows caution.
- **Teeth.** Baring, clenched teeth with a wrinkled nose signals imminent attack.
- **Tongue.** Tongue hanging loosely out of the mouth shows relaxation.

Using Scent

In addition to their bodies, dogs use scent to communicate. They operate with a whole world of fragrances that people can't even fathom. The olfactory glands of dogs are a million times more sensitive to odors than those of humans.

E-QUESTION

Why does my dog scratch at the ground after defecating?
By tossing his stools around while on a walk or even in your own yard, your dog is marking his territory and trying to spread his scent as far as possible.

While you might think you should correct your dog for sticking his nose where it doesn't belong, he's actually receiving information. Anal sacs just under a dog's tail contain secretions that are unique to each dog. Smelling these is like receiving a confidential e-mail from a friend. With one sniff your dog can find out another dog's age, sex, health, and whether or not he or she is altered or spayed.

By marking with their own urine, dogs can send many messages to other dogs. It's the reason why even a short walk with your dog can take so long. Every time your dog catches the scent of another dog, he has to mark the spot.

Verbal Cues

Dogs do more than just bark if they have something to say. They have whines, howls, yips, squeaks, growls, and even different volumes of barks. How your dog expresses himself depends on his mood and what he wants. To decipher what your dog is saying, evaluate the context.

Nothing gets another dog's attention faster than barking. It announces his territory, relieves stress, and expresses joy. High-pitched barks signal that your dog is lonely and wants your attention, a single bark is curiosity, and low repetitive barking will warn off an intruder if your dog is feeling protective.

There's no mistaking a growl. Dogs use it to warn away other dogs or humans, or if they're feeling frightened. Your dog can mix a verbal cue with a posture for added effect, such as combining a growl with a dominant or submissive posture.

When a dog wants to find another dog or a human, he will howl. It's a locator sound. Mournful howls signal distress, while a howl with high and low tones means your dog is playfully looking for another dog. There's no doubt that dog whining is annoying, but to a puppy it's an automatic attention-getter.

Your Posture

Now that you know how to read your dog, he needs to understand your body language too. If you carry yourself in a strong, upright position, your dog will interpret that to mean you are in charge. When you give your dog a command, keep your arms and hands at your sides. Raising them over your head may frighten your dog and distract him from following your request.

To lure him into a sit position, use a treat and raise your hands only slightly. Resist the urge to bend over your dog when he comes to you. Many dogs see that as an intimidating position and will back away.

Telepathic Communication

You probably already know how to talk to your dog. Most of the time you can tell that he's saying one of four things: "I'm hungry," "I want to go out," "come play with me," or "where's my toy?" But if you're searching for a more meaningful relationship with your canine companion, try conversing with him telepathically.

This involves having a two-way exchange with your dog that relies on your interpretations of his emotions, feelings, pictures, thoughts, and words. Think of it as a heart-to-heart discussion with a friend.

Discovering how to communicate with your dog is like learning to speak a foreign language. If you want to understand what he is trying to tell you, you'll need to assume that he wants to communicate with you, and to believe that conversing with your dog is possible. You just have to find the right words that you both understand. Of course, trusting your intuition or having a sixth sense definitely helps too.

ALERT!

An animal communicator does not predict your dog's future and should not give you a veterinary diagnosis or make health decisions for your dog. Although it may be tempting to ask, don't look to this practitioner for the answers to very specific questions you might have about your dog.

If you doubt your ability as a great animal communicator, there are pet psychics you can hire who will do the job for you. This paraprofessional should treat your dog with respect and will try to relay messages from your dog to you as accurately as possible. She should deliver insight and clarity about your dog's problems, but she can't force your dog to change, and doesn't read his mind. Many communicators handle most of their consultations via the telephone. They learn about your dog from your input but without the distraction of his physical characteristics.

Talk to the Paw

While telepathic communication isn't really a healing therapy, it does make you more responsive to your dog's needs. It can also help you:

- Discover your dog's preferences
- Ask how your dog's body feels and if he's sore
- Find out why he's misbehaving
- Learn if your dog has a message for you
- Receive feedback about your dog's bedding or food
- Find out if your dog does or does not like other pets in the house
- Learn if your dog is ready to be laid to rest
- Speak with a dog that has died

Finding a Communicator

To locate a pet psychic, ask your veterinarian or friends with dogs for referrals. There are many listings on the Internet, but trust your intuition about the person you contact. If you don't care for this individual during your initial conversation, chances are you're not going to like the results, so keep looking.

Interview the communicator by asking a few questions. These should include how long she has been an animal communicator and what animals she has worked with in the past. Some psychics specialize in just horses or only dogs.

Briefly tell her a little bit about the subject of your inquiry and find out if she has had experience with this topic before. Inquire about what preparation is needed before a session. Ask if there's a guarantee for her communication. Many psychics guarantee that they can establish a clear line of communication with a subject within the first fifteen minutes. If they can't, you shouldn't be charged.

CHAPTER 19

Getting Out and About

Letting your dog do what comes naturally will lead to many adventures for both of you. She's a curious creature and wants to see what the world has to offer. Luckily there's no shortage of dog-friendly things to see and do, from leaping over obstacles in agility competitions, to becoming a Canine Good Citizen, to visiting the sick, to traveling. Your job as a responsible dog owner is to make sure that your dog's safety comes first.

Age-Appropriate Exercise

One of the first things people want to do when they get a new dog is to take him out walking or jogging. It's fun and there are so many benefits to physical exercise for both of you.

Exercise improves cardiovascular conditioning, helps food digestion, reduces stress, tones muscles, strengthens bones, and stabilizes mood. This helps you and your dog shape up and builds a wonderful bond between the two of you that will last a lifetime. But before you head out the door with your dog's leash in hand, there are some things you'll need to do first.

To support your dog's good health and prevent any possible physical problems from popping up later on, your veterinarian should give him a thorough medical evaluation before you get started. This includes evaluating your dog's cardiovascular fitness and taking an X-ray of his hips and elbows. This verifies that your dog is physically able to handle the rigors of activity and is free of crippling hip or elbow dysplasia, which would result in painful movement in joints.

Running for Survival

Domesticated dogs aren't as sturdy as you might think they are. In the wild, they had to track down their own food if they wanted to eat. They were conditioned to be on the move at all times. This required skill, speed, and endurance for swimming, running, jumping, and climbing.

E-QUESTION

Should I feed my dog before or after exercise?
Feed your dog at least an hour before or an hour after exercising so she can digest and metabolize her food. Don't let her gulp a bowlful of water before or after working out; a few sips are okay. Too much to eat and drink may cause vomiting.

As companion animals, dogs have the luxury of receiving their food just for looking cute. They don't have to rely on their physical condition or contend with a harsh environment, extreme temperatures, or menacing predators to receive their two square meals a day. This probably explains why some dogs prefer resting on their laurels to seeking out adventure.

Getting Started

To improve health and avoid injury, hold off rushing out the door and doing any strenuous exercise with your dog until he has been properly conditioned. Regardless of how old your dog is or what canine sport you choose, he needs to slowly build up his strength, flexibility, and endurance. You can do this by walking your dog slowly at first, and gradually increasing the duration and intensity of the sessions.

Exercise for Puppies

If you have a puppy, begin taking your pup out on a leash for short walks lasting five to ten minutes. Gradually build up to a half mile, then a mile. Until your pup is older, limit outings to walking; forget strenuous, high-impact exercise such as jogging, hiking, or jumping.

It's okay if your pup chooses to run around on her own inside your home or a fenced-in yard. When her muscles begin to twinge from over exertion, she'll know when to stop. That's not the case when she's on a leash outdoors with you. She will push herself just to keep up with you and can injure her growing bones.

If you have a small breed, don't go for walks longer than a mile until your puppy's first birthday. For medium to large breeds, wait until they're at least eighteen months to two years of age. Their growth plates are still developing and musculoskeletal damage will occur if exercise is too strenuous.

Exercise for Adult Dogs

If you have an adult or overweight dog that hasn't been exercised, start with slow walking for ten or fifteen minutes, two or three times a week. In the beginning, your dog may seem slightly out of breath, but after a few sessions he should be able to handle the outing much more easily. When you see that he is able to go farther at a faster pace and is perhaps even pulling you on the leash, try increasing the length of the walk to thirty minutes and pick up the speed a little.

FACT

Warm up your dog prior to exercise. This helps prevent strained muscles and injuries. If you're going running, walk your dog for five minutes first. If you're going walking, give her legs and feet a light massage to stimulate blood circulation. Don't forget to cool your dog down after exercise by doing the same thing.

Dogs with every medical condition, including diabetes, heart disease, and irritable bowel disease, will benefit from regular exercise. For shy, fearful, hyperactive, and destructive dogs, continued outings provide both physical and emotional advantages. Exercise sessions give these dogs an outlet for their emotions, improve their moods, and generally help them relax and sleep better. Overweight dogs that exercise regularly and eat a quality diet will naturally lose some unwanted pounds.

Temperature Watch

Temperature extremes can be disastrous for your dog if she's outdoors without any protection from the elements. She can easily overheat and develop heatstroke or become frostbitten in very cold weather.

When the temperature is 80°F or higher and the humidity is high, your dog should not exercise or remain outside for longer than ten or fifteen minutes. Even if your dog just spends a few minutes outside in your yard during warm months, make sure there's adequate shade from trees or shade cloths.

Never leave your dog in a closed car. In hot or very cold weather, the temperature inside a closed car can climb even higher or dip even lower than the outside temperature, making both weather situations deadly for your dog. If you find her unconscious in the car, take her out immediately and get her to an emergency veterinary clinic.

First Aid for Heatstroke

When the body cannot keep the temperature in a safe range, the dog overheats. The dog's normal body temperature is between 100°F to 102.5°F. In moderate heatstroke the body temperature ranges from 104°F to 106°F. Severe heatstroke occurs when body temperature exceeds 106°F and can be fatal. The signs of heatstroke are rapid panting, bright red tongue, red or pale gums, thick or sticky saliva, depression, weakness, dizziness, vomiting, diarrhea, shock, and coma.

Cool your dog off by placing cool water, wet towels, or ice chips in the groin areas and underneath his arms at the chest. Take him to the emergency veterinarian right away. En route give him one dose of belladonna 30C. Heatstroke is usually deadly and you must take your dog to an emergency clinic immediately.

Cold Weather Precautions

Other than a few arctic breeds that were bred to live in the snow, dogs need protection from snowy and icy weather and should never be left outdoors for too long. Brief exposure to sub-zero weather can lead to frostbite of the feet, nose, or ears. Frostbitten skin is red, gray, or white and may begin to peel off. If your dog has frostbite, warm him up slowly with warm, moist towels. Transport him to your veterinarian immediately.

ALERT!

As soon as you return from cold-weather exercising, rinse your dog's paws, legs, and stomach with warm water before wiping off the snow and ice particles. Don't forget between his toes. This removes both the salt that irritates the pads and causes vomiting and diarrhea, and the poisonous antifreeze that he could ingest after licking his paws.

If you take your dog out exercising during the winter months, protect him by putting him in a coat or sweater with a high collar and protect his

CHAPTER 19: GETTING OUT AND ABOUT

feet in icy conditions. The clothing should cover the length of his entire body and his stomach.

Don't let your dog off leash in snow or ice and make sure he is wearing a collar with an identification tag and is microchipped. This will help you locate him if he becomes disoriented or loses his way in a snowstorm. More dogs disappear during the winter than at any other time of the year.

Should You Visit the Dog Park?

Some people can't wait to take their new dog to the dog park as soon as they bring him home. It sounds like a perfectly natural place to let the dog run off leash and play with other dogs, while the owner meets other dog owners and talks about their canine companions. But while it may be the ideal outing for some dogs, it can be a disaster for others.

Not every breed is suited to dog park play. Some dogs just don't like crowds and are naturally territorial, and others are not the rough-housing kind. Still others may have serious behavior problems with other dogs and people and need more socialization in a controlled environment, such as a training class, before they can reap the benefits of an off-leash community.

For dogs with a strong predator drive that have never been around small children before, tiny tots inside the dog park could mean trouble. Every dog that frequents the dog park should play well with others and should not be aggressive. It is up to owners to take responsibility for their dogs and know when to keep a dog away from the dog park. The last thing you want to have happen is a child or a dog injured in a fight.

Park Training

Your dog should be well socialized and should feel comfortable around people and other dogs before you visit the park. To accomplish this, take him to an obedience class or go walking around your neighborhood or outdoor shopping centers in your community where he'll encounter dogs and people and realize they're not threatening.

Basic obedience skills will also come in handy. You should always be able to have your dog obey instructions to wait, sit, stay, or come. Park manners are everything! If you ever feel afraid of another dog at the park, it's wise to leave.

Choosing a Healthy Park

Above all, dogs at the park should be healthy and free from communicable diseases and parasites that may affect other playmates. If you see that owners aren't cleaning up after their dogs' messes, politely remind them to do so or be prepared to do it yourself. You may also want to think about finding another place to play.

If you're contemplating your first visit to a dog park, here are a few simple rules that may help you and your dog have a safe encounter:

- Honestly assess your dog's personality to determine if it's suitable for this environment.
- When you arrive at the park, observe the dogs. If there's one who's coming on too strong with the other dogs, this isn't a safe place for your dog, so leave.
- Don't bring small children, reading material, hand-held computer games, or food with you. You need to pay attention to what your dog is doing and be ready to step in if there's a problem.
- Limit the number of toys and treats you give your dog inside the park. Your dog may not want to share his bounty with other dogs and this may trigger aggression.
- Leave your dog's collar on but remove his leash inside the park. A leashed dog could feel stressed and may want to protect himself if other dogs are not leashed.
- Take responsibility for your dog's actions. If your dog is getting too rough and someone complains about his behavior, apologize and take your dog home in order to avoid a conflict.
- If another dog is acting inappropriately, notify the owner. Be prepared to leave if the owner doesn't modify the offending dog's behavior.
- Always clean up after your dog.
- Observe the park rules.

Remember that your dog's health and safety comes first no matter where you take him. Never force a dog, especially if he is fearful, into a new situation or demand that he accept the touch of someone he fears. This invites aggression; your dog may feel the need to protect himself. Some dogs just need more time than others to feel comfortable, so be patient.

Don't coddle your dog. If he's shaking or trying to hide behind your legs when someone new approaches, resist the urge to comfort him and tell him it's okay. This sends the message that it's acceptable to act like this. It's better to ignore his reaction and prevent it by not putting him into a stressful situation in the future. Hopefully he'll pick up the cue from you that you're not worried and he shouldn't be either.

Always carry your cell phone with the number of the local animal control agency programmed in. You may need it if a problem arises, but don't use it to idly chit-chat with your friends or make business calls. After all, you brought your dog to the dog park to have a pleasurable outing away from your other responsibilities.

Dog Sports

If you want to add a performance title after your dog's name and are interested in competing with her in organized dog sports, there are plenty of possibilities to choose from. Before getting involved, have your veterinarian check your dog to make sure she doesn't have any joint pain or heart problems and is in excellent shape. To stay injury-free in competitive activities, your dog needs to be in top physical and mental condition.

E-QUESTION

Where can I find out about competitive dog sports?
To locate activities in your community, contact the AKC or ask your veterinarian or dog trainer. Check with local dog food supply stores or ask people with dogs that already compete. Your national and regional breed club can also provide information if your breed has a natural instinct for certain sports.

For small terriers and Dachshunds, earth-dog challenges are very popular. Bred to be hunting companions and to track small rodents, these breeds require little training for this event.

Pointing breed trials or competitions for Brittanys; English, Irish and Gordon Setters; Weimaraners; and Pointers test the dogs' ability to scent and find pheasant, partridge, grouse, and quail. There are also retriever field trials for Irish Water Spaniels and Labrador, Golden, and Chesapeake Bay Retrievers who have a natural affinity for locating fallen birds and fetching them from land and water, and for spaniels who live to hunt and retrieve game birds and waterfowl. There are hound trials for Beagles and Basset Hounds. The dogs are turned loose to find and follow a rabbit and are judged on how well they search.

Obedience Trials

Teaching your dog to sit and stay comes in handy around the house. It also builds a natural bond of trust between you and your canine companion. If you're interested in continuing her training after she's learned the basics, consider competing in obedience trials. The American Kennel Club first began holding obedience trials in 1936, and today there are obedience competitions at dog shows around the country.

FACT

In conformation dog shows, dogs are judged on how closely they match the ideal breed standard. In this sport, looks and attitude mean the world, and dogs must be well groomed and in excellent physical condition. Dogs earn points toward an AKC Championship (CH) title.

In this sport, the dog and the handler are judged on how well they complete a prescribed set of obedience exercises. It's all about accuracy and precision, but the natural movement of the handler and the dog's enthusiasm for participating are part of the performance.

There are three levels of competition that increase in difficulty: novice, open, and utility. In the novice class, a dog can earn an AKC Companion Dog (CD) title by heeling on and off a leash, coming when called, standing still when the judge performs a basic physical examination, and remaining in a sit and a down position with a group of dogs.

In the next level, dogs earn an AKC Companion Dog Excellent (CDX) title. The dog is evaluated on her ability to master even more exercises off leash and she must also retrieve and jump. A UD title in utility class tests the dog's ability for scent discrimination, directed retrieves, jumping, and hand signals. The most advanced title is an OTCH (Obedience Trial Championship).

These competitions enhance your dog's overall sense of well-being. She uses her intelligence to master a situation, her body to fulfill her expectations, and her ability to please you.

While some breeds don't like following directions and would rather reinvent the rules themselves, other dogs do better with boundaries. Excelling in this sport requires time and patience on your part, and you must use positive training techniques to motivate your dog to do her best.

Agility

If you enjoy perfecting your dog's sense of precision and timing, you'll especially like training and competing with him in agility trials. In this individual sport, you race against the clock as you guide your dog through an obstacle course. Competing in agility demonstrates a dog's natural athletic ability and his willingness to follow his owner's instructions. It requires conditioning, concentration, and training, as well as practice, practice, practice.

ALERT!

If your dog is limping during exercise, check the bottom of his feet for injury. The pads should be pink or black and never red, swollen, bleeding, or torn. Without gradual conditioning, running on concrete, asphalt, or rocky terrain will tear your dog's pads.

Agility began in England in 1978 as a demonstration during a halftime show at the prestigious Crufts dog show. It gained popularity, and the American Kennel Club decided to hold its first agility trial in the United States in 1994. Today it is the fastest growing dog sport.

Dogs earn titles by competing in different classes. In the standard class, dogs compete with such apparatuses as the dog walk, the A-frame, and the seesaw.

The other class is jumpers with weaves. In this competition, the dog jumps over tunnels and weaves through poles. There are increasing levels of difficulty in both classes and the dog can earn novice, open, and excellent titles. The highest title is MACH—Master Agility Championship. Every breed is eligible to compete and there are size-appropriate jump heights for every dog.

Tracking

Tracking is a noncompetitive individual sport where dogs demonstrate their natural instinct to follow a human scent trail. Dogs can earn a Tracking Dog (TD) title after only following one trail that is 440 to 500 yards long and between thirty minutes and two hours old. For an advanced title, known as a Tracking Dog Excellent (TDX) title, the dog must follow an 800- to 1,000-yard long trail that is three to five hours old. There may be twists and turns in the trail, and he may encounter physical obstacles and false scents along the way.

Dogs must be six months old to compete, although you can begin training your dog to track at any age. You'll need a nonrestrictive tracking harness and a twenty- to forty-foot leash. Some dogs are naturals at this sport and need little training, while others may need some coaching.

Flyball

This is the perfect sport for dogs that like speed and excitement. Flyball is a relay where teams of dogs race over four hurdles spaced ten feet apart. At the end of the jumps is a box with a lever. The dog jumps on the lever, which releases a tennis ball that shoots out of the box. After the dog catches the ball, he runs back over the jumps to the other side. As soon as he returns, the next dog in the relay races across the hurdles and repeats the drill. Teams keep score according to time and faults. While some breeds excel at this sport, all dogs love the excitement and have to be held back until their turn comes.

On Your Own

If organized sports are not your thing, you and your dog can enjoy individual outdoor activities such as jogging, hiking, backpacking, camping, and chasing a Frisbee. For dogs that enjoy water, swimming in the ocean, a lake, or your backyard swimming pool is great exercise. Swimming in warm water is especially beneficial for arthritic dogs because it helps alleviate stress on joints. There are even organized camps that are specifically planned for dogs and their owners.

Canine Good Citizen (CGC)

Your dog may be very well behaved at home, but if you want to prove it to the world, then a CGC title comes in handy. Developed by the American Kennel Club in 1989, the CGC program measures a dog's behavior and her comfort with strangers. Both purebreds and mixed breeds can earn a CGC title.

Many property managers require dogs to have this designation before they will rent to owners, and insurance companies will give homeowners insurance to previously excluded breeds if they have a CGC designation. If you want to become involved in therapy dog visits with children, the sick, or the elderly, your dog will need to pass the Canine Good Citizen test. Many agencies use this program to screen dogs before they are accepted into their programs.

While many dogs won't require any formal training to pass this test, some may need to attend a few obedience classes to brush up on their socialization skills. Kennel clubs and trainers in every community offer CGC instruction, and independent CGC evaluators administer the test. For more information about where and when the CGC tests are scheduled in your area, contact the AKC or your dog trainer.

There are ten simple requirements your dog needs to pass before she can earn a CGC:

- Accept the approach of a friendly stranger.
- Sit politely for petting.

- Have a healthy, well-groomed appearance and a willingness to be combed or brushed and examined by the judge.
- Walk nicely on a loose lead.
- Move politely through a crowd.
- Sit and lie down on command and stay in place when told.
- Come when called.
- Behave politely around other dogs.
- React without panic or aggression to common distractions, such as a chair dropping or a person running by.
- Stay nicely with a trusted person while the owner moves out of sight.

Every dog is more than capable of passing this test and earning a CGC title. All it takes is a little time and patience on your part to prepare your dog.

Becoming a Therapy Dog

Bringing comfort and joy to the sick, injured, and elderly is another activity you can do with your dog. Dogs of all shapes and sizes can bring a smile to the faces of children and adults in therapeutic facilities. You and your dog can be part of this special experience. All you need is time to volunteer and certification for your dog.

Getting Started

Most therapeutic facilities require that your dog receive obedience training, and dogs are usually screened for temperament before they are accepted. Many therapy programs require dogs to sit politely at the edge of a patient's bed and refrain from jumping up on people.

To find out what medical settings in your community need therapy dog visits, contact them first to learn what their requirements are. Most facilities prefer small groups of therapy dog teams rather than just one person with a dog.

It helps if you belong to a therapy dog organization. The three main organizations that provide certification for most therapeutic facilities are the Delta Society Pet Partners Program, Therapy Dogs International, and the AKC Canine Good Citizen Program. Many therapy programs provide their own training and certification, although the basic skills for all programs are pretty much the same.

Types of Programs

There are many different types of therapy work for dogs. While not every breed is suited to perform every task, you can probably find at least one that is a natural match for your dog.

In animal-assisted therapy, dogs can physically help people with tasks that require balance, bracing, or pulling. Assistance dogs can also be taught to open and close doors, turn light switches on and off, and retrieve items around the house.

For dogs with superior swimming ability, life-saving water rescue work is a natural activity. Strong water dogs are trained to tow a person to shore, take a life jacket to a drowning person, and tow a boat.

Canine Search and Rescue is a personally rewarding but highly intense activity that requires dedication and extensive training for you and your dog. Dogs are trained to search for and rescue missing people, and are deployed in emergency situations.

In classrooms, dogs can sit and listen to children who are struggling with reading aloud in a group. Studies show that when children read to a dog, it improves their reading skills.

Travel Safety

If you're going on an airplane or car trip and would like to take your dog with you, there are some precautions you should take to ensure that your canine companion is safe and comfortable. After all, this is an adventure for him too!

Leaving on a Jet Plane

You may want to think twice about putting your dog on a plane. Although airlines make every effort to keep you and your pet safe, today's erratic flight schedules mean that your pet may be stuck in an airport longer than is healthy for him. After all, there's no place in an airport for a dog to eliminate or to walk around and get some exercise while you're waiting to board your flight.

Bring bottled water or water from home especially for your dog to drink throughout your trip. Different water sources combined with the stress of travel may cause intestinal upset and diarrhea. Food from home is best for the same reason. Don't forget his food and water bowls! Some dogs won't use a different bowl that smells unfamiliar.

Toy dogs are usually permitted to stay with you in the cabin provided they remain in an airline-approved travel bag that you carry on board. Small, medium, large, and giant dogs must ride in airline-approved hard-sided kennels in the cargo compartment. There is a charge for taking your dog along and it's usually more expensive for dogs that ride in cargo.

Airlines have strict requirements that are constantly revised, so it's best to call the airline and speak to a reservation agent to verify the current rules before purchasing your own ticket. Some planes only have room for a few dogs on each flight and a reservation must be made for your dog when you book your own flight. Airlines may not accept dogs during certain times of the year or in extreme weather conditions.

All airlines require your dog to be examined by a veterinarian and to have a health certificate prior to travel, whether you carry him on or check him into the cargo area beneath the plane.

To reduce stress, your dog should be well-socialized around crowds and commotion long before you travel. You should also work to get him accustomed to spending several hours in an airline-approved kennel or carry-on bag. He should not be upset by altitude changes and motion.

Road Trip

To make your dog's journey as comfortable as possible and to reduce the chance of a stomach upset, don't feed her a meal on the morning of your trip. If she has never traveled in the car before, the first trip shouldn't be a long one. Plan ahead and begin taking your dog on short car rides around the neighborhood so she becomes accustomed to the motion of a car.

Some dogs are bothered with motion sickness even without being fed. If your dog becomes carsick, give her some peppermint capsules or a tablespoon of honey. You can also mix two drops of aspen, elm, scleranthus, and vervain Bach flower essences.

Your dog doesn't need to feel the wind on his face and should never be allowed to hang his head out the window while you're driving. If he does this, there's a good chance that debris or insects could fly into his eyes. This could cause mild eye irritation or even a scratched cornea. Open the windows only far enough for his nose to fit.

To protect her in case of a collision, she should always wear a pet safety restraint or ride in a travel kennel. Keep the leash on when she's not in the kennel so she can't run out when the door is opened.

Be sure that she has at least one and preferably two forms of identification—for example, a microchip and a collar with an ID tag—in case you become separated from her. A microchip is permanent and you don't have to worry about it falling off of your dog, but if the person who finds her doesn't have the special scanner to read the microchip, your reunion will take longer. A snug but comfortably fitting collar with a current waterproof identification tag with your name, address, and phone number helps the rescuer locate you immediately.

Bring some of your dog's bedding and toys from home so that she feels safer, and take a pet first-aid kit for emergencies. This should contain vitamin C and vitamin B-complex to help relieve stress. The B-complex will also prevent nausea if your dog develops motion sickness. Remember too to stop driving every few hours so that your dog can get out to eliminate and exercise her legs.

CHAPTER 20

Caring for the Senior Dog

It happens quickly. Your dog turns seven years old and is officially a canine senior citizen! Soon you'll start seeing a few gray hairs in his muzzle, a stiffer gait, and a few personality changes. Keeping his golden years golden will require a little more care than what you've given him in the past, but the effort is well worth it. Regular visits to the veterinarian, daily dental care, adjustments to his diet, and plenty of regular exercise will maintain his health and help him age gracefully.

Physical and Mental Changes

Dogs age. It's a fact. Your dog may still look and act like a puppy, but once he reaches his seventh birthday, he might as well apply for canine social security. He's a senior now even though he may or may not look like an old-ster for a few more years. Giant and large breeds show their ages sooner, sometimes around five or six years, while medium and small breeds may not appear "old" until age ten or twelve. Toy dogs tend to take longer to show their age.

One-third of your dog's life will be spent as a senior and he will experi-ence many physical and mental changes. As his owner, some of these are easier to deal with than others, and it's painful to watch your beloved canine slip into old age, but take heart!

Today, experts know more about caring for older dogs. Medical research-ers are constantly studying new ways to combat age-related health prob-lems, and it's no surprise that more natural therapies are becoming part of mainstream veterinary care.

Commercial food is available especially for seniors, and even pet prod-uct manufacturers are getting into the act of helping old dogs lead healthier lives. The latest designs in heated, orthopedic dog beds are just what stiff joints need, and there are indoor ramps for dogs that can no longer jump into the car or onto the bed or couch. Wheeled vehicles help dogs with rear legs that can no longer support them.

Physical Differences

The outward signs of old age come on gradually. Slower movements are the first hint that your dog is aging. It will take him longer to get up from a nap or go up or down stairs. Look too for a shift in your dog's weight, decreased muscle tone, and gray or lighter-colored hair on his muzzle and eyebrows.

His coat may have an odor, and it may be flaky, greasy, and thinner, with some bald spots. Regular bathing, brushing, and combing will help restore natural oils to the skin. Aloe vera gel applied directly to the skin will help soothe irritations from itching or biting.

Your dog will also need to urinate more often and may have stiff or pain-ful joints. Dental health becomes an issue in the golden years if good oral habits weren't established early. Your dog may have bad breath, sore and swollen gums, and loose or broken teeth, and he may be reluctant to chew his food.

Loss of the Senses

As your dog ages, his senses will dull. His sense of hearing, vision, and smell will all diminish. He may not hear the doorbell when it rings or wake up as quickly when you come home. Many seniors develop cataracts, a clouding of the lens of the eye that can cause partial or total vision loss. Although surgery can remove cataracts, it is expensive. Senior dogs also develop a more benign eye change called lenticular sclerosis, which is a normal aging change and does not require treatment. It looks like a cataract, but the veterinarian can make a definitive diagnosis.

FACT

Cancer is the number-one overall cause of death in dogs, and the incidence of cancer rises for senior dogs. According to the National Canine Cancer Foundation, one out of every three dogs are diagnosed with cancer; of those, nearly half the cases are fatal in dogs ten years or older.

Dogs do adapt to sensory changes and you can help your dog get around. If your dog has difficulty navigating around the house and he's easily disoriented in the dark, keep the furniture where it is. Now is not the time for a remodeling project. Go through the house to make sure there's nothing that can hurt him if he wanders, and regularly check the fence and gate so he won't get loose in the neighborhood.

Chronic Diseases of the Elderly

The geriatric years may also signal the onset and progression of chronic diseases such as arthritis, cancer, diabetes, hypothyroidism, kidney and liver failure, and heart problems. While medications are available to treat these problems, giving your dog the right diet, regular exercise, and holistic care all helps.

Mental Differences

Expect your aging canine to have a few senior moments as his mental capacities start to diminish. He may go into a room and stand there as if he's forgotten what he came in to do, or he'll prefer napping to going out in the yard. Maybe he won't be so anxious to scare off that squirrel on the fence that has taunted him for years, or he may have lost interest in warning the mail carrier to step away from your mailbox.

You may see other behavioral changes in your older dog. He may be confused, disoriented, and more sensitive to noise and sounds than he once was. Thunderstorms or smoke alarms make him tremble and cower. He may have been okay whenever you left him alone before, but now he suffers from separation anxiety and barks or becomes destructive in your absence. He may also have difficulty paying attention.

Cognitive Disorder

In everyday terms, people usually refer to cognitive disorder in dogs as doggie Alzheimer's or dementia. Despite all the jokes that they may make about senior dogs regressing and becoming absent-minded, canine cognitive dysfunction syndrome (CDS) is a real medical condition.

Many dogs that act old aren't really old at all. Rather, they could be suffering from kidney, thyroid, or adrenal gland disease, or osteoarthritis or periodontal disease. Once these conditions are diagnosed, treatment can help alleviate symptoms. Once the pain and infection subsides, the dog can feel a bit of his former youthful self return.

For most owners, CDS is usually a very difficult condition to live with. Seeing the shell of your formerly spry and loving dog spend hours sleeping or ignoring you when you come home is disheartening. On the one hand you can't help feel sad, but on the other, your beloved dog may have developed some new habits that can be extremely annoying, such as messing in the house or barking at inanimate objects.

E-QUESTION

What causes CDS?
Medical researchers don't know the reason why some dogs age more gracefully than others, but they do know that physical and chemical changes in the brain are responsible for CDS. Extracellular protein buildup within the senior canine brain is very similar to what people with Alzheimer's disease may experience.

While some dogs may begin developing this disorder as young as five years of age, others may be ten or eleven years or older depending on breed. In giant and large breeds, odd changes in behaviors can begin occurring at age five, while the onset of symptoms in small and toy breeds may not appear until the dog is twelve or thirteen years of age.

Personality Changes

There are several signs of CDS, and not every dog will have every symptom:

- Acting "old"
- Barking or howling for no reason
- Bathroom accidents in the house
- Disorientation
- Hearing loss
- Not recognizing familiar people or surroundings
- Pacing
- Sleeping more
- Standing in a corner
- Vision loss

Ways to Help

Although your dog has lived a long and full life, don't assume that a few problem behaviors automatically mean that it's time to say goodbye. You can take some measures to help him and preserve your sanity as well.

Try taking your dog outside for more frequent bathroom breaks and accept the fact that you'll just be cleaning up more messes in the house on a daily basis. Keep cleanup supplies where they are easily and quickly accessible. Now's probably not a good time to take an extended vacation with your dog or leave her behind with a house sitter or at a boarding facility. Your dog is accustomed to you and your routine and a new person or surroundings will disorient her even more.

Relief

There are effective medications for CDS, but like all drugs, these can have side effects. The natural approach uses antioxidants, L-carnitine, ginkgo, and Cholodin. Antioxidant nutrients such as vitamins A, C, and E; beta -carotene; and the minerals manganese, selenium, and zinc help slow down the aging process by protecting the body from free radical damage. Ginkgo biloba increases circulation to the brain and improves brain function.

If you're unsure whether or not your dog has CDS, your veterinarian can perform laboratory tests to rule out other diseases, such as kidney, thyroid, or adrenal gland disease that exhibit the same symptoms. Unfortunately, there is no single diagnostic test available that can diagnose CDS.

Coenzyme Q10, grape seed extract, bilberry, and cysteine may also be helpful, but ask your veterinarian which antioxidants he recommends and how much to give your dog. Studies reveal that choline supplements may prevent cognitive disorder and restore mental alertness.

Visiting the Veterinarian Regularly

Hopefully your dog already has a good holistic veterinarian whom you both like and feel comfortable with, because once your dog is a senior you'll be seeing the veterinarian a lot more frequently. Many veterinarians recommend that senior dogs have examinations about once every six months.

While this may sound like a lot of office visits, seeing the veterinarian often will help her spot any health problems, such as kidney disease, early while they're treatable. When dogs are up in years, their health changes rapidly. Don't assume that a health problem is simply old age. Holistic care is all about prevention.

The Senior Exam

It's a good idea to schedule the first geriatric exam when your dog turns seven years old. This helps establish a baseline workup to compare with results of future exams as your dog ages.

Your veterinarian will perform laboratory tests that include complete blood work and urinalysis to screen for kidney and liver function, infection, or anemia. A vaccine titer test to measure antibody levels and a heartworm test should also be done if your dog has not been on continuous heartworm preventative. Your veterinarian's senior physical exam will evaluate:

- Coat condition
- Condition of ears, eyes, mouth, teeth, and gums
- Diarrhea or constipation
- Heart and lungs
- Loss of or increase in appetite
- Skin and coat problems
- Stiffness in joints
- Weight gain or loss

You can help your veterinarian evaluate your dog's condition by keeping a written health log. By taking notes of any small changes in your dog's appearance and behavior, you'll be able to remember the details of anything unusual that comes up between appointments and report them to your veterinarian.

Keeping Teeth and Gums Healthy

Our four-legged friends also use their mouth and teeth to groom both themselves and their housemates. When it comes to moving things around in his environment—a bone, a blanket, a ball—a healthy mouth is a dog's best tool.

Providing regular dental care by brushing your dog's teeth once a day and giving him the right diet will help keep his teeth clean and free of infection. This also benefits self-grooming. Dogs use their front teeth to lick and bite close to the skin when there's an itch they just can't scratch any other way.

FACT

According to the American Veterinary Dental Society, 80 percent of dogs show signs of dental disease by age three. By the time they're five years old, most dogs already have gum disease and jawbone loss. Bad breath could be an early warning sign of gingivitis a dangerous gum disease.

Taking care of your dog's teeth helps prevent long-term health problems in other organs, such as the heart, kidneys, and liver. When bacteria and their toxins remain in the mouth they can enter the bloodstream, lungs, stomach, and intestines.

Periodontal Disease

Periodontal disease is one of the most serious health problems for older dogs. It suppresses the immune system and leads to other diseases, and the consequences can be life threatening. This doesn't happen overnight. After years of neglecting daily oral hygiene, plaque—a composite of saliva, bits of food, and bacteria—begins to accumulate on the surface of the teeth. These materials exert pressure on the gums and cause inflammation and receding gums. This creates a pocket between the gums and the teeth where debris can collect, which loosens the teeth and causes them to fall out. An abscess develops that can further destroy the root of the tooth.

Smelly Dog Breath

Ever kiss your dog and back away because he has really bad breath? If so, this is a signal that something has gone terribly wrong in his mouth. While this odor is common in many dogs, it doesn't mean that all is well. Far from it. Foul breath is a sign of periodontal disease.

Signs of Periodontal Disease

Red, swollen, or bleeding gums, excessive salivation, and heavy brown film or calculus on your dog's teeth are other symptoms of serious oral problems. The most obvious and serious indicator is if your dog refuses to eat or drops food out of his mouth while he's eating. This doesn't mean that he doesn't like his food. His mouth hurts and he'd rather go hungry than endure the pain. Once this happens, it doesn't take long for his weight to go down and his overall health to decline.

Small Breed Dental Trouble

Small dogs are especially prone to tooth trouble when they're young, and they need you to establish a good dental program for them early in life. Without it, by the time these tiny dogs are oldsters, they may not have any teeth left at all.

Healthy dog teeth are white or slightly yellow. Gums should be light pink. If there's plaque, you'll see a filmy coating with a heavier yellowish build-up from the base of the teeth. Heavy tartar is thick and hard and may be a darker yellow or brown. It's soft enough that you can brush some of it off or scrape it down with your fingernail.

Why is this? Although it doesn't look like it, small dogs have teeth that are proportionately larger than the size of their jaws. The teeth crowd and overlap one another and create odd spaces where food easily becomes trapped. Breeds with very short jaws have even worse problems as teeth turn every which way. The plaque deposits harden into calculus that can only be removed by your veterinarian.

Once this happens, the only way to save the teeth is through hand-scraping under anesthesia or with an ultrasonic cleaner. Many times it's too late and the teeth are too infected or too loose and must be extracted.

Anesthesia and Cleaning Teeth

Although holistic veterinarians acknowledge that it is expensive and there are occasional risks with anesthesia, they suggest using it even with older dogs because it's the only way to treat extreme dental problems. A dog with periodontal disease is more likely to die from the disease than from the anesthesia. A physical examination and laboratory tests should be given prior to surgery, and if everything is normal, the procedure can proceed.

E-QUESTION

How many teeth do dogs have?
Adult dogs have forty-two teeth; puppies have twenty-eight. They lose their baby teeth at around four months.

Anesthesia is much safer today than it once was. There have been tremendous advances in veterinary anesthesia in the last few years, and dogs awaken more quickly and experience fewer side effects. Isoflurane, an inhalation-type anesthesia that is quickly eliminated from the dog's body once inhalation stops, and propofol, a relatively new injectable anesthetic, are recommended for senior dogs. Be sure to ask your veterinarian about his monitoring equipment. Any anesthetic procedure should be monitored with a pulse oximeter, blood pressure monitor, and ECG. A pulse oximeter is especially important because it alerts the vet if the dog's blood oxygen level falls below the safe limit.

Post-Surgery

Following oral surgery, the gums will be sore and swollen, but a few herbal remedies will ease the pain. Try using purple coneflower. Boil it in water, strain it, and cool it slightly before applying it to the gums. Other herbs to try are goldenseal, myrrh, and plantain or the homeopathic treatment Silicea 30C as an alternative. Once your dog's mouth has healed, return to regular brushing.

Nutritional Support and Dental Care

Feeding your dog the proper nutrition helps all tissues, including gums, repair themselves; it also helps your dog maintain healthy teeth. A raw diet without preservatives or carbohydrates helps prevent bacterial and plaque buildup. Fruits and veggies are a great snack that will help keep oral membranes healthy. Raw bones scrape tartar off the teeth, but never give your dog cooked bones because these splinter after cooking and can cause injury.

While veterinarians once believed that eating canned food contributed to dental disease, a study in the *Journal of Veterinary Dentistry* found little difference between commercial dry and moist foods.

Treats and Teeth

Contrary to popular belief, most hard dog biscuits do little to keep the teeth clean. While they may give your dog something to keep him busy and exercise his jaw muscles, they don't remove tartar and may even contribute to tartar buildup when tiny bits of biscuit remain lodged at the gum line or between teeth.

Antioxidant Help

The following antioxidants give your dog's teeth a boost:

- Bilberry
- Coenzyme Q10
- Ester-C

- Gingko biloba
- Grape seed extract
- Lactoferrin
- Minerals: selenium, manganese, and zinc
- N-acetylcysteine
- Vitamins A, B, C, and E

Exercise Matters

When your dog was younger, getting enough exercise was probably never an issue. If she heard someone at the door, she would run to see who it was. If you threw the ball, she would chase it. She'd happily run beside you if went jogging, and she thought nothing about chasing after the squirrels in your yard. But for many senior dogs, moving from one couch to another to get as much sleep as possible is about all the exercise they want to get.

The geriatric canine set looks so comfortable and content snoozing all day that it's easy to let senior dogs lie. After all, your dog has done so much for you and she asks so little. There's no harm in letting her kick back all the time, right? Unfortunately, that's not the case. You're really doing her more harm than good by letting her lead a sedentary lifestyle.

If you ask your dog to get up and move around a little more, you can actually slow the progression of aging. Regular exercise will improve the quality of her life—physically, mentally, and emotionally.

Physical and Mental Benefits

Keeping your senior fit is one of the most important things you can do for her. There are so many physical benefits of routine activity—both for humans and for dogs. Being on the go benefits your dog's heart, lungs, and digestive system. Muscle use stimulates all tissues, increases circulation and blood flow, and helps rid the cells of toxins. Exercise helps improve bowel function and strengthens joints and muscles that will protect your dog from injury. Most importantly, regular exercise wards off obesity, which is the most common condition in senior dogs.

Getting out into the fresh air and seeing new sights also enhances your dog's mental well-being. Chances are she's lost interest in what's going on around her. If so, getting out and increasing her heart rate a little perks her up again and will help ward off depression. It will also make her want to move around a little more. You don't have to travel far or spend a lot of time in order for your dog to reap the benefits. A short walk in a new neighborhood, or a little car ride to stroll around an outdoor shopping center that your dog has never visited before, works wonders.

At-Home Exercise

Since older dogs don't tolerate extreme temperatures very well, consider staying home on very hot, very cold, or very wet days, and working out indoors. Make sure you have a carpeted area so your dog doesn't slip and fall, and begin slowly. Even small areas are conducive to playing indoor games.

ALERT!

Elderly, short-haired dogs are more sensitive to hot or cold weather than they were when they were younger. Don't take your dog out for exercise if it's too hot. Go early in the day or evening when it cools off. In cold weather, a dog coat or sweater and boots can help him stay warm.

Anything you can do to encourage your dog to get up and move will help. Use one of her favorite toys to interest her in a not-too-far-away game of fetch, rolling over a few times, light wrestling, or hide and seek. Just keep your program fun, easy, and not physically stressful.

Short But Sweet

Without enough exercise, the muscles weaken and begin to atrophy and lose function. Because it's painful, the dog doesn't move and her condition worsens.

If your dog hasn't been active recently, start out slowly and tailor her schedule to her condition. A few short walks of ten or fifteen minutes every day or every other day may be easier for her to tolerate and less stressful on her joints than one long session of thirty or sixty minutes.

If you're going out for thirty minutes, your schedule should begin with a short warmup of slow walking for about five minutes. For the next twenty minutes, increase the speed slightly but not so fast that your dog is panting or out of breath. End with a slower cool-down of about five minutes. Be sure your dog has water to drink following exercise. Unless your veterinarian specifically tells you not to exercise your dog, there's no reason to stop completely.

Signs to Watch

Although it is normal for oldsters to be a little stiff when they get up from a nap, limping or having difficulty getting up signals chronic pain or a problem with the heart or lungs. Watch your dog's breathing after exercise. If you notice extreme panting, take her to the veterinarian for a cardio-pulmonary checkup.

Altering the Diet

As your dog ages, his nutritional needs will change too. He's less active and doesn't need the same number of calories he once did. Now more than ever, it's critical to keep your dog at a healthy weight. Feed him the best food you possibly can, preferably a home-cooked diet.

FACT

New studies show that senior dogs need more protein in their diets than younger dogs. Protein supports the immune system and promotes cell replacement and enzyme activity, which begins to decline in old age. If your dog is overweight, cut down on the amount of fat in the diet, but make sure she gets 25 percent protein.

Be sure to include whole grains and fresh fruits and vegetables with dark colors, such as red grapefruit, green leafy vegetables, broccoli, beets, green beans, and peas. Don't forget the orange yams, carrots, and squashes; these are the best sources of antioxidant nutrients.

Don't overfeed him. Obesity will create even more health problems for him and shorten his life. If you notice that your senior suddenly looks thin or has a serious loss of appetite, take him to the veterinarian as soon as possible.

Feeding Schedule

Keep your senior on a regular feeding schedule so he knows when to expect his next meal. Feed him two small meals a day rather than one large one. It's easier for him to metabolize the food if he gets it in two installments.

Holistic Resources and Websites of Health-Related Organizations

Academy of Veterinary Homeopathy
P.O. Box 9280
Wilmington, DE 19809
866-652-1590
www.theavh.org

American Holistic Veterinary Medical Association
2218 Old Emmorton Road
Bel Air, MD 21015
410-569-0795
www.ahvma.org

American Kennel Club Canine Health Foundation
P.O. Box 900061
Raleigh, NC 27675-9061
888-682-9696
www.akcchf.org

American Veterinary Chiropractic Association
442154 E. 140 Road
Bluejacket, OK 74333
918-784-2231
www.animalchiropractic.org

ASPCA Animal Poison Control Center
1717 S. Philo, Ste. 36
Urbana, IL 61802
888-426-4435
www.aspca.org/pet-care/poison-control

Earth Animal
606 Post Road East
Westport, CT 06880
203-222-7173
www.earthanimal.com

International Veterinary Acupuncture Society
2625 Redwing Road, Suite 160
Fort Collins, CO 80526
970-266-0666
www.ivas.org

National Canine Cancer Foundation
5437 E. Sweetwater Ave.
Scottsdale, AZ 85254
866-262-0542
www.wearethecure.org

Tellington Touch (TTouch)
P.O. Box 3793
Santa Fe, NM 87501
866-488-6824
www.tteam-ttouch.com

Veterinary Botanical Medical Association
6410 Highway 92
Acworth, GA 30102
www.vbma.org

Veterinary Cancer Society
P.O. Box 1763
Spring Valley, CA 91979-1763
619-741-2210
www.vetcancersociety.org

**Veterinary Institute of Integrative
Medicine**
P.O. Box 740053
Arvada, CO 80006
303-277-8227
www.viim.org

Veterinary NAET
1637 16th Street
Santa Monica, CA 90404
310-450-2287
www.vetnaet.com

APPENDIX B

Additional Resources

Allegretti, Jan and Sommers, Katy, DVM. *The Complete Holistic Dog Book* (Berkeley, CA: Ten Speed Press, 2003).

Bell, Kristen Leigh. *Holistic Aromatherapy for Animals: A Comprehensive Guide to the Use of Essential Oils & Hydrosols with Animals* (UK: Findhorn Press, 2002).

Coates, Margrit. *Hands-On Healing for Pets: The Animal Lover's Essential Guide to Using Healing Energy* (UK: Random House, 2003).

Flaim, Denise. *The Holistic Dog Book: Canine Care for the 21st Century* (New York, NY: Wiley, 2003).

Fulton, Elizabeth and Prasad, Kathleen. *Animal Reiki: Using Energy to Heal the Animals in Your Life* (New York, NY: Ulysses Press, 2006).

Goldstein, Martin, DVM. *The Nature of Animal Healing* (New York, NY: Knopf Publishing, 1999).

Goldstein R., VMD, and Goldstein, S. *The Goldsteins' Wellness & Longevity Program* (Neptune City, NJ: T.F.H. Publications, 2005).

Hamilton, Don, DVM. *Homeopathic Care for Cats and Dogs: Small Doses for Small Animals* (Berkeley, CA: North Atlantic Books, 1999).

Holloway, Sage, and Callahan, Sharon. *Animal Healing and Vibrational Medicine* (Nevada City, CA: Blue Dolphin Publishing, 2001).

Knueven, Doug, DVM. *The Holistic Health Guide: Natural Care for the Whole Dog (Terra-Nova Series)* (Neptune City, NJ: T.F.H. Publications, 2008).

Lonsdale, Tom. *Feed Your Dog Raw Meaty Bones* (Wenatchee, WA: Dogwise Publishing, 2005).

Martin, Ann N. *Food Pets Die For: Shocking Facts About Pet Food* (Troutdale, OR: New Sage Press, 1997).

Messonnier, Shawn, DVM. *8 Weeks to a Healthy Dog* (New York, NY: Rodale Books, 2003).

Messonnier, Shawn. DVM. *Natural Health Bible for Dogs & Cats: Your A–Z Guide to Over 200 Conditions, Herbs, Vitamins, and Supplements* (New York, NY: Three Rivers Press, 2001).

Murray, Michael. *The Healing Power of Herbs: The Enlightened Person's Guide to the Wonders of Medicinal Plants* (New York, NY: Gramercy, 2004).

Pitcairn, Richard H., DVM, and Pitcairn, Susan Hubble. *Dr. Pitcairn's New Complete Guide to Natural Health for Dogs and Cats* (New York, NY: Rodale Books, 2005).

Schultze, Kymythy. *Natural Nutrition for Dogs and Cats* (Carlsbad, CA: Hay House, 1999).

Schwartz, Cheryl. *Four Paws Five Directions: A Guide to Chinese Medicine for Cats and Dogs* (Berkeley, CA: Celestial Arts, 1996).

Siegal, Mordecai. *UC Davis Book of Dogs: The Complete Medical Reference Guide for Dogs and Puppies* (New York, NY: Harper Collins, 1995).

Strombeck, D., DVM. *Home-Prepared Diets for Dogs and Cats* (Ames, Iowa: Iowa State University Press, 1999).

Tellington-Jones, Linda. *Getting in TTouch with Your Dog* (London: Trafalgar Square Publishing, 2002).

Index

W

Water, importance of, 67–68,
 158–59, 180–81, 209, 212. *See
 also* Dehydration
Water therapy, 143–44
Weight
 cancer and, 158
 exercise and, 82–83
 heart disease and, 200
Worms, 110–11. *See also*
 Heartworms

Y

Yin and yang, 53–54

THE EVERYTHING SERIES!

BUSINESS & PERSONAL FINANCE

Everything® Accounting Book
Everything® Budgeting Book, 2nd Ed.
Everything® Business Planning Book
Everything® Coaching and Mentoring Book, 2nd Ed.
Everything® Fundraising Book
Everything® Get Out of Debt Book
Everything® Grant Writing Book, 2nd Ed.
Everything® Guide to Buying Foreclosures
Everything® Guide to Fundraising, $15.95
Everything® Guide to Mortgages
Everything® Guide to Personal Finance for Single Mothers
Everything® Home-Based Business Book, 2nd Ed.
Everything® Homebuying Book, 3rd Ed., $15.95
Everything® Homeselling Book, 2nd Ed.
Everything® Human Resource Management Book
Everything® Improve Your Credit Book
Everything® Investing Book, 2nd Ed.
Everything® Landlording Book
Everything® Leadership Book, 2nd Ed.
Everything® Managing People Book, 2nd Ed.
Everything® Negotiating Book
Everything® Online Auctions Book
Everything® Online Business Book
Everything® Personal Finance Book
Everything® Personal Finance in Your 20s & 30s Book, 2nd Ed.
Everything® Personal Finance in Your 40s & 50s Book, $15.95
Everything® Project Management Book, 2nd Ed.
Everything® Real Estate Investing Book
Everything® Retirement Planning Book
Everything® Robert's Rules Book, $7.95
Everything® Selling Book
Everything® Start Your Own Business Book, 2nd Ed.
Everything® Wills & Estate Planning Book

COOKING

Everything® Barbecue Cookbook
Everything® Bartender's Book, 2nd Ed., $9.95
Everything® Calorie Counting Cookbook
Everything® Cheese Book
Everything® Chinese Cookbook
Everything® Classic Recipes Book
Everything® Cocktail Parties & Drinks Book
Everything® College Cookbook
Everything® Cooking for Baby and Toddler Book
Everything® Diabetes Cookbook
Everything® Easy Gourmet Cookbook
Everything® Fondue Cookbook
Everything® Food Allergy Cookbook, $15.95
Everything® Fondue Party Book
Everything® Gluten-Free Cookbook
Everything® Glycemic Index Cookbook
Everything® Grilling Cookbook
Everything® Healthy Cooking for Parties Book, $15.95
Everything® Holiday Cookbook
Everything® Indian Cookbook
Everything® Lactose-Free Cookbook
Everything® Low-Cholesterol Cookbook

Everything® Low-Fat High-Flavor Cookbook, 2nd Ed., $15.95
Everything® Low-Salt Cookbook
Everything® Meals for a Month Cookbook
Everything® Meals on a Budget Cookbook
Everything® Mediterranean Cookbook
Everything® Mexican Cookbook
Everything® No Trans Fat Cookbook
Everything® One-Pot Cookbook, 2nd Ed., $15.95
Everything® Organic Cooking for Baby & Toddler Book, $15.95
Everything® Pizza Cookbook
Everything® Quick Meals Cookbook, 2nd Ed., $15.95
Everything® Slow Cooker Cookbook
Everything® Slow Cooking for a Crowd Cookbook
Everything® Soup Cookbook
Everything® Stir-Fry Cookbook
Everything® Sugar-Free Cookbook
Everything® Tapas and Small Plates Cookbook
Everything® Tex-Mex Cookbook
Everything® Thai Cookbook
Everything® Vegetarian Cookbook
Everything® Whole-Grain, High-Fiber Cookbook
Everything® Wild Game Cookbook
Everything® Wine Book, 2nd Ed.

GAMES

Everything® 15-Minute Sudoku Book, $9.95
Everything® 30-Minute Sudoku Book, $9.95
Everything® Bible Crosswords Book, $9.95
Everything® Blackjack Strategy Book
Everything® Brain Strain Book, $9.95
Everything® Bridge Book
Everything® Card Games Book
Everything® Card Tricks Book, $9.95
Everything® Casino Gambling Book, 2nd Ed.
Everything® Chess Basics Book
Everything® Christmas Crosswords Book, $9.95
Everything® Craps Strategy Book
Everything® Crossword and Puzzle Book
Everything® Crosswords and Puzzles for Quote Lovers Book, $9.95
Everything® Crossword Challenge Book
Everything® Crosswords for the Beach Book, $9.95
Everything® Cryptic Crosswords Book, $9.95
Everything® Cryptograms Book, $9.95
Everything® Easy Crosswords Book
Everything® Easy Kakuro Book, $9.95
Everything® Easy Large-Print Crosswords Book
Everything® Games Book, 2nd Ed.
Everything® Giant Book of Crosswords
Everything® Giant Sudoku Book, $9.95
Everything® Giant Word Search Book
Everything® Kakuro Challenge Book, $9.95
Everything® Large-Print Crossword Challenge Book
Everything® Large-Print Crosswords Book
Everything® Large-Print Travel Crosswords Book
Everything® Lateral Thinking Puzzles Book, $9.95
Everything® Literary Crosswords Book, $9.95
Everything® Mazes Book
Everything® Memory Booster Puzzles Book, $9.95

Everything® Movie Crosswords Book, $9.95
Everything® Music Crosswords Book, $9.95
Everything® Online Poker Book
Everything® Pencil Puzzles Book, $9.95
Everything® Poker Strategy Book
Everything® Pool & Billiards Book
Everything® Puzzles for Commuters Book, $9.95
Everything® Puzzles for Dog Lovers Book, $9.95
Everything® Sports Crosswords Book, $9.95
Everything® Test Your IQ Book, $9.95
Everything® Texas Hold 'Em Book, $9.95
Everything® Travel Crosswords Book, $9.95
Everything® Travel Mazes Book, $9.95
Everything® Travel Word Search Book, $9.95
Everything® TV Crosswords Book, $9.95
Everything® Word Games Challenge Book
Everything® Word Scramble Book
Everything® Word Search Book

HEALTH

Everything® Alzheimer's Book
Everything® Diabetes Book
Everything® First Aid Book, $9.95
Everything® Green Living Book
Everything® Health Guide to Addiction and Recovery
Everything® Health Guide to Adult Bipolar Disorder
Everything® Health Guide to Arthritis
Everything® Health Guide to Controlling Anxiety
Everything® Health Guide to Depression
Everything® Health Guide to Diabetes, 2nd Ed.
Everything® Health Guide to Fibromyalgia
Everything® Health Guide to Menopause, 2nd Ed.
Everything® Health Guide to Migraines
Everything® Health Guide to Multiple Sclerosis
Everything® Health Guide to OCD
Everything® Health Guide to PMS
Everything® Health Guide to Postpartum Care
Everything® Health Guide to Thyroid Disease
Everything® Hypnosis Book
Everything® Low Cholesterol Book
Everything® Menopause Book
Everything® Nutrition Book
Everything® Reflexology Book
Everything® Stress Management Book
Everything® Superfoods Book, $15.95

HISTORY

Everything® American Government Book
Everything® American History Book, 2nd Ed.
Everything® American Revolution Book, $15.95
Everything® Civil War Book
Everything® Freemasons Book
Everything® Irish History & Heritage Book
Everything® World War II Book, 2nd Ed.

HOBBIES

Everything® Candlemaking Book
Everything® Cartooning Book
Everything® Coin Collecting Book
Everything® Digital Photography Book, 2nd Ed.

Everything® Drawing Book
Everything® Family Tree Book, 2nd Ed.
Everything® Guide to Online Genealogy, $15.95
Everything® Knitting Book
Everything® Knots Book
Everything® Photography Book
Everything® Quilting Book
Everything® Sewing Book
Everything® Soapmaking Book, 2nd Ed.
Everything® Woodworking Book

HOME IMPROVEMENT

Everything® Feng Shui Book
Everything® Feng Shui Decluttering Book, $9.95
Everything® Fix-It Book
Everything® Green Living Book
Everything® Home Decorating Book
Everything® Home Storage Solutions Book
Everything® Homebuilding Book
Everything® Organize Your Home Book, 2nd Ed.

KIDS' BOOKS

All titles are $7.95
Everything® Fairy Tales Book, $14.95
Everything® Kids' Animal Puzzle & Activity Book
Everything® Kids' Astronomy Book
Everything® Kids' Baseball Book, 5th Ed.
Everything® Kids' Bible Trivia Book
Everything® Kids' Bugs Book
Everything® Kids' Cars and Trucks Puzzle and Activity Book
Everything® Kids' Christmas Puzzle & Activity Book
Everything® Kids' Connect the Dots
    Puzzle and Activity Book
Everything® Kids' Cookbook, 2nd Ed.
Everything® Kids' Crazy Puzzles Book
Everything® Kids' Dinosaurs Book
Everything® Kids' Dragons Puzzle and Activity Book
Everything® Kids' Environment Book $7.95
Everything® Kids' Fairies Puzzle and Activity Book
Everything® Kids' First Spanish Puzzle and Activity Book
Everything® Kids' Football Book
Everything® Kids' Geography Book
Everything® Kids' Gross Cookbook
Everything® Kids' Gross Hidden Pictures Book
Everything® Kids' Gross Jokes Book
Everything® Kids' Gross Mazes Book
Everything® Kids' Gross Puzzle & Activity Book
Everything® Kids' Halloween Puzzle & Activity Book
Everything® Kids' Hanukkah Puzzle and Activity Book
Everything® Kids' Hidden Pictures Book
Everything® Kids' Horses Book
Everything® Kids' Joke Book
Everything® Kids' Knock Knock Book
Everything® Kids' Learning French Book
Everything® Kids' Learning Spanish Book
Everything® Kids' Magical Science Experiments Book
Everything® Kids' Math Puzzles Book
Everything® Kids' Mazes Book
Everything® Kids' Money Book, 2nd Ed.
Everything® Kids' Mummies, Pharaoh's, and Pyramids
    Puzzle and Activity Book
Everything® Kids' Nature Book
Everything® Kids' Pirates Puzzle and Activity Book
Everything® Kids' Presidents Book
Everything® Kids' Princess Puzzle and Activity Book
Everything® Kids' Puzzle Book

Everything® Kids' Racecars Puzzle and Activity Book
Everything® Kids' Riddles & Brain Teasers Book
Everything® Kids' Science Experiments Book
Everything® Kids' Sharks Book
Everything® Kids' Soccer Book
Everything® Kids' Spelling Book
Everything® Kids' Spies Puzzle and Activity Book
Everything® Kids' States Book
Everything® Kids' Travel Activity Book
Everything® Kids' Word Search Puzzle and Activity Book

LANGUAGE

Everything® Conversational Japanese Book with CD, $19.95
Everything® French Grammar Book
Everything® French Phrase Book, $9.95
Everything® French Verb Book, $9.95
Everything® German Phrase Book, $9.95
Everything® German Practice Book with CD, $19.95
Everything® Inglés Book
Everything® Intermediate Spanish Book with CD, $19.95
Everything® Italian Phrase Book, $9.95
Everything® Italian Practice Book with CD, $19.95
Everything® Learning Brazilian Portuguese Book with CD, $19.95
Everything® Learning French Book with CD, 2nd Ed., $19.95
Everything® Learning German Book
Everything® Learning Italian Book
Everything® Learning Latin Book
Everything® Learning Russian Book with CD, $19.95
Everything® Learning Spanish Book
Everything® Learning Spanish Book with CD, 2nd Ed., $19.95
Everything® Russian Practice Book with CD, $19.95
Everything® Sign Language Book, $15.95
Everything® Spanish Grammar Book
Everything® Spanish Phrase Book, $9.95
Everything® Spanish Practice Book with CD, $19.95
Everything® Spanish Verb Book, $9.95
Everything® Speaking Mandarin Chinese Book with CD, $19.95

MUSIC

Everything® Bass Guitar Book with CD, $19.95
Everything® Drums Book with CD, $19.95
Everything® Guitar Book with CD, 2nd Ed., $19.95
Everything® Guitar Chords Book with CD, $19.95
Everything® Guitar Scales Book with CD, $19.95
Everything® Harmonica Book with CD, $15.95
Everything® Home Recording Book
Everything® Music Theory Book with CD, $19.95
Everything® Reading Music Book with CD, $19.95
Everything® Rock & Blues Guitar Book with CD, $19.95
Everything® Rock & Blues Piano Book with CD, $19.95
Everything® Rock Drums Book with CD, $19.95
Everything® Singing Book with CD, $19.95
Everything® Songwriting Book

NEW AGE

Everything® Astrology Book, 2nd Ed.
Everything® Birthday Personology Book
Everything® Celtic Wisdom Book, $15.95
Everything® Dreams Book, 2nd Ed.
Everything® Law of Attraction Book, $15.95
Everything® Love Signs Book, $9.95
Everything® Love Spells Book, $9.95
Everything® Palmistry Book
Everything® Psychic Book
Everything® Reiki Book

Everything® Sex Signs Book, $9.95
Everything® Spells & Charms Book, 2nd Ed.
Everything® Tarot Book, 2nd Ed.
Everything® Toltec Wisdom Book
Everything® Wicca & Witchcraft Book, 2nd Ed.

PARENTING

Everything® Baby Names Book, 2nd Ed.
Everything® Baby Shower Book, 2nd Ed.
Everything® Baby Sign Language Book with DVD
Everything® Baby's First Year Book
Everything® Birthing Book
Everything® Breastfeeding Book
Everything® Father-to-Be Book
Everything® Father's First Year Book
Everything® Get Ready for Baby Book, 2nd Ed.
Everything® Get Your Baby to Sleep Book, $9.95
Everything® Getting Pregnant Book
Everything® Guide to Pregnancy Over 35
Everything® Guide to Raising a One-Year-Old
Everything® Guide to Raising a Two-Year-Old
Everything® Guide to Raising Adolescent Boys
Everything® Guide to Raising Adolescent Girls
Everything® Mother's First Year Book
Everything® Parent's Guide to Childhood Illnesses
Everything® Parent's Guide to Children and Divorce
Everything® Parent's Guide to Children with ADD/ADHD
Everything® Parent's Guide to Children with Asperger's
    Syndrome
Everything® Parent's Guide to Children with Anxiety
Everything® Parent's Guide to Children with Asthma
Everything® Parent's Guide to Children with Autism
Everything® Parent's Guide to Children with Bipolar Disorder
Everything® Parent's Guide to Children with Depression
Everything® Parent's Guide to Children with Dyslexia
Everything® Parent's Guide to Children with Juvenile Diabetes
Everything® Parent's Guide to Children with OCD
Everything® Parent's Guide to Positive Discipline
Everything® Parent's Guide to Raising Boys
Everything® Parent's Guide to Raising Girls
Everything® Parent's Guide to Raising Siblings
Everything® Parent's Guide to Raising Your
    Adopted Child
Everything® Parent's Guide to Sensory Integration Disorder
Everything® Parent's Guide to Tantrums
Everything® Parent's Guide to the Strong-Willed Child
Everything® Parenting a Teenager Book
Everything® Potty Training Book, $9.95
Everything® Pregnancy Book, 3rd Ed.
Everything® Pregnancy Fitness Book
Everything® Pregnancy Nutrition Book
Everything® Pregnancy Organizer, 2nd Ed., $16.95
Everything® Toddler Activities Book
Everything® Toddler Book
Everything® Tween Book
Everything® Twins, Triplets, and More Book

PETS

Everything® Aquarium Book
Everything® Boxer Book
Everything® Cat Book, 2nd Ed.
Everything® Chihuahua Book
Everything® Cooking for Dogs Book
Everything® Dachshund Book
Everything® Dog Book, 2nd Ed.
Everything® Dog Grooming Book

Everything® Dog Obedience Book
Everything® Dog Owner's Organizer, $16.95
Everything® Dog Training and Tricks Book
Everything® German Shepherd Book
Everything® Golden Retriever Book
Everything® Horse Book, 2nd Ed., $15.95
Everything® Horse Care Book
Everything® Horseback Riding Book
Everything® Labrador Retriever Book
Everything® Poodle Book
Everything® Pug Book
Everything® Puppy Book
Everything® Small Dogs Book
Everything® Tropical Fish Book
Everything® Yorkshire Terrier Book

REFERENCE

Everything® American Presidents Book
Everything® Blogging Book
Everything® Build Your Vocabulary Book, $9.95
Everything® Car Care Book
Everything® Classical Mythology Book
Everything® Da Vinci Book
Everything® Einstein Book
Everything® Enneagram Book
Everything® Etiquette Book, 2nd Ed.
Everything® Family Christmas Book, $15.95
Everything® Guide to C. S. Lewis & Narnia
Everything® Guide to Divorce, 2nd Ed., $15.95
Everything® Guide to Edgar Allan Poe
Everything® Guide to Understanding Philosophy
Everything® Inventions and Patents Book
Everything® Jacqueline Kennedy Onassis Book
Everything® John F. Kennedy Book
Everything® Mafia Book
Everything® Martin Luther King Jr. Book
Everything® Pirates Book
Everything® Private Investigation Book
Everything® Psychology Book
Everything® Public Speaking Book, $9.95
Everything® Shakespeare Book, 2nd Ed.

RELIGION

Everything® Angels Book
Everything® Bible Book
Everything® Bible Study Book with CD, $19.95
Everything® Buddhism Book
Everything® Catholicism Book
Everything® Christianity Book
Everything® Gnostic Gospels Book
Everything® Hinduism Book, $15.95
Everything® History of the Bible Book
Everything® Jesus Book
Everything® Jewish History & Heritage Book
Everything® Judaism Book
Everything® Kabbalah Book
Everything® Koran Book
Everything® Mary Book
Everything® Mary Magdalene Book
Everything® Prayer Book

Everything® Saints Book, 2nd Ed.
Everything® Torah Book
Everything® Understanding Islam Book
Everything® Women of the Bible Book
Everything® World's Religions Book

SCHOOL & CAREERS

Everything® Career Tests Book
Everything® College Major Test Book
Everything® College Survival Book, 2nd Ed.
Everything® Cover Letter Book, 2nd Ed.
Everything® Filmmaking Book
Everything® Get-a-Job Book, 2nd Ed.
Everything® Guide to Being a Paralegal
Everything® Guide to Being a Personal Trainer
Everything® Guide to Being a Real Estate Agent
Everything® Guide to Being a Sales Rep
Everything® Guide to Being an Event Planner
Everything® Guide to Careers in Health Care
Everything® Guide to Careers in Law Enforcement
Everything® Guide to Government Jobs
Everything® Guide to Starting and Running a Catering
    Business
Everything® Guide to Starting and Running a Restaurant
**Everything® Guide to Starting and Running
    a Retail Store**
Everything® Job Interview Book, 2nd Ed.
Everything® New Nurse Book
Everything® New Teacher Book
Everything® Paying for College Book
Everything® Practice Interview Book
Everything® Resume Book, 3rd Ed.
Everything® Study Book

SELF-HELP

Everything® Body Language Book
Everything® Dating Book, 2nd Ed.
Everything® Great Sex Book
**Everything® Guide to Caring for Aging Parents,
    $15.95**
Everything® Self-Esteem Book
Everything® Self-Hypnosis Book, $9.95
Everything® Tantric Sex Book

SPORTS & FITNESS

Everything® Easy Fitness Book
Everything® Fishing Book
Everything® Guide to Weight Training, $15.95
Everything® Krav Maga for Fitness Book
Everything® Running Book, 2nd Ed.
Everything® Triathlon Training Book, $15.95

TRAVEL

Everything® Family Guide to Coastal Florida
Everything® Family Guide to Cruise Vacations
Everything® Family Guide to Hawaii
Everything® Family Guide to Las Vegas, 2nd Ed.
Everything® Family Guide to Mexico
Everything® Family Guide to New England, 2nd Ed.

Everything® Family Guide to New York City, 3rd Ed.
**Everything® Family Guide to Northern California
    and Lake Tahoe**
Everything® Family Guide to RV Travel & Campgrounds
Everything® Family Guide to the Caribbean
Everything® Family Guide to the Disneyland® Resort, California
    Adventure®, Universal Studios®, and the Anaheim
    Area, 2nd Ed.
Everything® Family Guide to the Walt Disney World Resort®,
    Universal Studios®, and Greater Orlando, 5th Ed.
Everything® Family Guide to Timeshares
Everything® Family Guide to Washington D.C., 2nd Ed.

WEDDINGS

Everything® Bachelorette Party Book, $9.95
Everything® Bridesmaid Book, $9.95
Everything® Destination Wedding Book
Everything® Father of the Bride Book, $9.95
Everything® Green Wedding Book, $15.95
Everything® Groom Book, $9.95
Everything® Jewish Wedding Book, 2nd Ed., $15.95
Everything® Mother of the Bride Book, $9.95
Everything® Outdoor Wedding Book
Everything® Wedding Book, 3rd Ed.
Everything® Wedding Checklist, $9.95
Everything® Wedding Etiquette Book, $9.95
Everything® Wedding Organizer, 2nd Ed., $16.95
Everything® Wedding Shower Book, $9.95
Everything® Wedding Vows Book, 3rd Ed., $9.95
Everything® Wedding Workout Book
Everything® Weddings on a Budget Book, 2nd Ed., $9.95

WRITING

Everything® Creative Writing Book
Everything® Get Published Book, 2nd Ed.
Everything® Grammar and Style Book, 2nd Ed.
Everything® Guide to Magazine Writing
Everything® Guide to Writing a Book Proposal
Everything® Guide to Writing a Novel
Everything® Guide to Writing Children's Books
Everything® Guide to Writing Copy
Everything® Guide to Writing Graphic Novels
Everything® Guide to Writing Research Papers
Everything® Guide to Writing a Romance Novel, $15.95
Everything® Improve Your Writing Book, 2nd Ed.
Everything® Writing Poetry Book